The Living Work of Teachers:
Ideology and Practice

Edited By:
Karen Cadiero-Kaplan
Alberto M. Ochoa
Edward M. Olivos
James L. Rodriguez
Natalie Kuhlman

California Association for Bilingual Education
Covina, California

This book is dedicated to our SDSU Policy Studies in Language and Cross-cultural Education Department colleagues and tireless campaigners for social justice in education—their contributions and dedication have enriched our lives:

Cristina Gomez	(1956 - 2002)
Henry Trueba	(1931 - 2004)
Russell Young	(1956 - 2005)
Bea Gonzales	(1942 - 2005)
René Nuñez	(1936 - 2006)

The Living Work of Teachers: Ideology and Practice

A critical perspective has always occupied a central role in the work of the California Association for Bilingual Education, and this edited volume by Alberto Ochoa and Karen Cadeiro-Kaplan is a testament to the organization's ongoing commitment to publish excellent works to this end. Accordingly, our vision statement "Biliteracy and Educational Equity and Excellence for All Students" cannot be accomplished *unless* the community of scholars, activists, educators, and parents actively engage in critical examination and participation to ensure that this vision is fully actualized.

Advocacy for language diverse students' educational rights has been the essence of CABE's work since it first began in 1976. It is our belief that schools must operationalize the following principles to ensure that all students are academically successful and participate fully in our society. Students must be: 1) academically prepared; 2) multilingual; 3) knowledgeable about the diversity of our multicultural global society; 4) information and technology literate; and 5) civically oriented and active advocates for their communities.

This book, *The Living Work of Teachers: Ideology and Practice*, represents CABE's social justice orientation through the contribution of its authors whose critical investigations represent and document the voices of parents, teachers, and students. This volume simultaneously unveils injustices, as well as depicts resistance to oppressive policies and practices so that readers may be encouraged to act for the rights of our children. It is meant for practitioners, scholars, policymakers, and advocates, and is part of CABE's ongoing commitment to disseminate vital critical works that reflect our mission to "Promote and Support Educational Excellence and Social Justice for All.

Magaly Lavadenz, Ph.D.
Immediate Past President and
Chair, Publication and Information Committee
Loyola Marymount University

Albert Ochoa and
Karen Cadiero-Kaplan
San Diego State University
Published by

 **California Association
for Bilingual Education**
16033 E. San Bernardino Rd.
Covina, CA 91722

Library of Congress Catalog Card Number: TXu 1-261-512

ISBN 1-889094-03-X

Table of Contents

Preface

by Alberto Ochoa and
Karen Cadiero-Kaplan
San Diego State University

This publication presents a series of articles that examine the ideological, belief, and value systems of bilingual educators, parents, and school leaders in addressing the educational development and attainment of English language learners. It also examines the existing assumptions about education, as well as the tensions these assumptions pose in relation to the lived experiences that linguistically diverse school communities encounter with the school systems' policies and practices in California and across the United States.

The articles in this volume collectively point to the tensions in our democracy and processes that continue to evolve. These tensions existfor many teachers who, after many years of education both inside and outside the classroom, come to the conclusion that the principles of democratic schooling drive their ambition to teach. Yet, democratic schooling is larger than the confinements of a classroom. It is the very idea that education is a vital part in the process of a democratic society. The notions of freedom, equity, community involvement, critical thinking and participatory citizenship are major components of any democratic society.

Over the last 100 years, as capitalism has evolved, schools have taken on a major role in the growth and development of our children. As a result, the educational system has become a pivotal institution within society at large and its role has become increasingly significant. In a country such as the United States, whose self identity claims to be profoundly democratic, it becomes crucial for our educational system to support this concept or else face the consequences of its contradictions.

An honest evaluation of our school system today would expose contradictions to democracy at large. With the ongoing implementation of regulated state standards enacted by politicians, unequal funding of school districts, and biased curricula based on dominant cultural norms; it is apparent that the current educational system design is flawed in its efforts to maintain the status quo. Although they can be found sporadically, the most fundamental factors necessary for democratic schooling are missing in the educational arena. Theories from prominant educators all bring to light profound concepts of social justice and effective teaching and learning which have the ability to fundamentally change our schools as well as our society as a whole. These educators include Dewey (1944), Bowles & Gintis, Herbert (1976), Vygotsky (1978), Freire (1990), Apple (1993), Macedo (1994), Cummins (1995), Delpit (1995), Kincheloe, Steinberg & Gresson (1996), Sleeter (1996), Feinberg & Soltis (1999), Spring (1999), and Wink (2000)

Paulo Freire in his book *Pedagogy of the Oppressed* speaks to the theory of the 'banking concept' and states that teaching has become a depository of information that requires no thought or critique. The expectation of the educational system is that students will accept the information conveyed as absolute. This type of teaching necessitates the teacher as the authoritarian figure and the student as the ignorant object in need of being taught. Although it is true that teachers may have much to offer students in terms of learning, the idea that teachers are all knowing leads to a type of autocratic classroom in which, the balance becomes unequal because teachers have all the power and student are at the mercy of their benevolence.

Freire's theory suggests that there is an alternative way to approach teaching where the teacher and the student both have something to share with each other and are co-learners and co-teachers. The notion of one's consciousness being directly interconnected to the world around them gives the student as equally valid a perspective as the teacher. With this premise, the student also has something that the teacher could learn from. Freire refers to this idea as true educational freedom, which includes active communication between both parties.

The publication begins with an introduction by Dr. Antonia Darder and is followed by four sections: Ideologies of Teaching and Literacy, Teachers Beliefs and School Context, Language Policy and Education, and Parent Voices. A brief overview of each section provides the reader with the issues presented by each contributor.

Introduction

In the opening section, Dr. Antonia Darder calls for educators to defend the rights of English language learners. She points to linguistic inequalities and their relationship to schooling as central concerns for educators who profess a commitment to both critical literacy and a democratic society. Darder suggests that the development of literacy is as much a cultural, political and economic concern, as it is an academic one. For these reasons, neither academic issues of language nor the politics of literacy can be fully understood outside of their historical relationship to colonization, national power, class struggle, and the ideologies that sustain mainstream educational policies and practices, often at the expense of linguistic minorities. She notes that although the right to become literate in students' language of origin and the dominant language of the society in which they reside represents a key tenet of linguistic rights around the globe, this precept has often been ignored. For example, in the U.S., with first the passage of Proposition 227 in California and later the institutionalization of *No Child Left Behind,* fundamental attention to linguistic rights has taken a back seat to so-called *accountability* measures. These accountability measures, promoting a teach-to-the-test curriculum—particularly in low-income schools where the large majority of English language learners attend, place a greater emphasis on high-stakes test scores, than on the critical literacy skills that will enhance democratic participation and social empowerment.

Dr. Darder argues that critical educators must come to terms with the fact that injustice "is not an unfortunate aberration of capitalism, but an inescapable outcome and an essential condition of its successful economic functioning." Given this reality, it is unfortunate that so many theories and practices of literacy development function conveniently to perpetuate existing social controls that create disempowering social and economic conditions in our school communities.

Section: I. Ideologies of Teaching & Literacy

The first article entitled *"Literacy Ideologies: Examining Curricula for English Language Development and Biliteracy"* authored by Dr. Karen Cadiero-Kaplan examines existing literacy theory and guides those concerned with the achievement of English language learners in an exploration of ideological constructions of the curriculum designed to teach English to bilingual students. She argues that in order for teachers to engage in the teaching of literacy for English language learners as well as native language speakers of English, there is a need to examine not only one's own ideology towards literacy, but that of materials, processes, and programs that are most often promoted in schools for the teaching of language and literacy. Dr. Cadiero-Kaplan argues that ideology has the most profound impact on the resulting policy and curricula decisions made from federal to state and local levels of schooling.

The second article is authored by Dr. Larry Emerson and is entitled *"Emerging Diné Decolonization Theory and Its Application to a Language of Decolonization."* This article focuses on micro level (personal) decolonization theory development and proposes that as an Indigenous community, the Diné, like many Indigenous, non-western communities, are in a unique political and cultural position to gain insights into decolonization theory and practice. Diné decolonization theory is relatively new in the field of Diné studies. This article examines the relationship of colonialism theory to a 2002 study by the author regarding Diné (Navajo) emerging notions of decolonization. An opportunity for the Diné exists to rely on a politic of *hozho* (e.g. harmony, beauty, balance, respect) as a basis for its political action regarding conscientization, language recovery, and decolonization. The author assumes that colonialism is a fact of Diné existence and cannot be described as a "thing of the past". Instead, it is an ever-present phenomena and living reality that affects how, Diné, live their lives within the "Diné Nation" or within the "Navajo Reservation".

The third article entitled *"Developing Ideological Clarity: A Case Study of Teaching with Courage, Solidarity, and Ethics"* is authored by Dr. Cristina Alfaro. The article begins with a discussion on the preparation of teachers of language minority students. Dr. Alfaro is concerned with the issues that revolve around the standards for the teaching profession and best practices to address students' linguistic and academic development. The article focuses on the importance of examining the role of teacher's political and ideological clarity in working with language mi-nority and other subordinated minority student groups. A case study is provided of a teacher that goes through an ideological border cross-ing journey. In this journey he acknowledges that he must gain both political and ideological clarity in order to increase the chances of academic success for his students. This teacher, in addition to implementing pedagogically sound strategies, responsive to the needs of his language minority students, also engages in the rigorous process of developing ideological clarity in order to effectively create a classroom environment with critical praxis.

Section II. Teachers Beliefs & School Context

The fourth article authored by Dr. Yvette V. Lapayese is entitled *"Racism and Language Minority Students: A Critical Race Theory Approach to Explore Oppositional Acts by Latino Educators working with Spanish-speaking Students."* The article discusses the racist climate in California and sets the stage for examining the experiences of Latino teachers working with Spanish-speaking students. This article discloses that Latino teachers are critically aware of racial discrimination, racial segregation, and racial inequities that systematically disadvantage Spanish-speaking students and engage in oppositional acts that can serve as transformational instances of resistance. These oppositional acts provide concrete strategies for other Latino teachers and critical educators interested in challenging the structures of oppression that govern our schools. Lastly, in light of Latino teachers' experiences and perspectives, the article also suggests changes in teacher preparation programs to better meet the needs of Latino educators invested in transformational resistance.

The fifth article authored by Dr. Antonella Cortese is entitled *"Teachers' Self-knowledge of their Personal and Professional Epistemologies as Seen Through the Teaching of Writing."* This article documents beliefs that teachers bring to the classroom and how they approach the teaching of writing. How the teaching of writing, or any subject matter, is characterized is not as simple as a teacher objectively following an instructional method. What teachers bring into their classroom practice—their personal political, social, cultural, and linguistic perspective(s) fundamentally impacts their students at the academic level. The purpose of this article is to illuminate why and how teachers make the choices they do by providing a space for teachers to dialogue and reflect upon their practice in writing instruction from a multi-faceted perspective—social, political, cultural, and pedagogical—to both see and look at how their prevailing ideologies on a personal level and their resulting pedagogical theories are expressed and illustrated through views on the literacy process and teaching of writing. The voices of two teachers are documented with regards to their classroom activities and their personal reflections of their teaching.

The sixth article is entitled *"Taiwanese Student Teachers' and Teachers' Views on Efficacy of English Preparation Programs"* and is authored by Dr. Shu-Ching Chu. This international focus provides insights on the current teacher preparation programs in Taiwan that are designed to prepare Taiwanese English teachers. Dr. Chu documents the perceptions of student teachers and classroom teachers toward teacher preparation of elementary school English teachers in a non-English-speaking country. This work is written from an international perspective, the voices and perceptions of student teachers and experienced classroom teachers are discussed with regards to pedagogical practices, resources, and professional development support needed for English teacher preparation programs in Taiwan. The findings, while particular to Taiwan, point to similar conditions experienced by teachers in the United States, namely, the importance of curricular training and the need of support systems to assist teachers in their professional development. Chu argues, based on her results, that Taiwanese pre-service teachers need more practical and effective teacher education in order to improve the quality of English education for children whose primary language is not English.

Section III. Language Policy and Education

The seventh article entitled *"Who Says? Dynamics of Post-Proposition 227 Language Policy In a California School —1998-2004: Multiple Perspectives and Multiple Positions"* is authored by Dr. Tamara Collins-Parks. The article documents a micro-political case study of the district level dynamics surrounding the implementation of Proposition 227. In 1998, Proposition 227 mandated Structured English Immersion as the automatic placement for English Language Learners unless they submitted a yearly waiver petition. The context of the study is the implementation of English-only instructional policy in a white dominated but majority Latino district. The district denied almost all waiver petitions and implemented an English-only instructional policy. Through the voices of parents, community members, teachers and administrators, the author illustrates the variety of perspectives towards the district policy, including support, opposition and neutrality. The study contributes to a greater understanding of the dynamics of communication, conflict and cooperation surrounding the implementation of new policy impacting ethnolinguistically diverse students. The study indicates a need for better communication with the impacted community, including inclusion of stakeholders, and democratic implementation of policy.

The eighth article entitled *"Indigenous Language Loss and Revitalization: The Case of the Kumeyaay in Baja California"* is authored by Paula Meyer and Jon Meza Cuero. The article documents an approach to language revitalization and explores the reasons why the languages of Indigenous peoples are resistant to revitalization efforts. The authors look at the social, political and economic factors that have played a part in the demise of the languages and that continue to affect revitalization attempts. They describe the socio-political situation of an Indigenous community in Baja California and the many types of loss that the community has suffered and continues to suffer. They conclude that without dialogue among the community and significant people from outside the community, these losses will continue to impede language revitalization efforts. Through genuine dialogue, the community will pave the way to the power that they need to revive their language and their culture. They can thus affirm a positive identity as separate from the dominant society and so be able to participate as equals in that society.

Section IV. Parent Voices

The ninth article entitled *"A Useful Symbology for Modeling Critical Interactions among Stakeholders in Education"* is authored by Dr. Georges Merx. The article documents the tensions and conflicts that arise when parents and educators of differing backgrounds interact and attempt to collaborate. Such relations are often complex, subtle, and difficult to discern outright. In addition to textual descriptions, the author's use of graphic organizers provide a means to categorize, generalize, and illustrate these complex relationships and interactions. The approach discussed in this chapter illustrates a suggested methodology for the visualization of educational interactions and to illustrate the multi-dimensional scenarios such as parent-educator interactions.

The tenth article is entitled *"Operationalizing a Transformational Paradigm of Parent Involvement: Parent Voice and Participation"* and is authored by Drs. Edward Olivos and Alberto Ochoa. The article outlines what the authors describe as a *Transformational Paradigm of Parent Involvement.* The authors argue that despite educational research supporting parent involvement, most school efforts tend to be aimed at mere volunteerism and low-impact rhetoric leading to superficial engagement, particularly when involving bicultural parents. Olivos and Ochoa propose that efforts must be made to critically analyze the current modes of engagement that exist in the school system in an attempt to move parent involvement toward a more transformational orientation. The authors further suggest that bicultural parents can be transformational agents of school reform/change and cultural democracy and offer examples of transformative parental involvement efforts in San Diego County, California.

Questions for Reflection

The editors of the publication suggest that you keep in mind the following questions as you journey through the articles—as we seek educational practices that promote democratic schooling and prepare children, youth, educators, and parents to address increasingly complex and interrelated issues resulting from the global economy, diversity in all its forms, multilingualism and social justice.

- How can we provide teachers with ideological clarity? In order for teachers to engage in the teaching of literacy for English language learners as well as native language literacy development, there is a need to examine not only one's own ideology towards literacy, but that of curriculum and processes that are most often promoted in schools for the teaching of language and literacy. For it is ideology that has the most profound impact on the resulting policy and curricula decisions made from federal to state and local levels of schooling.

- How do you get teachers to engage and broaden student experience? How does a teacher promote critical thinking and reflection in students? Lastly, how do teachers give up structure to facilitate student interaction within their environments to promote learning?

- How can the power of language, literacy, and pedagogy provide an emancipatory literacy? How does critical pedagogy address the concept of cultural politics by challenging students' experiences and perceptions that shape the histories and socioeconomic realities that give meaning to how students define their everyday lives? How do students construct what they perceive as truth? How can literacy be about the ability to decode text, while also being conscious of the world through personal liberation? How can literacy address more than just reading the word, but also foster the confidence to speak, question, think critically, be inventive, and empowered to promote change? We believe one must have access to learn to become a citizen in all communities.

- How can the practice of critical pedagogy, dialogue and analysis serve as the foundation for reflection, dialogue, and action namely praxis for parent involvement in our schools and school transformation? It is this educational strategy that supports a problem-posing approach to education where the relationship of students to teacher and teachers to parent is, without question dialogical, with each having something to contribute and receive. Students learn from the teachers; teachers learn from the students and parents, and parents from teachers and from the voices of youth.

References

Apple, M. (1993). <u>Official Knowledge: Democratic Education in a Conservative Age</u>. New York: Routledge Press.

Bowles, Samuel and Gintis, Herbert (1976). <u>Schooling in capitalist America: educational reform and the contradictions of economic life.</u> Basic Books, Inc. Publisher.

Cummins, J. (1995). Empowering minority students: A framework for intervention. In O. García & C. Baker (Eds.), <u>Policy and practice in bilingual education: Extending the foundations</u> (pp. 103-116). Clevedon, Avon, England: Multilingual Matters, Ltd.

Delpit, L. (1995). <u>Other people's children: Cultural conflict in the classroom</u>. New York: The New Press.

Dewey, J. (1944). <u>Democracy and Education.</u> New York: The Free Press.

Feinberg, W. and Soltis, J. F (1999). <u>School and Society</u>. New York: Teachers College Press.

Freire, P. (1990). <u>Pedagogy of the oppressed</u>. New York NY: Continuum.

Freeman, D. & Richards, J. (1996). <u>Teacher learning in language teaching</u>. Cambridge University Press.

Hinchey, P. (1998). <u>Finding Freedom in the Classroom</u>. P. Lang.

Kincheloe, J. L., Steinberg S R. & Gresson III A. (1996). <u>Measured Lies: The Bell Curve Examined</u>. New York: St. Martin's Press.

Macedo, D. (1994). <u>Literacies of Power: What Americans Are Not Allowed to Know</u>. Westview Press.

Spring, Joel. (1999). <u>American education,</u> 9th ed. Mc Graw-Hill, Inc.

McLaren, Peter &Leonard, Peter. (1993). <u>Paulo Freire: A critical encounter</u>. Routledge.

Sleeter, C. E. (1996). <u>Multicultural Education as Social Activism</u>. New York: SUNY Press.

Vygotsky, L. S. (1978). <u>Mind in society: The development of higher psychological processes</u>. Cambridge, MA: Harvard University Press.

Acknowledgements

Special recognition to the California Association for Bilingual Education (CABE) for providing literary space for scholarly voices working on the conceptualization of multiliteracy and democratic schooling and the opportunity to create this text of recent research. Our gratitude to Drs. Antonia Darder, Natalie Kuhlman, James Rodriguez, Edward Olivos, and faculty scholars, involved in the San Diego State University Center for Equity and Biliteracy Education Research (CEBER), for assisting in the editing of this publication. We also thank Ms. Martha Pedaroza for her work in the copy editing process, and a special thanks to the San Diego County Office of Education WRITE Project for sharing their artwork and the artist Mr. Barajas.

Karen Cadiero-Kaplan & Alberto Ochoa
San Diego State University

Introduction
by Antonia Darder
University of Illinois Urbana-Champaign

I

> Although language is a potent symbol of class, gender, ethnicity, religion and other differences, disputes involving language are not really about language, but instead about fundamental inequalities. [1]

It is impossible to contemplate the process of schooling outside the realm of language and its relationship to our formation as literate human beings. From the most personal to the most theoretical, the question of language raises both profound and difficult questions that must be thoughtfully considered and critically engaged. In our efforts to seriously interrogate literacy development, issues of language rights and its relationship to culture, identity, class, and citizenship must remain ever at the forefront of our inquiry. Yet, no matter where such a discussion begins or where it leads, what cannot be denied is the political nature of language and, in particular, its powerful influence in structuring the lives of language minority populations. Hence, linguistic inequalities and their relationship to schooling are central concerns for educators who profess a commitment to both critical literacy and a democratic society. In saying this, I wish to suggest that the development of literacy is as much a cultural, political and economic concern, as it is an academic one. For these reasons, neither academic issues of language nor the politics of literacy can be fully understood outside of their historical relationship to colonization, national power, class struggle, and the ideologies that sustain mainstream educational policies and practices, often at the expense of linguistic minorities.

It is significant to note that although the right to become literate in students' language of origin and the dominant language of the society in which they reside represents a key tenet of linguistic rights around the globe, this precept has often been ignored. For example, in the U.S., with first the passage of Proposition 227 in California and later the institutionalization of *No Child Left Behind*, fundamental attention to linguistic rights has taken a back seat to so-called *accountability* measures. These accountability measures, which more often than not promote a teach-to-the-test curriculum—particularly in low-income schools where the large majority of English language learners attend—place a greater emphasis on high-stakes test scores, than on the critical literacy skills that will enhance democratic participation and social empowerment.

In response, critical educators have challenged the misguided notion that elevated test scores automatically translate into highly literate and critically conscious students. Contrary to the rhetoric of *No Child Left Behind* advocates, high-stakes testing is not the panacea for improving literacy and academic achievement among English language learners, nor even working-class students in general. Instead, it represents a significant step backward in educational policy and practice—a situation that should particularly concern administrators, teachers, parents and education activists within all low-income communities. In fact, the success of proposition 227 or the *English for the Children* campaign in California (and in its revised formulation in States like Massachusetts and Arizona) represents the tip of the iceberg in neo-liberal efforts to "turn back the clock" on linguistic rights. This represents a disingenuous effort by conservatives to preserve structures of inequality and social exclusion in the United States, in the name of national unity and economic imperatives.

Yet, it is as a direct consequence of U.S. foreign economic policies in Latin America and other parts of the globe that many immigrants have been forced to flee their countries as a direct outcome of regional wars and economic impoverishment. U.S. foreign trade agreements, such as GATT and NAFTA, have generated a decline in living standards both in this country and abroad. In the last decade, thousands of jobs have disappeared as factories have closed down shop and exported jobs to cheap labor markets around the world. The outcome of geopolitical economic crisis in Latin America has been particularly visible in California, which has historically served as a port-of-entry for a large percentage of Spanish-speaking immigrants.

Nearly 50 percent of the 40 million Latinos residing in California today are foreign born. In Los Angeles County alone, over 4.2 million are Latino. And although the largest percentage is from Mexico, there is a growing number of immigrants from other Latin American countries, including El Salvador, Nicaragua and Argentina. Latino and Asian populations are expected to experience the greatest growth, more than doubling their numbers by 2040. Meanwhile, population projections estimate that by the year 2020, Latinos will become the largest ethnic group in the state. This echoes national projections that "minority" residents will very soon become the majority of the population in most large urban centers, a reality that is already a fact in many large U.S. cities today. Moreover, the 2000 census documented an astonishing increase in Latino immigrants in the Deep South, showing Latino population increases of nearly 300 percent in North Carolina, Arkansas, Georgia and Tennessee.

It is not surprising then that the increasing demographic diversity of California's student population should raise pedagogical questions and concerns for educators committed to the linguistic rights and literacy need of all students. However, these concerns surface not because of the newness of the situation, but rather the reality that, except in few instances, Latino student achievement has lagged considerably behind that of their white counterparts. Even more disconcerting is the fact that low educational attainment by Latino students cannot be simply explained away as the result of recent immigration. Rather, it must be noted that U.S. born, English-speaking, working-class, students from Latino, African American, Asian and Native-American and even poor Euro-American communities across the country have consistently experienced lower high school and college completion rates than students (of all ethnicities) from more affluent neighborhoods. Hence, the issue of literacy as an educational concern might potentially serve to galvanize political efforts for educational justice and democratic schooling.

However presently, statistics on academic achievement point to the persistent practice of the U.S., as a modern nation-state, to blatantly racialize language minority populations within our borders—particularly when such actions are judged by the dominant class to be in the interest of national security or economic well being. More often than not, the move to obtain cultural and class dominion over a nation's diverse population has rendered minority language speakers problematic to capitalist accumulation. To ensure that the "Other" was (and is) kept in line with the system of production, a variety of racialized institutional policies and practices have been implemented during the nation's history—policies and practices that have led to the widespread deportation, assimilation, incarceration and even genocide of minority populations.

Tove Skutnabb-Kangas,[2] a leading international biodiversity and linguistic rights advocate, argues that the majority of language communities over the last 100 years have become victims of linguistic-geno-cide—that is, where the language is killed rather than the person. With-out question, she associates this genocide to the destruction of potential competition for political and economic power, in order to eliminate any claims to nation-state rights among indigenous and minority popula-tions. This view provides a hint to the linguistic genocide associated with the plight of African Americans who were separated from their families and forced into slave labor; the Dine stripped of much of their land and their children arbitrarily removed to English-speaking board-ing schools; and Mexican, Puerto Rican and Chinese workers who were exploited for cheap labor and subjected to substandard housing and schooling. Similar mechanisms of language loss are at work today in public schools where students are systematically ushered into Eng-lish-only environments, not only preventing them from developing lit-eracy in their home language, but socializing them into an inadequate literacy process that does little to promote their cultural and material empowerment.

Given the pressure and strain to survive such conditions, many stu-dents have now lost much of their linguistic connection to their ances-tral culture. Again, key to this discussion is the manner in which rac-ism, manifested through linguistic genocide, is intricately linked to po-litical economic power, control of natural resources, and the subordina-tion of those inferiorized as the "the other" within U.S. society. As job opportunities decline, policing the barrios, anti-immigrant sentiments, and English-only campaigns intensify, tightening the very controls that were loosened at an earlier time when the need for cheap, unskilled labor existed. This intensification is fueled by the debates of conserva-tive political gatekeepers who allege that undocumented immigrants take away jobs from citizens, lower property values, threaten law and order, consume education and welfare resources, and, now, constitute a national security risk.

Current anti-immigrant sentiments and efforts to thwart bilingual-ism are every bit as politically vicious as they were in the earlier de-cades of the twentieth century—fueled by similar political alliances and the xenophobic nativist rhetoric of conservative policy makers and big business. Specific conditions that parallel both these historical eras include increasing immigration, burgeoning student enrollments in ur-ban centers, economic decline and overt military spending overseas. Assimilative policies and practices developed then continue to shape the hidden barriers that stall the implementation of critical literacy edu-cational reform today.

However, differences in the impact of these policies across different immigrant groups may be best explained as a difference in the racialization process experienced by Europeans v. non-European immigrants. For example, despite the initial experiences of racialization suffered by Irish, Italian, Polish, and Russian immigrants, it was always presumed that these European immigrants could be absorbed into the cultural definition of the American nation-state. No such presumptions were held for non-European populations. Joseph Check argues that:

> Racial "indigestion" caused by European immigrants arriving faster than they could be absorbed may have been unpleasant, but at least it presumed that in time, through schooling, they could be absorbed and the dilution on "our national stock" reversed. This presumption rested, in turn, on an implied kinship between all Europeans, whether "noble" Anglo-Saxons or "degenerate" Irish, Italians, Poles, or Russians. No such kinship was presumed to exist with non-European groups: Native Americans, Asians, Puerto Ricans, and African-Americans. There was no argument for assimilation-through education, and so widespread exclusion from mainstream activities (including education) or relegation to second-class status was a common practice for these groups.[3]

This raises the idea of kinship and its relationship to linguistic preservation and literacy development. The use of a shared language (or dialect) is one way in which a sense of kinship is constituted and participation in communal life guaranteed. Kinship here includes cultural processes that make social relations meaningful, including forms of address, modes of reckoning and story telling.[4] It is through linguistic practices that kin subjects are produced or incorporated as members of a collective subjectivity, while providing them with a sense of identity and belonging.

In cases of cultural and linguistic subordination, contact with school power and authority is used to erode students' cultural values and linguistic practices, resulting in generational alteration in the practices and collective life of the group. One of the tactics most often employed by the dominant society in transforming and administering diverse communities of working-class immigrant populations is to restrict their movement within society and access to opportunities. The key here is to create institutional conditions by which communal surplus labor (or participation) can be redistributed, in order to outlaw or obstruct participation away from communally shared rituals and practices designed to reinforce and reproduce the original kinship structures[5]—thus, redirecting identity, participation and loyalty to the State.

Institutional efforts to obstruct minority language development and its uses, as well as curtail rituals or cultural practices, are all implicated here. Again, such practices tend to become most severe during times of imperial expansion or economic decline, when the "other's" language and culture are determined to be a detriment to national unity and the process of capital accumulation. Over time, institutional assimilative practices and policies, tied to restriction within both schools and the labor market, function to normalize the loss of primary culture and language among immigrant and indigenous populations. Meanwhile, local manifestations of racism in the guise of language and cultural subordination within schools are intricately linked to the movement of capital and the consolidation of political power. Hence, the struggle for an emancipatory education in general, and a critical bilingual literacy education, in particular, must be grounded in an understanding of the contemporary political economic contexts that shape the lives of English language learners, their families, communities, and teachers.

II

> There is no unity between school and life, and so there is no automatic unity between instruction and education. In the school, the nexus between instruction and education can only be realized by the living work of the teacher.[6]

Critical literacy is intricately tied to the *living work* of the classroom teacher. This is so because literacy and ideology are linked by the very relationships that sustain material inequality and exclusionary social forces within schools and society. More simply put, ideology shapes the legitimation of knowledge within schools and underlies the hidden curriculum of literacy instruction. This constitutes an important factor, as we consider the values and beliefs of classroom teachers and the educational formation that they have received in teacher education programs.

Unfortunately, despite the increasing diversity of the U.S. population, many of the traditional assimilationist pedagogical notions persist. These notions essentially incorporate, on the one hand, the belief that cultural and class differences are a malady that must be remedied or stomped out in order for students from subordinate populations to achieve academically. While, on the other hand, students who are considered to be the "other" are deemed intellectually suspect, unable to accommodate to academic expectations. As a consequence, there are few curricular materials for literacy instruction that fundamentally respect the cultural and class values and beliefs that students bring to the classroom. Instead, teacher perceptions of English-language learners and other students considered outside the mainstream, along with the pedagogical materials they employ often function to perpetuate notions of deficit and structures of inequality—despite their well-meaning efforts.

If teachers, then, are to engage effectively in the literacy instruction of English language learners, they must be prepared to examine their personal views and perspectives related to how minority students use language, their accents, and their variant speech patterns. Yet, this alone is not enough. Beyond individual reflection, teachers must also become cognizant of the ideological dimensions that underscore the curriculum and educational processes that are most often promoted in schools for the teaching of language and literacy skills. They must learn to decode the racialized, gendered, class, homophobic, and other oppressive meanings that are encoded in curricular materials that appear neutral and benign, yet carry real consequences of social exclusion.

It is also important that teachers understand the manner in which ideology has a profound impact on educational policies and curricular decisions made by federal, state and local policymakers. Ideology, with its unexamined assumptions, functions as an interpretive lens to both determine and sustain relations of power, as well as the distribution of authority, resources and opportunities within schools. As such, ideology is central to the material subordination of working class populations, including language minority communities. In this respect, linguistic and cultural formations represent significant material forces that are meaningful in light of the racialized conditions of inequality faced by oppressed populations.

If teachers are to become effective in their classroom literacy efforts, they must rigorously interrogate the consequences of literacy policies and practices in the lives of the students they teach. The unwillingness of many teachers to step outside the familiar terrain of mainstream literacy instruction converts them into just another problem that students must contend with in the course of their public school education. To counter this phenomenon, teachers must embrace, as part of their *living work*, a willingness to question critically the consequences of their literacy practice. They must interrogate the consequences of the curriculum they are implementing and pursue with students and their parents possible alternatives that can function to create opportunities for "getting real" about the literacy development needs of English language learners. "Getting real" here also means that teachers recognize cultural, cognitive, and linguistics differences as central to a dynamic and stimulating educational environment and an authentic democratic body politic. In addition, teachers must take note that differences in culture and cognition are also tied to class differences and alternative strategies for survival, within the context of not only a highly diverse but economically unjust society.

In order for teachers to contend successfully with the differences in problem-solving and communication styles that their students bring to the classroom, they must work to create a living classroom experience of democracy, where oppressive structures can be courageously challenged and transformed. Unfortunately, the failure to engage with the realities of students' lives results in an educational process that is abstracted and disconnected. This ultimately functions to further alienate English language learners not only from their relationship with their teachers, but from their ability to participate actively in the knowledge construction necessary to become empowered and literate human beings.

In making a case for a critical literacy instruction that engages stu-dent experience as a central component does not mean that this is where the educational process ends—for this is actually the beginning. Critical literacy constitutes an approach where the intimacy of learning established between teachers and students opens the field for examining and re-examining together their particular and shared views of the world. In this way, they learn to affirm, question, resist, challenge and transform their views, through an experience of knowledge construction grounded in a democratic process of participation, voice and action within their everyday lives.

When teachers utilize a critical approach to literacy development that integrates issues associated with culture, language and class, they are better able to infuse vitality into the emancipatory dynamics of their teaching. By so doing, English language learners are challenged to consider in meaningful ways the experiences and perceptions that shape their cultural histories and class realities. This is tied to assisting students to explore the manner in which they ascribe meaning to their everyday lives and how they construct what they perceive as knowledge and truth. Literacy here becomes more than just simply a functional process of learning to read and write. Instead it becomes an opportunity for students not only to learn about themselves and their histories in ways that are meaningful and in concert with the struggles they face each day, but also to become critically literate about the manner in which power and privilege operates. They learn through their personal engagement with texts and the world how, why, by whom, and for whom knowledge is constructed. This speaks to a literacy development that fosters the confidence of students to openly question, think creatively, become inventive, and hence, more expansively explore and name their world.

Inherent in a critical approach to literacy development is also the expectation that reflection, dialogue and action—namely praxis—within the classroom will also function as the foundation for establishing school involvement among the parents of English language learners. Through an emphasis on critique, dialogue and conscientization, a critical pedagogical approach to literacy supports a problem-posing pedagogy, in which the relationship of students to teachers and teachers to parents is, unquestionably, dialogical in nature. Within the context of critical dialogue, there must exist an implicit faith in the capacity of teachers, students and parents to participate collaboratively in the process of schooling, with each having something to contribute and gain through their participation. It is through meaningful interactions and working collectively for the benefit of students that teachers and parents construct intimate relationships of solidarity and school-community coherence.

Lastly, ethics, civic responsibility and literacy as a moral imperative must also be central to how teachers comprehend the significance of critical literacy, particularly in the lives of disenfranchised students who must constantly resist the oppressive structures and practices that defile their dreams. Whether to affirm, resist or transform their lives, English language learners must develop the skills for voice and participation—skills that can be garnered only through their development as ethical and moral subjects of history. It is for this reason that Paulo Freire[7] repeatedly insisted that ethics had to occupy an increasingly significant role in our pedagogy and our scholarship. As critical educators of literacy committed to democratic principles of everyday life, ethics must be understood as a political and pedagogical question—that in the final analysis constitutes a moral one. For without morality, education becomes an instrument of oppression. Here, we must not mistake morality for moralism. Instead, being moral is to explore deeply the texture and quality of human behavior, ideas and practices in the living—which cannot be done by abstracting our students from their social surrounding, from their culture, from their language, or from their histories of survival. This requires instead that we interweave the pedagogical with the moral and political, where literacy development recognizes that "ethics is about excelling at being human, and nobody can do this in isolation." [8]

Along the same vein, the pernicious legacy of racisms—the multiplicity of ideologies, policies, and practices that result in the racialization of populations and the destruction of linguistic rights—must be understood in the context of everyday struggles and the formation of student identities. Here, identities are often conditioned by a capitalist-inspired language curriculum, fueled by fabricated consumer sensibilities of gendered, racialized, homophobic, and nationalist patriotic notions of "the good life." Moreover, it is this core ideological process that sustains the ravages of globalization and that must be challenged and dismantled, if poverty and human suffering are to be eradicated.

In light of this, critical educators must come to terms with the fact that injustice "is not an unfortunate aberration of capitalism, but an inescapable outcome and an essential condition of its successful economic functioning. Capitalism is—and this is surely as clear today as it ever was—a social system based on class and competition."[9] Capitalism functions as a globalized system, which requires as its prerequisite, the deep impoverishment and exclusion of three-quarters of the world's population. Given this reality, it is unfortunate that so many theories and practices of literacy development function conveniently to deaden and annul opposition to the capitalist order, while existing social con-trols are conserved, even in the wake of increasing impoverishment and incarceration. Meanwhile, the marketplace continues to move people away from few, modest needs to the creation of many false needs, through the use of advertising and the belief that consumption equals happiness.[10] Oftentimes, these beliefs are carefully hidden behind the assimilative notions and ideas that masquerade as literacy education in the United States.

Additionally, capitalism disembodies and alienates our daily existence within the larger society and within classroom life. As the consciousness of teachers and students becomes more and more abstracted, they become more and more detached from their material bodies. For this reason, it is absolutely imperative that critical educators acknowledge that the origin of emancipatory possibility and human solidarity resides in our bodies. And as such, language constitutes the vehicle by which the body's needs, wants, desires, fears, joys, aspirations, and hopes are expressed. Given the relationship of the body to a student's linguistic faculties, critical literacy development cannot effectively take place in the absence the body's full participation. This is only possible when students' expressions are engaged in ways that communicate to them that they matter in real and meaningful ways.

With all this in mind, this volume represents a significant effort by critical educators and scholars in California concerned with the current conditions that English language learners face today, within a post-227 school context. What they share in common is a deep commitment to an emancipatory pedagogy, consistent with a political project for social justice, human rights and economic democracy. Most clearly, their teaching and scholarship entail a critical understanding of literacy development, grounded in the mutuality and interdependence of our collective existence as cultural citizens of the world and living subjects of our own histories.

Footnotes

[1] Nettle, D. and S. Romaine (2000). *Vanishing Voices: The Extinction of the World's Languages*. London: Oxford Press (19).

[2] Skutnabb-Kangas, T. (2000). *Linguistic Genocide in Education—or Worldwide Diversity and Human Rights*. New Jersey: Lawrence Erlbaum Associates.

[3] Check, J. (2000). *Politics, Language and Culture*. Westport, Conn: Praeger (50).

[4] Amariglio, J.L., S.A. Resnick, and R.W. Wolff (1988). "Class, Power and Culture" in C. Nelson and L. Grossberg (eds.) *Marxism and the Interpretation of Culture*. Chicago: University of Illinois Press.

[5] Ibid.

[6] Gramsci, A. (1971). *Selections from the Prison Notebooks*. New York: International Publishers (35).

[7] *Freire, P.* (1970) Pedagogy of the City *(New York: Continuum)*
——————— (1996). Pedagogy of Hope. *New York: Continuum*.
——————— (1998) Teachers as Cultural Workers. *Boulder, CO: Westview*.

[8] Eagleton, T. (2003). *After Theory*. New York: Basic Books (142).

[9] Gindin, S. (2002). "Anti-Capitalism and Social Justice." *Monthly Review*, Vol.53, No.9 (3).

[10] *Brosio, R. A. 1994*. A Radical Critique of Capitalist Education. *New York: Peter Lang*.

Chapter 1

Literacy Ideologies: Examining Curricula for English Language Development & Biliteracy

by Karen Cadiero-Kaplan, Ph.D.
San Diego State University

Abstract

The intent of this chapter is to guide those concerned with the achievement of English language learners in an exploration of ideological constructions of the curriculum designed to teach English to bilingual students. The author argues that in order for teachers to engage in the teaching of literacy for English language learners as well as native language speakers of English, there is a need to examine not only one's own ideology towards literacy, but that of materials, processes, and programs that are most often promoted in schools for the teaching of language and literacy. This chapter defines functional, cultural, progressive, and critical ideologies and their relationship to teacher practice and implications for student learning.

"There can be no disinterested, objective, and value-free definition of literacy: The way literacy is viewed and taught is always and inevitably ideological. All theories of literacy and all literacy pedagogies are framed in systems of values and beliefs which imply particular views of the social order and use literacy to position people socially."
(Auerbach, 1991 p 71)

In order for teachers to engage in the teaching of literacy for English language learners as well as native language speakers of English, there is a need to examine not only one's own ideology towards literacy, but that of materials, processes, and programs that are most often promoted in schools for the teaching of language and literacy. For it is one's ideology that has the most profound impact on the resulting policy and curricula decisions made from federal to state and local levels of schooling.

Schooled literacy ideologies are at the center of political debates regarding definitions of what it means to be a 'literate' person in school
and society. However, such discussions are not engaged by teachers
and curriculum developers when considering what materials will be
utilized or programs to be implemented to teach English, language,
and literacy. Such processes of critical discussion are particularly important when considering the cultural diversity of the student population in schools across the country and specifically in California, as ideologies of schooled literacy are "generally acquired outside one's primary social network" and are "used for gauging success or failure
within the institution" (Powell, 1999, p. 24). According to Galindo
(1997), "ideologies are systems of ideas that function to create views
of reality that appear as the most rational view; a view that is based
on 'common sense' notions of how the social world ought to be." (p.
105). As a result, any approach to literacy is based on an assumption of
normative practice.

From a social political standpoint the 'normative practice' is the most
prevalent system of ideas that underlies and informs social and political action (Jary & Jary, 1991), with social and political action being state
adopted curriculum and teaching methods for literacy and language
development in schools. For example, in California two commonly
used state approved curriculum series that have been adopted by many
school districts are the Houghton-Mifflin *Reading* series and the *Open
Court* series by McGraw Hill. Thus, the narrowing down to these two
curricula choices reflects the standard or norm from which all teachers
at a particular school or district will teach and in turn use to develop
reading literacy for their students. Processes of curricula decisions such
as these most often occur without any discussion of the ideologies that
inform each curriculum and related materials. So, from all the literacy
and language arts options, practices, and possibilities for teaching Language Arts in a large urban school district, in most instances only one
or two programs are selected to meet the needs of all students in the
school district, even if the district has students from diverse language,
culture and socio-economic backgrounds.

As a former school teacher, and now university professor, I continually see how many teachers and teacher educators rarely consider
or discuss their orientations, beliefs, values, or processes for literacy
instruction from political or ideological perspectives. What often occurs is that teachers and educators discuss their own beliefs about literacy and language development, but may not readily notice that their
practices or beliefs are not reflected in the materials or teaching meth-

ods presently adopted as 'best practices' by schools. At the same time teachers are in the position to continually respond to curricula shifts for language and literacy instruction without engaging in further interrogation of the ideologies that inform the materials, methods or practices or policies that inform the curriculum.

This chapter attempts to engage these 'normative assumptions' of both English superiority and the 'best' literacy practices, which are present within language development and English Language Arts programs. In this chapter when speaking of curriculum and methods of teaching language and literacy it is important to recognize that any approach or way of defining what it means to be 'literate' is based on ideological constructs, and as such has the possibility of positioning literacy and outcomes in several ways. One, for "individual empowerment and personal voice, basic morality and skill" or for "rudimentary 'functional' job skills" are designed to serve the interests of maintaining the status quo (Luke, 1990). Depending on ones ideology, literacy in English is deemed either to empower learners as critical thinkers who are capable of understanding and communicating information critically and analytically in one or more languages, or literacy is a skill that is necessary in order for one to be able to decode words, comprehend written and oral directions and function in English within society with the skills necessary to perform specific job tasks. Both of these ideological approaches are found presently within the English curriculum utilized for teaching English language learners in schools. In this chapter the focus will be on how English literacy is taught and language developed in schools where most students are learning English as a second or third language.

Curriculum Defined

In order to engage 'ideology' of curriculum it is important to first understand what is meant by the word curriculum. Kincheloe (1998) relates an important concept about how we define curriculum in terms of the etymology of the word. The noun 'curriculum' is derived from the Latin verb, 'currere' which means running a race course, an action. However, in education, the interpretation of the word is reduced to the noun form, which means 'the track'. This difference in definition is crucial for it implies that curriculum, as it is commonly used, is dictated and static, not fluid or changing. According to Kincheloe (1998), who references Patrick Slattery,

Mainstream educators forget that curriculum is an active process; it is not simply the lesson plan, the district guidebook, the standardized test, the goals and milestones, or the textbook. The curriculum, Slattery continues, is a holistic life experience, the journey of becoming a self-aware subject capable of shaping his or her life path (Kincheloe, 1998; p. 129).

When this interpretation is applied to the literacy curriculum in schools it is far too easy to see how the noun form has flourished when we look at the instructional practice of tracking or ability grouping. This occurs in the English curriculum when students are grouped according to their reading levels, and in English as Second Language (ESL) classrooms, where students are grouped according to language proficiency, thus dictating which 'curriculum' they will 'receive'. This definition of curriculum as an object is reflected in the current federal mandate of No Child Left Behind (NCLB) which advocates a curriculum that is specific and measurable with success being defined by a single test score. Additionally, and most importantly, such groupings and mandates are a form of social control which function to "provide differential forms of schooling to different classes of students" (Giroux, 1983 p. 47).

To work towards this understanding of the literacy curriculum, I will define and describe the four common *ideologies of literacy* that inform pedagogy and practice: **functional literacy, cultural literacy, progressive literacy and critical literacy**. Since these are definitions of literacy it is important to note that all of these forms are understood in contexts where oral language, reading and writing occur and address questions that go beyond skill level to aim, purpose, audience, and text (Macedo, 1987; Luke, 1988; Gee, 1990; Williams & Capizzi-Snipper, 1990). In this chapter I consider them to represent various forms of *schooled ideologies* because each literacy is "a discourse that carries with it certain expectations for thinking, behaving, and using language" (Powell, 1999, p. 24).

Table 1: School Literacy: Ideology & Practice

Literacy Ideology	*Common Teaching Practice Approach*
Functional	Grammar Method; Phonics & Skills English Immersion; Standardized Instruction; Decoding; Phonics
Cultural	Great Books (Bloom); Cultural Literacy (ED Hirsch) English Submersion/Transition Programs
Progressive	Maintenance Programs; Whole Language (Edelsky); Communicative Approach (Krashen); Student Centered; Constructivist (Vygotsky)
Critical	Democratic Practice (Dewy); Critical Pedagogy (Freire)

As can be seen in Table 1, each of the four ideologies of literacy is linked with common approaches for reading and language instruction, and related to specific curriculum models. For example, a Functional Ideology is related to the Phonics Skills Method of language instruction, a commonly used method in the teaching of English in many classrooms. The purpose of the table and the review that follows is to illustrate the connection between the ideology, which informs curriculum and practice, and the resulting practice we often see in classrooms. You will note that few models exist for the critical ideology. As will be illustrated, this form of literacy while not considered a 'common' practice within mainstream educational settings, is in fact a schooled literacy concept that functions to reveal the underlying assumptions of text, literacy and language development that exist within the sociopolitical structure of schools. The intent here is to place literacy in a school context in which individuals can critically reflect on their own beliefs about literacy and the processes they utilize within their practice. It is important to note that the intent is not to position one form of literacy over the other, but rather to examine each form critically within the context of lived realties and schools.

Schooled Literacy Ideologies

A *functional literacy* ideology is reflected in a curriculum that teaches students the skills deemed necessary to participate in school and society successfully. A person who is functionally literate is generally considered an individual who has the ability to read and write "well enough to understand signs, ads, newspaper headlines, fill out job applications, make shopping lists, and write checks" (Williams & Capizzi-Snipper, 1990), most often this is considered to be a fourth to sixth grade level of competency. According to Myers (1996) the functionally literate curriculum was originally defined under the premise of *English for All* and focused on "sequential reading skills, grammar skills, and some of the 'basic' cultural information usually found in literature with an emphasis on decoding and analyzing parts of texts-as-objects" (p. 34).

In this practice, reading is focused on decoding words and analyzing text by answering specific reading comprehension questions both orally and in writing. Comprehension is focused on being able to understand vocabulary, directions, and meaning from text (Oakes, 1985; Shannon, 1989). As such, the functional literature curricula and related instructional practices are "pre-packaged and restrictive; with a pedagogical focus that is individualistic, behaviorist, and competitive" (Kelly, 1997, p. 10). Such instruction does not encourage students to challenge the texts or ideas presented and "reduces the concept of literacy...to the pragmatic requirements of capital; consequently, the notions of critical thinking, culture, and power disappear under the imperatives of the labor process and the need for capital accumulation" (Giroux, 1983, pp. 215-16).

Historically, functional literacy was most prevalent during the Industrial Revolution (1870-1960) and is equated with the 'school as factory' model (Giroux, 1983; Myers, 1996) which continues to be part of most curriculums, and has recently gained conservative support in the development of state standardized testing and the "back to basics movement" (Luke, 1988; Apple, 1995) and most recently as part of NCLB mandates. This curriculum is traditionally found in many elementary, junior and senior high school pull out programs for English language development and remedial English classes that include a high number of English language learners. In many schools these classes are referred to as 'accelerated or academy' which are labels that reflect not 'high expectations and achievement' but a form of tracking for lower performing students. In these classrooms teachers focus on basic skill instruction including phonemic awareness, spelling, and specific reading skills including comprehension and discrete writing tasks (Giroux, 1983; Oakes, 1985; Apple, 1995). At the same time, the functional literacy curriculum reinforces job related skills and behaviors, not only by teaching students how to respond to individual questions and form, but in praising compliance to classroom rules and procedures and tasks.

One noticeable and disturbing distinction in such classrooms is that student representation tends to fall along ethnic and class lines, in that the majority of students found in functional literacy classrooms tend to be ethnic minorities and/or are from poor or working class neighborhoods (Giroux 1983; Oakes, 1985). The functional literacy curriculum is the focus that drives Title I school programs, where "functional literacy all too often becomes the schools' tacit educational objective for non-native English speakers" (Williams & Capizzi-Snipper, 1990, p. 6). As such, "nonstandard literacies of minority groups and the poor are regarded as deficits or deprivations rather than differences" (McLaren, 1988a, p. 214). Presently, many school programs serving high numbers of language minority students have implemented functional literacy curricula, such as *Open Court* by McGraw Hill Publishers. This reading curriculum includes the "systematic direct instruction in phonemic awareness and phonics, grade-appropriate decodable text" (American Federation of Teachers, 2001).In this practice, reading is focused on decoding words and analyzing text by answering specific reading comprehension questions both orally and in writing. While these are skills deemed necessary for 'learning to read' such processes utilized uncritically may do little to engage students' native language, culture and voice, since processes are teacher directed and require single correct responses.

A *cultural literacy* ideology focuses on the teaching of morals and values, with a curriculum that includes the classics or 'Great Books' (Bloom, 1987; Hirsch, 1988; Ravitch, 1985; Myers, 1996). In contrast to a functional ideology, a cultural ideology places priority on the information readers bring to discourse. That is, members of a society need to have a common background knowledge in order to understand messages through conversation, newspapers, and other media that report on historical events or engage ideas from world literature and history (Hirsch, 1988; Williams & Capizzi-Snipper, 1990). In order to be successful and competent citizens of society and the world, there is specific cultural knowledge that all Americans need to know in order to be successful and competent citizens. Specifically, this literacy consists of a network of information that all proficient readers possess (Hirsch,

1988). Individuals who support and promote a cultural literacy ideology (Bloom, 1987; Hirsch, 1988; Bennett, 1995) assume that this knowledge is part of the Western upper middle-class culture. They write that in order for those from lower socio-economic classes and/or linguistically and ethnically diverse groups to be successful in school and to have access to the 'mainstream' culture, they must be taught this 'cultural knowledge'. Critical theorists refer to cultural knowledge as 'cultural capital'. "Cultural capital refers to Pierre Bourdieu's concept that different forms of cultural knowledge, such as language, modes of social interaction, and meaning, are valued hierarchically in society" (Leistyna, Woodrum, & Sherblom, 1996, p. 334). This cultural literacy focus is highly embedded in standardized test measures that are part of state and federal accountability systems as well as testing used for higher education as part of the entry criteria for college admissions (e.g., GRE, SAT).

According to Hirsch (1988) "cultural literacy constitutes the only sure avenue of opportunity for disadvantaged children, the only reliable way of combating the social determinism that now condemns them to remain in the same social and educational condition as their parents" (p. xiv). As such, it is believed that by gaining this knowledge students from marginalized communities, including those who speak a language other than English, will be able to more successfully partici-pate in oral and written discourses of the mainstream culture (Bloom, 1987; Hirsch, 1988; Williams & Capizzi-Snipper, 1990). While this concept may seem altruistic and seems to provide all with a common ground for communication, it is problematic as it negates individual and community experiences. The issue is that this "common knowledge' is defined by an elite group of individuals. This network of knowledge consists of "a descriptive list of the information actually possessed by literate Americans" (Hirsch, 1988, p. xiv). Gee (1990) states that

> cultural models are the basis on which choices about exclusions and inclusions and assumptions about context are made; every word in the language is tied to a myriad of interconnecting cultural models. It is entirely unlikely that anyone could overtly teach the whole network of cultural models for any one culture. It is also unlikely that anyone learns any very significant cultural model just by overt instruction, by being told about it (p. 90).

However, it is just such a process that the ideology of cultural literacy advocates. To be 'culturally literate' students are taught common core values, morals, and culture, specifically the 'dominant culture' through mainstream history and the 'Great Books' (Giroux, 1988). This type of curriculum is deemed by critical theorists as "closed and elitist; its pedagogy is authoritarian, humanist, and universalizing (Kelly, 1997, p. 10). Aronowitz & Giroux (1993) state, that the curriculum of cultural literacy

> has long been invoked as an argument for the reproduction of elite's. It is a position that advocates a social system in which a select cadre of intellectuals, economically privileged groups, and their professional servants are the only individuals deemed fit to possess the culture's sacred canon of knowledge, which assures their supremacy (p. 26).

The curriculum of cultural literacy reflects an ideology based in the Western traditions and which attempts to control not only the spaces where knowledge is produced, but to make a certain core knowledge 'legitimate'. Such literacies are linked to positions of power. As Giroux (1983) states, reading (in this tradition) is a process of understanding and further reduces the notion of understanding to "learning content deemed appropriate to the well-educated citizen" (p. 212). Within this conservative perspective the individual experience, if different from that espoused by the canon, is not valued. Thus, the knowledge that is deemed 'literate' by proponents of cultural literacy is one that

> "portrays a nation propelled by a harmony of interests, despite internal and external pushes and pulls, that in the end work out of the good of all. De-emphasized in this harmonious view is labor history, women's history, immi-grant history, class discord, challenges to capitalism, political dissent, and the continuous struggle over the purposes of the nation" (Coles, 1998, p. 104).

The curriculum of cultural literacy can be found in Advanced Placement English classes, College Preparatory courses, and in many private high schools. This curriculum is designed to prepare students for positions of power and as such, rejects individual experience while discrediting or ignoring the influences of popular cultures, ethnic and racially diverse cultures, and cultures grounded in sexual communities (i.e., feminist, gay) all of whom, it could be stated, reject Christian-Judeo ethics which serve as the cornerstone of appropriate morality in such 'elite cultures' (Aronowitz & Giroux, 1993).

In this practice, the individuals for whom the cultural literacy curriculum is supposedly designed are not the ones receiving it. I contend it is because those students who 'lack the cultural knowledge' are most often found in schools or classrooms that focus primarily on functional literacy, where the emphasis is on skill and drill. As such, the ideology of cultural literacy, while advocating for the disenfranchised, is positioned to maintain societal inequity. Such an elitist ideology deems alternative cultural and linguistic discourse communities within this society as illiterate, since literacy is determined solely on the basis of knowing and being able to converse, read, and write about those topics that make one literate (McLaren, 1988). However, this ideology does not dismiss the ideology of functional literacy. On the contrary, those advocating for a cultural literacy recognize that the functional skills of decoding and comprehension are necessary in order to be successful in reading and having access to cultural knowledge.

As Hirsch (1988) states "it (cultural literacy) takes no position about methods of initial reading instruction beyond insisting that content must receive as much emphasis as skill" (p. 1). Therefore, cultural literacy does little to engage the ideology that informs functional literacy; rather it indirectly supports such methods that serve to maintain the status quo. Cultural literacy however, is in contrast to progressive literacy, where value is placed on individual experience as a mode of acquisition of skills and knowledge. It is towards this ideology I now turn.

A *progressive literacy* ideology "advocates personal discovery with a curriculum that is student centered and liberal" (Kelly, 1997 p. 10). The goal of teachers of progressive literacy during the 19th century was to "integrate literacy instruction into the curricula based on children's interests, needs, and inclinations; that is to make literacy a natural consequence of children's study of their physical and social environment" (Shannon, 1989 p. 10) This curriculum is based on many of the democratic ideas postulated by John Dewey (1916) that include the free interchange of ideas between students and educators and the notion of a student-centered curriculum. Such a curriculum attempts to "affirm and legitimize the cultural universe, knowledge, and language practices that students bring into the classroom (McLaren, 1988a, p. 215). A progressive literacy ideology requires students and teachers to engage in the process of learning to read and write based on themes and topics of interest to students, with vocabulary related to the lives of students (Shannon, 1989). This ideology is seen in the whole language curriculum which is derived from constructivist and cognitive views of learning.

Constructivism is the belief that people are active seekers and constructors of knowledge and thus come into the classroom environment with innate goals and curiosities (Nicaise & Barnes, 1996). This practice views social discourse as part of learning, and most importantly, views students as agents over their learning (Randolph & Everston, 1994; St. Pierre-Hirtle, 1996). Unlike cultural or functional ideologies, that define set skills or knowledge bases to 'access' literacy, a progressive approach values the literacy or knowledge discourse the individual brings to text, which can be seen in the theory of whole language learning.

This approach views reading as an intellectual process, "where the comprehension of text is deferred to the development of new cognitive structures which can enable students to move from simple to highly complex reading tasks" (Macedo, 1991, p. 152). This is not to say the <u>mastery</u> of technical skills of decoding and comprehension is not important, rather skills are developed with the "explicit recognition of the importance of some form of shared cultural knowledge" (McLaren, 1988a). Where the functional approach supports teaching the parts that make up the whole, a whole language theory

> exemplifies a constructionist view of learning, according to which concepts and complex processes are constructions of the human brain; therefore, research suggests, the greater the intellectual and emotional involvement in learning, the more effective the brain learns, uses, and retains what is learned (Weaver, 1998, p. 7).

Thus, a progressive literacy is found within a constructivist curriculum that begins to recognize the voices of linguistically and ethnically diverse students.

Accordingly, a progressive ideology supports whole language processes since the basic principles of a whole language approach include the belief that literacy is best developed when individuals make many of their "own decisions about what to read, write, and learn" and further will "learn to read and write by being supported in actually reading and writing whole texts-not by being required to do limited activities with bits and pieces of language" (Weaver, 1998, p.7). In contrast to functional literacy, which reduces reading to a technique of 'learning to read', progressive forms of literacy support a process of 'reading to learn'. Thus literacy, reading, writing, listening, speaking, and thinking develop in an integrated manner (Au, 1998). McLaren (1988a) cites a passage from Shirley Brice Heath that articulates the importance of reading to learn, she states:

> Readers make meaning by linking the symbols on the page with real-world knowledge and then considering what the text means for generating new ideas and actions not explicitly written or said

> in the text. The transformation of literacy skills into literate behaviors and ways of thinking depends on a community of talkers who make the text mean something. For most of history, such literate communities have been elite groups, holding themselves and their knowledge and power apart from the masses (from McLaren, 1988a, p. 215).

The progressive ideology, while valuing the knowledge of the individual, still postulates a curriculum that remains apolitical and unexamined from a critical perspective (Freire & Macedo, 1987; McLaren, 1988; Macedo, 1991). This concern falls within the ideology of critical literacy. Within a critical literacy approach, educators and learners work in community to fully develop the academic skills of ethnically and linguistically diverse students and their community. To accomplish this task requires literacy approaches that,

- Promote the use of first and second language for full literacy development;
- Encourage processes of reading the world and the word;
- Include the use of dialogue, texts, and multiple discourses inside and outside the classroom to inform curriculum and learning;
- Engage learners in critical debates so they become well informed about their world;
- Take up literacy from the perspective of student lives in relation to their present experiences;
- Provide literacy experiences beyond written text to social action and empowerment;

The ideology of *critical literacy* is defined by Kelly (1997) as "a literacy of social transformation in which the ideological foundations of knowledge, culture, schooling, and identity-making are recognized as unavoidably political, marked by vested interests and hidden agendas" (p. 10). This literacy, although student centered, expands on the progressive notion of personal discovery in that it places both the teacher and student in a historical context and requires both to interrogate the curriculum, which, in this literacy, is that of the everyday world (Macedo, 1994; Kelly, 1997; Powell, 1999). Students involved in a critical literacy curriculum read the world and the word, by engaging through dialogue, texts, and discourses that occur both inside and outside the classroom.

Aronowitz and Giroux (1993) take the critical literacy perspective and apply it to the canons of cultural literacy articulated above and remind educators that "the democratic use of literary canons must always remain critical... and must justify themselves as representing the elements of our own heritage" (p. 38). It is within this critical approach that literacy curricula are the most powerful and transforming because such practices take on the texts and discourses of cultural literacy by placing them within a historical and cultural context, providing a sense of place through historicity. Within a critical environment, historicity allows students to read any text or discourse from the perspective of their lives in relation to their present experience (McLaren 1988; Darder, 1991). Thus, a critical literacy curriculum includes historicity as a core element in reading cultural literacy. This approach requires that students (and teachers) not read history as an unfolding of 'Absolute Spirit' and record, but as a record told from one perspective that can be held up for examination from other perspectives (Apple, 1995; Freire, 1998). Through this critique students (and teachers) uncover the myths of 'civilization' which places the cultural literacy canon in real world contexts and rather than revered, are transformed. Powell (1999) supports such engagement and transformation, and states that a new definition of literacy is needed. A definition that acknowledges the hegemonic power structure while valuing the discourses of groups that have traditionally been marginalized,

> such a literacy would enable students to question and to engage in critical dialogue so that they might be educated for participation in a democracy. It would provide a means for identifying and reflecting upon those ideological and social conditions that serve to profit a few at the expense of many (p. 20).

Therefore, critical literacy moves beyond text to social action. Based on the above review of functional, cultural, and progressive literacy ideologies, it could be argued that critical literacy is not a schooled ideology, since it is designed to engage the individual in evaluating and demystifying school texts found in both functional and cultural literacy perspectives. However, in order for students to have access to any one particular ideology or form it is within the context of schools that such critique and engagement should and must occur. In this sense then critical literacy is a schooled concept and should be considered in any discussion surrounding literacy curriculum and practice. Thus, while I support more critical and progressive ideologies of literacy, I acknowledge the use of functional and cultural literacy, as they have the potential to inform engagement in text and also the potential to redefine 'cultural' literacy to include the culture of the many as opposed to the few.

As teachers and educators, we do not typically view literacy as both pedagogy and social action; rather literacy is typically viewed as a method which is apolitical (Cadiero, 2001). Based on this review of literacy ideologies it is "evident that schools have not traditionally been encouraged to teach all discourses; rather they have been commissioned to teach a particular discourse, or form of literacy—a literacy that is sanctioned by dominant groups" (Powell, 1999, p. 13). Thus, schools have not readily accepted the teaching of critical literacy for it reveals the underlying hegemony in literacy practices and further, within school practices and curriculum. Giroux (1987) states that

> Gramsci viewed literacy as both a concept and a social practice that must be linked historically to configurations of knowledge and power, on the one hand, and the political and cultural struggle over language and experience on the other. For Gramsci, literacy was a double-edged sword; it could be wielded for the purpose of self and social empowerment or for the perpetuation of relations of repression and domination (p. 1-2).

Thus, literacy curricula decisions are most often the result of conscious choices that are tied to the political and economic structures of our country. Further, they are inherently ideological in that they are "qualified by the context of assumptions, beliefs, values, expectations, and related conceptual material that accompany their use by particular groups of people in particular socio-historical circumstances" (Knoblauch & Brannon, 1993, p. 15). As a result, the manner in which literacy, and further language, is taught is based in a particular ideology that clearly defines 'literate' acts through reading, writing and engagement with text (Powell, 1999). In the case of ethno-linguistic students, the nation's language policy for literacy curricula and practice is presently functional at best. This practice provides for the very basic skills of English language development. Therefore, teachers and educators must be cautious not to confuse '*what is* with *what must be*' and not fail to recognize that "common practices come not from divining decree, but from choices made sometime, somewhere" (Hinchey, 1998, p.7) within specific historical and cultural contexts that support both political and economic structures. One way teachers can begin to analyze and engage in unveiling their ideological approach and that of their curriculum and practice is through critical literacy practices. How can every day student language, activities, and experiences be used to create critical thinking and reflection?

Critical Literacy in Practice

In response to recent conservative ideological policies such as NCLB and policies towards literacy that are narrow and limit student voice and achievement, many teachers and researchers have responded by articulating critical practices and policies for literacy curricula and programs. Powell (1999) states that "what is needed in our society is a different definition of literacy-one that acknowledges the hegemonic power structure and that values the discourses of groups that traditionally have been marginalized" (p. 20). Critical teachers and teacher researchers have begun to rise to this challenge in practice by valuing student voice, linguistic diversity, cultural pluralism, and democratic schooling while emphasizing literacy, biliteracy and multi-literacy competencies as processes of empowerment. Freire and Macedo (1987) point out that,

> A central assumption of critical literacy is the recognition that knowledge is not merely produced in the heads of experts, curriculum specialists, school administrators, and teachers. The production of knowledge is a relational act. For teachers this means being sensitive to the actual historical, social and cultural conditions that contribute to the forms of knowledge and meaning that students bring to school (p. 15).

Critical teachers support and promote the creation of classrooms where student voices, experiences, and histories are a valued part of the course content. At the core of such practice, or praxis, is Paulo Freire's concept of 'consciensization'; the ability of teachers to take on both 'exposition and explanation' as elements of critical dialogue (Freire, 1998). And, as such, teachers provide critical classroom activities that "help students analyze their own experiences so as to illuminate the processes by which those experiences were produced, legitimated, or disconfirmed" (McLaren, 1988 p. 217). In such an engagement, teachers are no longer dispensers of knowledge, promoting only one canon or belief, but become agents of change in assisting students in seeing themselves within the larger historical, political, cultural, and economic structures where student voices exist.

Shor (1992) advocates for participatory problem-posing as a way to transform academic knowledge into themes accessible to students. Such a curriculum "involves a two-way transformation of subject matter and discourse" (p. 77). In such classrooms the subject matter is introduced by the teacher as a problem for students to reflect on from their cultural-historical perspective and in their own language. In presenting the curriculum in this manner, students (who come to class with their own universe of words, themes, and experiences) are challenged to go beyond themselves, into a new territory not generated from their backgrounds. As a result, the role of the teacher is that of a democratic problem poser (Shor, 1992). The following is one example of how two educators put critical problem posing into practice in an inner-city high school English class.

In Linda Christensen's (1998) high school English class, students blamed themselves and/or their teachers for their poor performance on a pre-university entrance exam. One student stated "well, if you'd taught us subject-verb agreement instead of writing, I'd have a better score on the verbal section" (p. 41). Rather than let such comments go, Christensen and her colleague, Bill Bigelow, asked students to write about a test they had taken. Both teachers also wrote papers on the topic as well. The following day the students and teachers read their papers, while seated in a circle, to the class. In doing this the teachers became part of the community, and as Christensen states "if we didn't write and share, we would (have held) ourselves above and beyond the community we (were) trying to establish". The members of the community noted common themes among the stories and then began to question why they all came away from their testing experiences feeling threatened and stupid. It is important to point out that comments such as these are prevalent in K-12 settings across the state of California as students take state mandated tests including the California Achievement Test (CAT-6) or the State Tests of Academic Achievement (STAR). The teachers felt that while the students could see similarities across experiences in the class, there was little solace because now they all felt they should/could have done better. This is the place where, I believe, most educators leave such discussions and, in doing so, fail students and perpetuate the hegemonic structures of ability groupings.

However, Christensen and Bigelow saw immediately that the students needed "a broader context in which to locate their feelings...they needed to explore where these so-called aptitude and achievement tests originated and whose interests they served" (p. 43). In response to this, Christensen and Bigelow introduced students to the creators of intelligence testing through books and writings on the Intelligence Quotient (IQ) and Educational Testing Service (ETS) testing histories and philosophies. From these readings students maintained dialogue journals and completed a historical study of standardized testing. Some facts the students discovered were that "SAT questions measured access to upper-class experience, not ability to make appropriate analogies" and the "vocabulary did not reflect the everyday experience of these inner-city kids" (p. 45). This lesson shows how students were able to engage in dialogue and research and begin to reveal hegemonic structures and, as a result, students were able to see more clearly how the test did not take into consideration their experiences, and lead students to an awareness of what 'knowledge' was required to pass such exams.

Christensen (1998) points out that while this activity allowed students to "break down their sense of isolation and alienation, while they pushed toward a greater knowledge of how this society functions, they were moved less often to hope and action and more often to awareness and despair" (p. 46). This observation is critical because, while the teacher felt this was a positive activity, she was able to recognize that in order to foster change and empowerment among students, further interrogation was required. Christensen met with her colleague and engaged in a dialogue about how the lesson could be handled in the future and together they determined that in another lesson she could "put kids in touch with real people who haven't lost their hope, who still fight and plan to win" (p. 46).

The curriculum activities described were guided by teachers to promote praxis and consciensization, one key to implementing a critical literacy curriculum in the classroom. This lesson further demonstrates that reflection must occur not only during the process of dialogue with students, but also beyond the lesson with other teachers. In this manner real attitudinal change and empowerment can and does occur. Catherine Walsh (1996) sums up best the realities and challenges critical literacy educators face when constructing and implementing curriculum that has as its focus the transformation of school curriculum and society:

> Really becoming involved in the reshaping of our society and schools is difficult not only for the work it entails but because it challenges us to deal with uncomfortable, threatening, tension-producing concerns that are personal as well as social in nature. It necessitates a thoughtful consideration of our individual perspectives and positions including how they came to be as well as a thoughtful consideration of our pedagogy and practice in and out of the classroom. Such a process requires that as educators, we become more cognizant of the differences between our students and ourselves racial, ethnic, cultural, economic, residential, and generational (growing up in today's world vs. when we were children) of the overt and hidden ways that some students' voices are trivialized and denied, and of the ways that the policies,

relations and instructional, and language practices of our classrooms and school reproduce the power and ideology of the broader society (p. 227-228).

In order to truly change literacy curricula in our schools teachers must be willing not only to engage in a critical dialogue with each other and school administrators, but become activists for democratic schooling, facing both the risks and rewards such an endeavor entails. Although the course may be lengthy and arduous, it is only through such activities that the hegemonic structures of ability grouping and tracking can begin to be revealed and dismantled. Once such oppressive tracks are removed then more students may have the opportunity to explore, create, critique and transform curriculum within environments that value and encourage individual voices through dialogue, reflection, and action. This formative curriculum approach is not only more academically and socially demanding, but also promotes biliteracy, critical consciousness and principles of democratic schooling.

Author Note: This chapter is derived in part from my text "The Literacy Curriculum and Bilingual Education: A Critical Examination" Published by Peter Lang, New York (2004).

References

Apple, M. (1995). Education and power. New York, NY: Routledge.

Aronowitz, S. & Giroux, H. (1993). Postmodern education: Politics, culture & social criticism. Minneapolis, MN: University of Minnesota Press.

Au, K.H. (1998). Social constructivism and the school literacy learning of students of diverse backgrounds. Journal of Literacy Research. 30, 297-319.

Auerbach, E. (1991). Literacy and ideology. In W. Grabe (Ed.), Annual review of applied linguistics (pp. 71-85). New York: Cambridge University Press.

Bennett, W. J. (Ed.). (1995). The children's book of virtues. Needham Heights, MA: Simon and Schuster Publishing.

Bigelow, B. (1998). The human lives behind the labels-The global sweatshop, niki, and the race to the bottom. In W. Ayers, J. Hunt, & T. Quinn (Eds.), Teaching for social justice: A democracy and education reader (pp. 21-38). New York, NY: Teachers College Press.

Bloom, A. (1987). The closing of the American mind: How higher education has failed democracy and impoverished the souls of today's students. New York, NY: Simon & Schuster.

Cadiero-Kaplan, K. (2002). *Literacy Ideologies: Critically Engaging the Language Arts Curriculum*. Language Arts Journal, 79 (5), 372-392.

Cadiero-Kaplan, K. (2004). The literacy curriculum and bilingual education: A critical examination. New York, NY: Peter Lang.

Christensen, L. (1998). Writing the word and the world. In W. Ayers, J. Hunt, & T. Quinn (Eds.), Teaching for social justice: A democracy and education reader (pp. 39-47). New York, NY: Teachers College Press.

Coles, G. (1998). Reading lessons: The debate over literacy. New York, NY: Hill & Wang Publishers.

Darder, A. (1991). Culture and power in the classroom: A critical foundation for bicultural education. Westport, CN: Bergin & Garvey.

Dewey, J. (1916). Democracy and education. New York, NY: Free Press.

Freire, P. (1998). Pedagogy of freedom: Ethics, democracy and civic discourse. New York, NY: Rowan & Littlefield Publishers.

Freire, P. & Macedo, D. (1987). Literacy: Reading the word and the world. Westport, CT: Bergin & Garvey

Galindo, R. (1997). Language wars: The ideological dimensions of the debates on bilingual education. Bilingual Research Journal, 21 (2 & 3), 103-141).

Gee, J. P. (1990). Social linguistics and literacy. New York, NY: Falmer Press.

Giroux, H. (1983). Theory and resistance in education: A pedagogy for the opposition. Granby, MA: Bergin & Garvey Publishers.

Giroux, H. (1987). Literacy and the pedagogy of empowerment. Introduction in P. Freire & D. Macedo. Literacy: Reading the word and the world. Westport, CN: Bergin & Garvey. 1-29.

Giroux, H. (1996). Living dangerously: Multiculturalism and the politics of difference. New York, NY: Peter Lang.

Hinchey, P. (1998). Finding freedom in the classroom: A practical introduction to critical theory.

Hirsch, E. D. (1988). Cultural Literacy : What Every American Needs to Know. New York, NY: Vintage Books.

Jary, D. & Jary, J. (1991). The Harpers Collins Dictionary of Sociology. New York: Harper Perennial.

Kelly, U.A. (1997). Schooling desire: Literacy, cultural politics, and pedagogy. New York, NY: Routledge.

Kincheloe, J. (1995). Meet me behind the curtain: The struggle for a critical postmodern action research. In P.L. McLaren, & J.M. Giarelli (Eds.), Critical theory and educational research. New York, NY: State University of New York Press.

Knoblauch, C.H. & Brannon, L. (1993). Critical teaching and the idea of literacy. Portsmouth, NH: Heinemann.

Leistyna, P., Woodrum, A., Sherblom, S. (1996). Breaking Free: The transformative power of critical pedagogy. Cambridge, MA: Harvard Educational Review.

Luke, A. (1988). Literacy, textbooks and ideology: Postwar literacy instruction and the mythology of Dick and Jane. New York, NY: The Falmer Press.

Macedo, D. (1991). The politics of an emancipatory literacy in Cape Verde. In C. Mitchell & K. Weiler (Eds.) Rewriting literacy: Culture and the discourse of the other. Westport, CN: Bergin & Garvey.

Macedo, D. (1994). Literacies of power: What Americans are not allowed to know. San Francisco, CA: Westview Press.

McLaren, P. (1988)a. Culture of Canon? Critical pedagogy and the politics of literacy. Harvard Educational Review. 58, 2. 213-234.

McLaren, P. (1988)b. Life in schools: An introduction to critical pedagogy in the foundations of education. New York, NY: Longman Press.

Myers, M. (1996). Changing our minds: Negotiating English and literacy. Urbana, IL: National Council of Teachers of English.

Nicaise, M. & Barnes, D. (1996). The union of technology, constructivism, and teacher education. Journal of Teacher Education, 47, 3, 205-212.

Oakes, J. (1985). Keeping Track: How schools structure inequality. New Haven, CN: Yale University Press.

Powell, R. (1999). Literacy as a moral imperative: Facing the challenges of a pluralistic society. New York, NY: Rowman & Littlefield Publishers.

Randoloph, C.H. & Everston, C. (1994). Images of management for learner centered classrooms. Action in Teacher Education. 16, 1, 55-63.

Ravitch, D. (1985). The schools we deserve: Reflections on the educational crises of our times. New York, NY: Basic Books.

Shannon, P. (1989). Broken promises: Reading instruction in 20th century America. Granby, MA: Bergin & Garvey Publishers.

Shor, I. (1992). Empowering education: Critical teaching for social change. Chicago, IL: University of Chicago Press.

St. Pierre-Hirtle, J. (1996). Constructing a collaborative classroom. Learning & Leading with Technology, 23, 7, 19-21.

Walsh, C. (1996). Making a difference: Social vision, pedagogy, and real life. In C. Walsh (Ed.), Education reform and social change: Multicultural voices, struggles, and visions (pp. 223-239). Mahwah, NJ: Lawrence Erlbaum Associates.

Weaver, C. (1998). Reconsidering a balanced approach to reading. Urbana, IL: The National Council of Teachers of English.

Williams, D. & Capizzi Snipper, G. (1990). Literacy and bilingualism. White Plains, NY: Longman.

Winterowd, W.R. (1989). The culture and politics of literacy. New York, NY: Oxford University Press.

Chapter 2
Emerging Diné Decolonization Theory and Its Application to a Language of Decolonization

by Larry W. Emerson
Native American House
University of Illinois Urbana-Champaign

Abstract

This article focuses on micro level (personal) decolonization theory development and proposes that as an Indigenous community, the Diné, like many Indigenous, non-western communities, are in a unique political and cultural position to gain insights into decolonization theory and practice. Diné decolonization theory is relatively new in the field of Diné studies. This article examines the relationship of colonialism theory to a 2002 study by the author regarding Diné (Navajo) emerging notions of decolonization.

Introduction

Diné decolonization theory is relatively new in the field of Diné studies. It ascribes that two dimensions of decolonization exist: the macro that applies nationally and the micro that applies personally. This chapter will focus on micro level theory development and will propose that as an Indigenous community, the Diné, like many Indigenous, non-western communities, are in a unique political and cultural position. An opportunity for the Diné exists to rely on a politic of *hozho* (e.g. harmony, beauty, balance, respect) as a basis for its political action regarding conscientization, language recovery, and decolonization.

I will be assuming that colonialism is a fact of Diné existence and cannot be described as a "thing of the past". Instead, it is an ever-present phenomena and a living reality affecting how we, Diné, live our lives within the "Diné Nation" or within the "Navajo Reservation". We define and term our geopolitical location, as a "nation" or "reservation", based upon our historical, political, and cultural orientation.

Who are the Diné?[1]

The Navajo Nation, also called *Diné bikeyah* (lands of the Diné), is roughly 25,000 square miles in size and is situated inside what the Diné call the Four Sacred Mountains. Two of these mountains are in Colorado: the eastern mountain, called *Sisnaajinii*, near Alamosa and the northern mountain, called *Dzil Dibenitsaa*, near Durango. The southern mountain, called *Tsodzil*, is near Grants, New Mexico and the fourth, the western mountain, called *Dook'o'osliid*, is near Flagstaff, Arizona. If these Four Sacred Mountain boundaries are strictly applied, then the area is much larger than the 25,000 square miles presently defining Navajo Nation boundaries. The present Navajo political boundaries are located in northeastern Arizona, southeastern Utah, and northwestern New Mexico.

There are more than 290,000 tribal members according to 2002 population data, and 110 communities, also called "chapters," organized in five "agencies" or administrative districts within the Navajo Nation. There are an estimated 88 clans grouped in ten clan families. Diné creation stories describe the origin of four clans that have expanded to the present number. Clan groupings also reflect the incorporation of various tribal and non-Indian groups such as the Mexican, Ute, Pueblo, or Bilagáana (white people). I prefer to use the word *Diné* rather than "Navajo" because the word *Diné* is our own word. The word *Navajo* is more than likely a Spanish derivative.

Diné origins are in continual dispute. On the one hand, anthropologists and linguists point to cultural and linguistic similarities to Athabaskans of the Alaskan region and to migration data which suggests that Diné are relative newcomers to the American southwest having traveled to the present site from areas now known as Canada and Alaska as early as 900 A.D. and as late as 1200 A.D. Diné traditionalists dispute these findings indicating an origin within the Four Sacred Mountains. Both sides could be right. One has to be flexible in defining what origins, intermarriage, clan histories and stories, and communal consciousness mean. In any event, Iverson (2002a) says the argument is irrelevant since it hardly matters what historic geographic relations Diné come from. The Diné have created their community within this particular environment. Anything that might have happened before what happened in their present location is prelude. There were no "Navajos" at that time. At the same time "[W]ithout this place, there could be no Diné" (Iverson, 2000a, p. 6).

Issues Working Against Traditional
Indigenous People

It has been estimated that "of the 120 military conflicts in the world (as of 1987), three-fourths involved *native nations* seeking to hold off or free themselves from larger, occupying *nation-states*..." (Mander, 1991, p. 342). Indigenous rights extend to both domestic and international arenas. The following is a list that represents typical problems and issues faced by Indigenous peoples. A typical list of issues for Indigenous people include (Barreiro 1999):

1. Being landless in terms of whole tribes, communities or groups.
2. Being politically, culturally, socially, economically, linguistically, and spiritually marginalized.
3. Responding to imperialism through self-determination efforts.
4. Having to claim sovereignty despite imperialism and colonialization efforts by nation-states.
5. Having to proclaim the right to be consulted regarding western or modern efforts at "development."
6. Having to define cultural and spiritual rights against corporate commodification of plant medicines, "cultural and archeological artifacts", songs, prayers, and ceremonies, language, or against the codifying of genetic structures and pools primarily by corporations, aided by governments.
7. Having to define hunting, fishing, and other subsistence rights.
8. Having to define religious rights to protect languages, songs, ceremonies, and prayers.
9. Having to engage in all issues of cultural difference which includes ones aspirations, interests, and choices.
10. Having to define human rights which come out of an experience of dehumanization, discrimination, murder, land theft, and genocide.
11. Having to wrangle with international law and United Nations bureaucracy.
12. Seeking political autonomy that embraces economic, social, and cultural jurisdiction that is unique and specific to each Indigenous group and its relationship to a nation-state.
13. Seeking financial and other aid or resources to assist in self-determination efforts (e.g. land recovery).
14. Having to seek redress for ill effects of imperialism and colonization on physical, mental, emotional, and spiritual health of the people.

15. Having to defend ecological and environmental concerns within Indigenous territories or areas considered as sacred sites.
16. Having to articulate opposition to the monocultural assumptions of modernization or westernization in its pedagogical form so that Indigenous traditional knowledge can develop more culturally and spiritually appropriate educational experiences for its members, and
17. Having to contend with language shifts and losses caused by genocidal practices.

The Diné people face, and have faced, similar issues, making colonialism and imperialism a constant and consistent theme in Diné history.

Micro and Macro Colonialism

In studying colonialism, one tries to make sense of the historical, political, social, cultural, and economic responses of both the colonizers and the colonized to the phenomena of conquest, control, oppression, imperialism, and domination. One studies both the resistance to and maintenance of colonialism. Issues such as gender, class, race, ideology, identity, hybridity, or indigeneity are integral parts of the colonialization – decolonization theoretical framework. In the study of colonialism, one observes a dialectical or oppositional relationship between the colonizer and the colonized.

Macro decolonization is characterized by formal agreements in which colonizer governments release political control over a colonized people. Formal decolonization, culminating after fierce anti-colonial struggle, was a major theme of the 1900s. Notable are the 93 or so decolonizations that occurred after 1945 (i.e., India, Pakistan, Burma, West Africa, Algeria, Senegal). These agreements involved geography and political destiny. The themes underlying these decolonizations rested on three main destinies: (1) to restore an imprisoned nation by allowing it to see its own history, (2) resistance is an alternative way of seeing history, and (3) to reject separatist nationalism in favor of an integrated human community (Said, 1993).

Micro-level decolonization occurs with individuals or small groups. Micro decolonization is a conscious and deliberate attempt to heal from colonialism's historical, intergenerational traumatic effect on ones emotional, physical, intellectual, and spiritual being. Many Indigenous forms and processes of decolonizations are possible and are being developed and recorded by activists and scholars (Colorado 1999;

Whelshula 1999; Hibbard 2001; Johnson 2001; Woodworth 2001; Burgess 2002). Processes tend to involve culture, stories, and traditional knowledge and are employed to uncover old and new ways to heal, decolonize, transform, and mobilize oneself and ones community, while developing new modes of political and cultural self-determination (Smith 1999).

Decolonization studies can inform us on how we can engage a decolonization practice and critical awareness of our lives, particularly at the local level. Indeed, it is possible for one person or for a community to acknowledge, understand, and reject many hundreds of years of accumulated colonized behaviors, beliefs, attitudes, and practices.

History of Indian/Native Education

Colonialism and education are linked since schools and education were used as colonizing tools to control the Diné and other Native tribes. I am going to ascertain how colonization has operated in schooling and education, so that the notion of decolonization might have better meaning.

Colonization through education, beginning with the 1868 Treaty, took several forms: the ignoring of Indigenous cultures; the manner in which colonizer educators limited educational opportunities through lack of funding or adequate facilities; elitist policies that presumed to spread education to the masses; the use of education as a tool for assimilation; and the use of European languages as the instructional language for Indigenous peoples (Albach 1995).

Colonial education took place in two forms: missionary or religious schooling and later public schooling (Smith 1999). However, with Native American peoples, there was another layer of colonial schooling: the role of the U.S. Congress and executive branch which took paternalistic and imperialistic responsibility to research, finance, plan, design, implement and evaluate schools for Native children through its national boarding schools. At times U.S. policy favored mixing Christianity with schooling Native children. (Adams 1995; Reyhner and Eder 2004).

In terms of Native American and Diné education and colonization, Iverson (1978) writes that the historical events between the United States and Indian nations include the project of educating Native Americans. These periods or eras are termed *'civilization" to removal, extermination, incorporation, assimilation, revitalization, termination, and self-determination.* The notion of formal education of Native peoples is embedded in the ideology of each of these eras. According to Iverson (1978) the consistent policy, despite all these eras, has been that of *American-ization*. American Indian education has always been for the purpose of promoting order in the larger American society through an ideology promoting mobility of Indian children to the American mainstream.

Iverson (1978) also explores the legal and other complexities in the colonization of Native Americans: Natives were considered "domestic dependent nations" in 1832 by the U.S. Supreme Court; of having Native lands declared reservations to be held in trust by the U.S. governmentforits"wards" (i.e. the Nativepeoples);andthecomplexjurisdictional problems between states, federal, and tribal levels of government. She suggests that the establishment of a Jesuit school for Florida Indians in Havana in 1568 was a starting point in Indian education, followed by the opening up of free common schools for Natives in 1645, and a 16th century era of Christianization using schools as sites for religious conversion (Iverson 1978). Colonizers described Native people as savages, devils, pagans, heathens, and the like. This indicates Euro-American racism which was the underpinning for educational efforts on behalf of Native peoples (Iverson 1978).

There was also resistance: Handsome Lake's proposal in 1820 that Iroquois educate Americans; under Tecumseh the rejection of schools in the War of 1812; and the emergence of the peyote religion and Ghost Dance ceremony in the mid 1800s all indicated firm rejection of Americanization. The Cherokee response in the 1800s was an attempt to peacefully adapt Cherokee ways to American notions of education. Seqoyah developed a Cherokee alphabet in the mid 1800s. However, despite Cherokee innovations, they were forcibly removed from their aboriginal territories through the 1830 Indian Removal Act (Iverson 1978). Diné parents' response in the late 1800s to the mid 1900s was simply to hide their children from school officials.

In 1850 the Congress created a "Civilization Fund" which provided a subsidy to religious schools. "Manual labor schools" to provide "education in Christianity" did not work well either. (Trennert 1988). If there was a lapse in assimilation efforts towards Native people, it might have been during the Civil War. The "Friends of the Indians" tried to influence new policies and to make the Indian a "useful factor in our [American] body politic" (Iverson 1978). An Indian Peace Commission in 1867-1868 recommended the establishment of an effective way to resolve the Indian "problem" through the use of schooling (Trennert 1988).

The Carlisle Indian School, established in 1880, was developed as a vo-cationally-oriented, military-style boarding school in Carlisle, Pennsyl-vania to systematically school Native youth in the direction of Ameri-canization, Christianization, and Eurocentric notions of civilization. Key aspects of the Carlisle Indian School were the assimilation of the Native students into the American economy, and the use of English as the only language of instruction. The 1890s also brought unprec-edented U.S. sanctioned efforts to Christianize Native youth using the tool of education (Iverson 1978). In 1899 Indian Commissioner Thomas Morgan wrote that "Indians must conform to the white man's ways, peaceably if they will, forcibly if they must." Such words tended to be the guiding philosophy behind much of Indian education (Trennert 1988).

The Phoenix Indian Industrial Boarding School, Phoenix, Arizona between 1891 and 1935 is an example of a boarding school institution with assimilationist ideals that was neither a success nor failure. In 1891 the school, under the leadership of the federal government, began in an old hotel by enrolling 31 Pima and 10 Maricopa male youth, initi-ating a "Soap precedes Godliness" policy of assimilation through baths, new clothes, and a new militarized schedule of life. Local business-men, mainly farmers, saw opportunities to use Indian youth as farm laborers, although school officials discouraged the idea of Indian youth's mixing with the white race because, in the school's eyes, the role of Indian youth was to go home to civilize their own people. The Phoenix Indian School was seen early on as the tool by which 35,000 Indian people of the Arizona region would eventually be civilized (Trennert, 1988).

Federal officials, from the Commissioner on Indian Affairs in Wash-ington D.C. to the local school, were responsible to oversee the school's leadership, administration, funding, curriculum, evaluation, and poli-cies. The Office of Indian Education was created within the Bureau of Indian Affairs (BIA) to implement federal Indian education policy that created standardized rules for all Indian schools under federal control. Indian Commissioner Thomas Morgan in the late 1890s believed Indi-ans could be assimilated in one generation.

Between the early 1900s and 1930 federal policy made little chang-es. Trennert (1988) reports that in 1928 the Merriam Report, which was a detailed study condemning the BIA's poor performance and activities in politics, economics, and education, pleaded for vast changes in the BIA's educational policies of forcing Indian children to schools far away from home, towards policies in favor of local schooling for Indian children in their home environment. The report castigated the BIA for allowing Indian child labor programs that allowed students to go to school half of the time and work the other half; for instituting school jails; and for policies and practices of brutality. Indian school facilities were outdated and dilapidated. The report argued that there was a need for better trained teachers, a better curriculum, less oppressive discipline policies, better health and sanitation practices, better safety standards, and better dormitory standards which advocated for shutdown of bay areas that were large sleeping rooms in favor of individualized dorm rooms. The mid 1900s brought little change. Boarding schools reflected the need to industrialize, assimilate, acculturate, Americanize, and Christianize Native youth. The 1928 Merriam Report to the U.S. government reported mass cases of the kidnapping of children by schools and other abuses.

The 1934 New Deal era attempted to incorporate Native culture and language in its BIA curriculum. However, World War II, the Korean War and the American conception of itself as a world power did little to change American political notions that the Indian people needed to be civilized. For the Navajo, in 1946 the Bureau of Indian Affairs (BIA), located within the Interior Department, called their policy the "Special Navajo Education Program". This Special Education program (not to be confused with PL 94-142) eventually grew into a federal project that placed thousands of Diné children from Arizona, New Mexico and Utah into boarding schools. In 1946, the BIA estimated that there were 24,000 Navajo children of which 6,000 were in school.

There were Indian responses throughout the years to the civilization effort. Many Indian children fought back at teachers, resented the alien environment of the boarding school, resented the schools for forcibly separating them from parents and community, and fought back concerning humiliating punishments instigated by school officials. Students ran away from school in great numbers, conspired to set school buildings on fire, or simply embarked on passive resistance campaigns (e.g. work slow downs, defiance, pranks, disrupting school routines, or displays of pride in cultural and traditional ways). Parents also resisted compulsory attendance policies, poor health conditions at schools, and likely equated white encroachment with school policies (Adams 1995).

In the 1950s, U.S. Congressional legislation culminated in various efforts either to assimilate or destroy Native people. Assimilation came again in the form of education policy, but an early 1950s Indian termination policy, aimed at disintegrating Native governments and lands, added fuel to the "Indian problem" fervor. "Termination" meant to end U.S. government–tribal relations through the official destruction of legal ties of "Indian tribes" to the U.S. government by giving individual title to land, hence destroying "nations" reservations.

The 1960s and 1970s brought heated Indian protests against the schools and other policies, particularly after a 1969 Senate Subcommittee release of an Indian education report entitled, *Indian Education: A National Tragedy, a National Challenge*. Indian students under BIA tutelage consistently scored lower then non-Indian students, generally received a less than quality education, and continued to suffer abuses under federal school policies.

By 1960 there were some 50,249 Navajo students in boarding schools in places like Sherman Indian School, Riverside, California, Chilocco Indian School in Oklahoma, Phoenix Indian School in Arizona, the Cheyenne-Arapaho Indian School in Oklahoma, Steward Indian School in Nevada, Chemawa Indian School in Arizona, Haskell Indian School, the Riverside Indian School in California, and the Fort Sill Indian School in Oklahoma, and the Intermountain Indian School in Provo, Utah. From 1946 to 1959 the Intermountain Indian School enrolled a total of 20,232 Navajo youth (Roessel 1979).

By the 1970s many Native youth were now in public schools, and in 1973, about 70 percent of the 250,000 students were in public schools, compared to 1926 when some 4/5ths of students were in federal boarding schools. The U.S. policy to terminate the legal status of Native tribes resulted in causing Native youth in certain states to switch to state public school education. Needless to say, in the 1970s the dropout, basic skills, parental participation in schools, student health, and student behavioral statistics and rates for Native youth were deplorable (Iverson 1978). A shift or transfer of schooling from the federal to state governments, while ignoring tribal potentials for educating their own, is a sign of colonization.

In the 1960s two Diné communities as a way of resisting U.S. education policies and trying to adapt to them, created "community schools" in which they attempted to balance the curriculum between Americanization and a pro-Diné curriculum. This effort eventually helped influence U.S. education policy towards the Native people through the 1975 Indian Self-Determination and Educational Assistance Act. The Indian Self-Determination Act promoted the take-over of educational programs operated by the Bureau of Indian Affairs (BIA) by local community groups.

Today most Native students (estimated at 80%) are in public school-shat are "close to home." Most Native students receive schooling under a typical public school process. The rest (some 20%) are being schooled in biculturally oriented and federally funded "community, contract or grant schools."

A Study of Diné Notions of Decolonization: 19 Markers

In a 2002 Shiprock, Navajo Nation study (Emerson 2002) partici-pants (called "relatives" in the study) engaged in a colonialization-decolonization dialogue for an average of 36 classroom hours. There was a high focus and concentration around three (3) recurring themes, issues, and concepts. These were in regards to (1) traditional modali-ties[2], (2) decolonization, and (3) the dichotomy between traditional and modern worlds in a colonial context. There were seven (7) additional node areas of critical importance as well, judging from participant con-versations. These surfaced in regards to (1) components of colonialism, (2) Diné cultural values in relation to colonialism, (3) gender issues in relation to colonialism, (4) neocolonialism, (5) healing in relation to in-tergenerational trauma and colonialism, (6) concerns with hierarchal structures as examples of colo-nialism, and (7) follow-through actions regarding what to do with the colonial-decolonization framework in-formation.

Relatives also identified nineteen (19) critical markers pertaining to their notions of Diné micro-scale decolonization. Relatives chose to express these nineteen (19) markers of decolonization by imagining decolonization taking place and shifting from one type of social struc-ture to another. These structures are the hierarchy and heterarchy. The Relatives felt that hierarchy best represents a colonial structure, while heterarchal structures in a circular relationship to one another exem-plify Diné precolonial traditional society. They felt that other Diné could benefit by knowing these areas through the study of decolonization.

A summary of these nineteen areas follows as expressed in sum-mary form by research participants.

1. *INQUIRY, RESEARCH, AND LEARNING*.
   V.K. The need to use inquiry, research, and learning to go beyond what the everyday self knows regarding oppression and methods to free oneself from it. Only by engaging oneself in this manner can one decolonize.

2. *DECOLONIZATION: RECOGNIZING AND BRINGING ABOUT AWARENESS TO YOURSELF.*
V.K. Teaching oneself and learning about traditional knowledge[3] and methods because you have to figure out where you're at, how acculturated you are. You have to recognize this first. Then start from there. That's the first step to looking at decolonizing yourself. Because if you're not aware of it, you may not know if this is the right thing or the appropriate way to be. You could be acting more through a colonization mode of being. The first step in decolonization is awareness.

3. *SHAME-BASED ISSUES IN DECOLONIZATION.*
M.B. I was always wondering why Navajos carry a lot of shame (laughter), carry a lot of shame no matter what. I didn't really understand its intergenerational aspects. Being colonized, colonization theory helps explain where shame came from and how it brought a lot of change. We're not so consciously aware of it. We're not really aware of it.

4. *HEALING: FROM GENERATIONAL TRAUMA TO PRESENT TRAUMAS.*
V.K. The reason I chose healing is because we went through a lot of traumas from our ancestors on. Our ancestors lived with trauma. Being traumatized by the Europeans, our way of living, was really harsh. Our treatment by them wasn't at a humanistic level. We weren't allowed to be human, to be who we are. It forced us to be not human. I think we've been through a lot of that generationally. Decolonization healing is really important in order to heal our spirits, to heal our minds, to heal our physical, and to heal our emotions. Because the only way we can heal is to learn though our own healing. We all have needs too to have that healing from colonization. There is no room for that and that healing will lead to setting you free from oppression.

5. *IGNORING GREED, POWER (DECOLONIZATION).*
G.G. Acting out something that you're not…is a result of shame. Acting out in a way as when showing off, you are not really acting your true self. In doing so we ignore where we, as Indigenous people, came from. Because of colonization, we are ashamed of our hoghans (traditional homes). We call people that come from there "*na'a'ah.*" Some of those principles and teachings from which we learn–like being

uncivilized - and that is what we ignore. In our traditional way, because we're trying to be human, we're not trying to be the "show off."

6. *RESISTING COLONIZATION.*
    A.L. Mine is on resisting colonization. That's what I learned. I can deal with colonization. Recognizing it and resisting it, I can be who I am. I can be very cultural. I did grow up on the reservation and have lived in the sheep camp. I had the whole nine yards. I do speak my language which I wish I could speak well. That's what I want to do. Also I want to be better in English. I can't write either. But, I'm o.k. with it too, as a second language. And the part is I am making an effort. That's what counts.

7. *POSITIVE AND NEGATIVE EFFECTS OF TEACHING TOOLS.*
    G.G. At one time we just put our kids in school not really knowing what school was. We hadn't been too aware of it. [Today,] people just put kids in schools and a lot of teachers say "we're not babysitters." A lot of people say that. But now, we have a good understanding of what school is and how we want our children to turn out. And what we'd like them to focus on and what we'd like them to learn. Although the negative things, the bad things, that it has, we understand that now and we can point those out.

8. *LIBERATION AND EQUALISM.*
    V.K. I think that's part of decolonizing, meaning that learning to have respect no matter- there's no such things as categories, or stereotyping, and all that, judgmental criteria, qualifications. Decolonization is being equal and working together in energy in liberation and being free from all that... having internal happiness. I think that's the first thing -the spiritual is the first thing we look for to find that happiness.

9. *HUMILITY.*
    M.B. After you recognize who you are as a Navajo person, you have to kind of get back into where you came from, like she was saying *"hazho'o joogaal"* (where are you going in life?). It's all part of being humble. *Adahaznidzingo, t'aa doole'i* - you have to be humble... in that rat race, trying keeping up with the Jones', it isn't our concept. Knowing who you are and being ok with yourself.

10. <u>*REVERENCE FOR SELF; FAITH IN SELF; SOUL SEARCH (SELF).*</u>
G.G. *Adaholdizin* (self-care, self-respect, to hold the self in sanctity). We don't know how to do that anymore. *Adaholdizin dooleel* (to cause care, respect). In order to do that you have to have faith in yourself. Faith is not just believing in like a higher power. But, it's having faith in yourself, believing yourself, about who you are. It all comes back to who you are.

It all falls back on *"haadee'shi joogaal"* (where is one coming from). *Bahajooba'jijiyaanidi, doo ya't'ehii adahholdizin dooleel* (to have compassion, to have a sense of well being can be an attainment). In order for you to figure out you have to have faith in yourself and you have to go soul searching for yourself too. *Ha't'iisha' eiya bike'neizhghei ?* (Where is the hurt or pain?) *Ha't'iisha' eiya jooglogo anali?* (Where is the happiness?) *Ha't'iisha' eiya hanaa' k'eizh to' anali?* (Where are the tears?) *Hashit'ehi jiiyigoo ei analniizchaad?* (Where is your physical health?) All that has something to do with your soul searching. *Haadee'shii ajoogaal nidee'eibinashji bee adaholdilzin.* (It is these from which self-respect, self-knowing, self-sanctity comes from).

And that reverence and faith and soul searching? *Nizhonigo bee joogaal bee nijighao eiya* (Only if you walk in beauty) . . . you're not easily persuaded. You're not even going to be persuaded. You have your boundaries up. *Ei t'aa bahoziniyee'* (That is obvious). What you want is where you're going.

11. <u>*EARTH, SKY, SUN, DAY, MOON, NIGHT - OUR KINSHIP.*</u>
G.G. *Ei eiya, jo aawiiji nhazdzaan bi kaa' t'aa doo yadilhil, aadoo jinahoogleel, do k'e nahoo. (on ohoogleel.* (Our mother earth, our father sky we will attain a sense of kinship relationship) As the sun goes down we age. As the moon changes, too, throughout the month, we age. *Ako, nahazdaan bikaa' yeedaligii, t'aa anit'ee' nizhonigo bee nihahonidzin* (On the surface of our mother earth we all walk in beauty from being dressed that way). Every last inch of us, our humanity...*johanaa'ei do' akot'e.* The sun as well, *aldo', adinidiin, nilchi', ei akot'e ako. Eit'aa ayisii bee needaadoo, ei bee hwoni'na, joni* (So, too, with the sun, the moon, the wind, we walk and live our lives). . . in the ceremonies, and in the songs, and in the prayers, there healing process that's going through. The healing process, eiya, those are the main deities that they talk to. *Nda'jookahigii. Nahazaan bikaa' adahoot'ehigii, a'at'ehii*

(we ask, we plead, and desire, all from the surface of mother earth) so, when the ceremonies are going on, *aa naagha. Doo bahozinda. 'ha'atiishii bee adilji doodzil* (something from somewhere we get our strength of mind, body). A lot of times there's no medicine for it. *Bee'adoolnilgo, doo biighada. Doo at'iidah. Aadoo, doo alchinda. Doo bahoozinda. Do bichi nahwi' naago, k'e na (inaudible)* But you know that person is going down. *Ha'tishba* (inaudible), physically *doo bahozinda Ahotd'eiigaal nidi.* But through ceremonies, *ha'atiishii,* every little thing, down to the last thing, *azee baholo, jini.* Some of the ceremonies, *t'a nilei* But, yet, *kodiyaa. Ahaadidah doo naah nįį'hoolzhiayaa. Ahaadidah doo anaago dee'shii,* there are new things that are happening. They are so different than what happened a long time ago. Now, these new things are happening because of colonization. *Ei yaa agii, azee' eedi lahgo anih.* That's the part of healing that I think that we're going to have to go back to. *K'ad aajoo nahoolzhish, k'ad aajoo nat'aa Diné nida nd'eestii… ba' adaalne' k'ad,* it's getting different. At the same time, *la'doo atiida.* Those things are happening.

12. *HUMANISTIC LEVEL: SPIRITUALITY.*
    V.K. On that part, I think spirituality plays an important role in decolonizing. I think that helps balance out things on who you are. And being Diné means that everything's connected. The way colonization is disconnected is by (inaudible), but spirituality brought in everything (inaudible). The part that I'm really struggling now with colonization is spirituality. . .

13. *EQUALITY.*
    A.L. Equality means regardless of what way we were, we're all equal. We're all human and that's the way decolonization is. The way others look at it is that we're less than. But in the spiritual way, we're human and equal. That's our traditional concept … With the way my spirituality (inaudible), that's where my self-esteem came in. I was taught that everybody's equal. … in there the medicine told that that everybody's equal. Everybody has a say. Everybody's gifted. You're no better than, no less than anyone. That's the way we are taught. So with that, when I got out of the reservation and working in the medical [field] with all these doctors and nurses who were Bilagáánas, working there, and here I was a Navajo.

Some looked down on me, but actually what I was told through my [culture] is be proud of who you are, you're not going to be (inaudible). They started off somewhere just like you. They left home and this is where they ended up. They just didn't become doctors in one week. They worked so hard to get there. And you can do the same thing. There's nothing wrong with where you're at. So that's where I kind of thought of how the Bilagáána is. It doesn't phase me anymore after that. I guess I'm the type of person who needs to do more research on that. You know, finding that reality. Just like now. That's why I'm taking this class. To learn more about it, instead of just saying that's good enough for me. That's not me. I like to do more in-depth research before I actually say, oh yeah, that's true. I find out there's a clarity of what's it really about? That's the way my thoughts are.

14. *LANGUAGE AND VOICE . (how tone, inner, empathy, compassionate, ethics, ceremony go with decolonization).*
G.G.   The reason why I put that is because how you use your language and the tone of your voice. It came through my father. I tried to figure out how he set me in line. How he did that and how I could recognize that and how my other brothers turned out, going into boarding school and all that stuff. It has to do with the language and words he used when he trying to discipline us. And also the tone of voice that he used. And it is not only just him, but other relatives as well. And the reason why, is because words can be bitter and tough and it can teach discipline that's why the language and voice is really important . . . it comes from the inner portion. Has to have compassion . . . and that goes specific to ethics . . . and the ceremonies that they go through. Also, the everyday common language that we go through, language at the family and kinship level), at that level, it changes. Eventually, you will arrive at a ceremony and will notice the change in language there too. The atmosphere changes.

15. *CULTURALLY ORIENTED.*
A.L. I don't know, but maybe I'm in-sensitive now or whatever, but to me I've learned [to appreciate] the positive and negative. Everything is o.k. with me, even if it's a negative response? I learn from it. I'm not hurt or agonized by nega-tivity. The words that comes out, the teaching, the lesson, if it comes out, if it means something to me, it's o.k. That's the way I look at it. To me ever since I lost my

son, it seems I'm into another level of being. I am open to anything, negative and positive. There's a strength in a negative response. And also in the positive way, too. So, culturally, any culture I'm open. There's a lot of... anywhere around the world, wherever I'm at there is so much teachings. I don't have to be doing everything. In a spiritual way, too, I did my journey. One thing I learned is that I will never get all the answers I want. There are certain things I will never know. There is limitations, too. And then there is an answer. Maybe because where I am at spiritually I am not ready or something.

16. <u>REACQUAINTING ONESELF WITH TRADITIONAL KNOWL-EDGE.</u>
M.B. You have to experience something like what GG was saying once. Using all your senses. Getting back in touch with some of your feelings that were just sitting there. Dormant? Reawakening that somehow. The emotions are there somewhere in other generations. That's the way I'm looking at it.

LE: The way I'm understanding it that colonization can put us to sleep.
MB: Yeah.
LE: It can make us numb, dumb to the world out there. A traditional modality has the capacity to at the center of the senses (touch, smell, taste) at that level ... to awaken someone who has been going through the colonization process. It can awaken at that level. In order to respond to the evils of colonization, it takes a traditional modality which is a nonwestern, non-modern learning and spiritual activity. That's what it takes to go to the core of that. That's what can be a resistance and form a healthy response to the assault of colonization.

17. <u>COLONIZATION - DECOLONIZATION.</u>
F.Y. I find colonization interesting because it impacts the lives of the Native people. And the same with decolonization, very interesting to me. That's what we need to learn, to decolonize. I think in order to decolonize we need to learn what colonization means. How it operates and how it's used by the colonizers. Those are the two main points I have that have become an interest to me. And I think I'll be using more of those terms, definitions, and the concepts of these two words.

18. <u>MODERNISM.</u>
    F.Y. Modernism comes in third. It pretty much goes hand in hand
    with traditional knowledge, traditional knowledge being the old
    school of how the Indigenous people came to live. Modernism, I
    see as a phenomena in a way as long term. Pretty much everything
    is coming back towards traditional knowledge. Traditional knowl-
    edge was left behind for a while, but, I think that's what is needed
    to prolong the living, life, here on earth.

19. <u>*INTERGENERATIONAL TRAUMA.*</u> F.Y. Intergenerational trauma
    is the greatest or one of the issues that has the most impact on In-
    digenous people. It stems from colonization and intergenerational
    trauma is a big factor in why we have not progressed as much as
    we should. And it is also important to know about and to start to
    use traditional modalities to overcome intergenerational trauma.

Conclusion

   The Diné relatives (or research participants) quite willingly described
nineteen (19) markers by which they could determine that
decolonization is possible. It was not an easy task; however, because the
study of colonialism in one's history and back (or front) yard is largely
a painful and difficult one. They were able to consciously generate the
19 markers partly because classroom time and space was used to fully
engage the colonization–decolonization framework. They were able
to generate the information because they felt safe and free to do so. The
relatives had received no prior schooling or information regarding colonialism and its impact on the Diné.
   The study of Diné colonization entails many hours of investment in
dialogue and in the study of collective Diné history. Additionally, it
requires looking inward into one's own experiences regarding the effects of colonialism that is a reality in contemporary Diné society. The
process reflects one's inner search for concepts and a language that frees
oneself from colonial oppression. It is the process of identifying "what's
right" based on "what went wrong" historically.
   Decolonization involves consciously and intelligently naming what
needs to be named in order to give birth to a language and way of ex-
pression that is opposed by colonialism. Eventually, a culturally specific language could be developed that pinpoints a new location from
which oppressed people can speak. Not all decolonization languages

need be the same. The languages can be as diverse as Indigenous peoples are today.

For Indigenous peoples, that language can be inherent in the Native tongue or in newer, non-Native languages ushered in by colonialists. One obvious location from which to speak is the precolonialized or the space of traditional, non-modern knowledge. When one assumes this and in fact "goes there", he/she finds old knowledge and visions of humanity very comforting since, as in the Diné example, it speaks of a world of an inner beautitude of identity and well being (called *hozhoji* in the Diné language). The politics and process of decolonization theory and practice can be accessed and experienced from this place.

It is a decolonization process when this new or restored naming of the inner beautitude of oneself and one's community takes place because the thought ushers in the possibilities of a politic of *hozho* (e.g. harmony, beauty, balance) as opposed to a politic of mere power.

References

Adams, D. W. (1995). Education for extinction: American Indians and the boarding school experience. Lawrence, Kansas, University Press of Kansas.

Albach, P. G. (1995). Education and neocolonialism. The post-colonial studies reader B. Ashcroft, G. Griffiths and H. Tiffin. London and New York, Routledge: 452-456.

Barreiro, J. (1999). "Hemispheric Digest." Native Americas: hemispheric journal of Indigenous issues XVI(3 & 4): 3-7.

Burgess, P. L. H. F. (2002). Processes of decolonization. Reclaiming Indigenous voice and vision. M. Battiste. Vancouver, BC, Canada, UBC Press.

Colorado, P. (1999). Recovery of the Indigenous mind. CIIS, San Francisco, Ca, California Institute for Integral Studies.

Emerson, L. W. (2002). Hozhonahazdlii': towards a Diné practice of decolonization. Education. San Diego, California, San Diego State University: 237.

Hibbard, P. N. (2001). Remembering our ancestors: recovery of Indigenous mind as a healing process for the decolonization of the western mind. School for Transformative Learning, Traditional Knowledge Doctoral Program. San Francisco, Ca, California Institute for Integral Studies: 91.

Iverson, K. (1978). Civilization and Assimilation in the Colonized Schooling of Native Americans. Education and colonialism. P. G. Altbach and G. P. Kelly. New York, NY, Longman, Inc.: 149 - 180.

Johnson, K. K. (2001). On the path of the ancestors: kinship with place as a path of recovery. Integral Studies and Philosophy. San Francisco, Ca, California Institute for Integral Studies: 189.

Reyhner, J. and J. Eder (2004). American Indian education: a history. Norman, Oklahoma, University of Oklahoma Press.

Robert A. Trennert, J. (1988). The Phoenix Indian School: forced assimilation in Arizona, 1891-1935. Norman, Ok, University of Oklahoma Press.

Roessel, R. A. J. (1979). <u>Navajo education, 1948 - 1978: It's progress and its problems</u>. Rough Rock, Az, Navajo Curriculum Center.

Smith, L. T. (1999). <u>Decolonizing methologies: research and Indigenous Peoples</u>. Dunedin, New Zealand, University of Otago Press.

Whelshula, M. (1999). Healing through decolonization: a study in the deconstruction of the western scientific paradigm and the process of retribalizing among Native Americans. <u>Division for Transformative Learning, Traditional Knowledge Doctoral Program</u>. San Francisco, Ca, California Institute for Integral Studies: 200.

Woodworth, W. (2001). The Morning Star: it is bright, Tawennawetah Teyohswathe: traditional ways of knowing and cultural responsibility. <u>School of Consciousness and Transformation</u>. San Francisco, Ca, California Institute for Integral Studies: 242.

Footnotes

[1] Throughout this writing, I will be using written Navajo that has been transcribed directly from tape recordings. I did not attempt to standardize the pronunciations and tried to write Navajo as I heard the speaker speak it. Because of printing restrictions, I left out diacritic markings as well.

[2] The term "traditional modalities" was borrowed from the Yup'ik Native Alaskans who use the term as a means to distinguish their modes of subsistence from more western or Americanized modalities of living.

[3] Traditional knowledge can be described as non-modern knowledge or in some sense precolonial knowledge. It can be defined in relationship and sometimes in opposition to knowledge that evolves from the modern world.

Chapter 3
Developing Ideological Clarity: A Case Study of Teaching with Courage, Solidarity, and Ethics
by Cristina Alfaro
San Diego State University

Abstract

Discussions about how to best prepare teachers of language minority students revolve around the standards for the teaching profession and best practices to address students' linguistic and academic development. Whereas this focus is important, it is equally critical to interrogate the role ideology plays in how teachers work with language minority and other subordinated minority student groups. This chapter focuses on a case study of a teacher that goes through an ideological border crossing. On this journey he acknowledges that he understands both the politics and their related ideologies that inform his teaching practices, he does this in order to increase the chances of academic success for his students. This teacher, in addition to implementing pedagogically sound strategies that are responsive to the needs of his language minority students, chose to engage in the rigorous process of developing ideological clarity in order to effectively create a classroom environment with critical praxis.

Introduction

What keeps a person, a teacher able as a liberatory educator is the political clarity to understand the ideological manipulations that disconfirm human beings as such, the political clarity that would tell us that it is ethically wrong to allow human beings to be dehumanized…One has to believe that if men and women created the ugly world that we are denouncing, then men and women can create a world that is less discriminating and more humane. (Freire, 1997, p. 315)

Over the past years, as a teacher educator, it has always been difficult to observe dynamic and enthusiastic teacher candidates that passionately exclaim, during their pre-service work, that they have entered into this career so that they could make a difference; yet, a few years later to see them, in their own classrooms caught within the dominant ideology—perpetuating the existing educational system, they so strongly denounced and proclaimed they would fight, not tolerate. Having said this, I began to think about my own experience as a prospective teacher, practicing classroom teacher and then teacher educator. In so doing, it wasn't until I seriously began to critically analyze myself—my own ideology, based on Paulo Freire's work, that I understood the absolute necessity for teachers to first and foremost develop *ideological clarity*, a personally-based philosophical position which would engage not only how teachers view the world but what that means in their identifying who they are as individuals in the larger society. This has led me to study both prospective and practicing teachers in their pursuit of becoming critical educators. That is to say, teachers engaged on a personal and socio-political level that sustains and guides them in their work with language minority students and other subordinated minority student groups where such ethical commitment, courage, solidarity and dedication is needed.

The Importance for Teachers to Develop Ideological Clarity

For me, it is not easy to think of ideology or what kind of ideology we should develop without first asking myself a fundamental question about precisely what it means to have ideological clarity. For a teacher of language minority students, ideological clarity can best be understood as the framework of thought that is used in the classroom to give order and relevance to a curriculum that is politically driven by dominant ideologies. Bartolomé (2002) states that

> [...] *ideological clarity requires that teachers' individual explanations be compared and contrasted with those propagated by the dominant society. It is to be hoped that the juxtaposing of ideologies forces teachers to better understand if, when, and how their belief systems uncritically reflect those of the dominant society and support unfair and inequitable conditions*
> (p. 168).

As a pedagogical tool, a teacher's ideological clarity serves as a starting point for questioning and critically examining the theories that inform their thinking and related classroom practices. As such, an understanding of the need and how to develop ideological clarity gives teachers the means to name, interrogate, critique, and question why they accept or reject aspects of the educational curriculum they utilize. This process enables teachers to critically understand and question the hegemony embedded with the dominant class ideological views of curriculum. These conservative hegemonic views are what legitimate and outright support the curriculum thwarting democratic education and silencing the voices and histories of their students. It is important to recognize that developing ideological clarity is an ongoing process of struggle. Moreover, the process of developing ideological clarity points to the powerful connections between economics, politics, culture, language, and pedagogy which exist both inside and outside schools. Within this context, teachers of language minority students must recognize their responsibility to create a paradigm shift in their classrooms that will transform the hegemonic processes that perpetuate the dominant ideologies that marginalize subordinate student groups. To this end, Macedo (2003), argues that the most important aspect of effective teachers, is the *color* of their ideology for it is a teacher's ideological clarity that "announces or denounces" teaching for equity and social justice. Besides the countless teaching strategies and methods to reach all students' diverse learning styles and the like, a teacher's ideological clarity is the one necessary dimension that will allow her or him to navigate through the political agendas that exist in the educational arena. Ideological clarity is the beacon that guides teachers in negotiating and teaching in a democratic manner that enables them to continue with the struggle for equity and social justice.

Teacher Preparation and Professional Development Programs

Common threads throughout teacher education programs clearly depict the lack of an explicit connection between ideological clarity and teaching. Teacher education programs, for the most part, focus their teaching methodology on the implementation of state standards for the teaching profession without critical reflection upon the oppressive nature of a "one size fits all" model (Brisk, 1998; Ladson-Billings, 1994). This is depicted by the textbooks used and types of activities undertaken by pre-service teachers in college and university programs throughout the U.S. (Troyna & Rivzi, 1997). The teaching standards taught, for the most part, reflect the basic literacy skills, classroom management, record-keeping, tracking, and testing that support the dominant curriculum ideologies.

Educational institutions typically follow a traditional curriculum that has a scope and sequence, or road map, that dictates the teacher certification process. This process is based on the completion of a certain number of required courses and teacher performance expectations and exams that have clearly defined outcomes. Such teacher preparation coursework usually stresses the attitudes and values held by the dominant society and have as common principles the reproduction of a set of canons that are monolithic and non-inclusive (Bell & Munn, 1999-2000). These principles tend to perpetuate the values and social stratification existent in American society so teacher education becomes a tool that promotes the reproduction and legitimization of the world view of the dominant majority. Such views, however, ignore the perspectives held by people of color (Darder, 1991; Delpit, 1995; Smith & Zantiotis, 1989). Teacher education programs, in order to "stay in business", are expected to embrace the state legislators' efforts to "professionalize" teachers. According to Freire (1997),

> [...] they do this with the appearance of considering themselves up-to-date and able to transcend "old ideologies". They speak of the great need of professionalizing pedagogical programs even if they are empty of any possibility to understand society critically (p. 41).

It is my strong belief that given the characteristics of our world and society, teacher education programs must extend their programming beyond the tapestry of "standards". Paramount at the onset of their preparation, teachers must be able to negotiate their sociocultural position based on the political and ideological dimensions of the educational system in which they will work (Ochoa, 2002). In this manner, the goal of teacher preparation programs, that promote biliteracy/multi-literacy, is to provide situational learning experiences and dialogical interactions that will expose and allow teacher candidates to view their world through multiple realities and cross-cultural lenses. Only through these multiple lenses will they begin to struggle to construct their own *ideological* and political clarity.

International Teacher Education Program Framework

This chapter examines and documents how teachers develop ideological clarity within the context of an international teacher preparation program (ITE), situated in Querétaro, Mexico, designed to prepare teachers for diverse classrooms with large populations of English Language Learners (ELLs), whose first language is Spanish (Kuhlman, Alfaro, Attinasi, Driesbach, Merino, 2003).

Prospective teachers in this ITE program experience a range of four different teacher preparation contexts or stages: Stage 1: Participation in coursework in California and Mexico, Stage 2: Observing and teaching children in a private and public school settings in Mexico, Stage 3: Teaching practice in an indigenous school and community setting, and Stage 4: Student teaching in a California public elementary Dual Language Schools. These four contexts create the space and pathway for teachers to critically analyze the dimensions necessary to develop their ideological clarity. For the purpose of this study I focused on the following dimensions: personal values, personal freedom development, cross-cultural comfort, and social consciousness. These four areas of personal growth are examined as they relate to the process teachers engage when developing ideological clarity.

Teachers' Journeys toward Ideological Clarity: Purpose

My intent is to further research in this area by highlighting the pedagogical obstacles in the preparation of teachers of English Language Learners. This goal stems from my own childhood educational struggles and from many years of experiencing and observing the inequities in education. According to Dewey (1938),

> [. . .] education has to be embedded in the real life experience of the learner […]. [It] has to connect with the past of the individual as well as propel him or her into the future […]. Experience is the product of the interaction of the individual with his or her environment. (p. 2)

The research project that informs this chapter specifically focused on how teachers develop and reflect on the process of developing "ideological clarity" and how it connects to their teaching practices (Alfaro, 2003). That is, the moment teachers engage in the journey of developing ideological clarity, is the moment they will also understand education in a different way. In order for teachers to begin to gain ideological clarity they require a space, and an infrastructure that will both support and impose upon them the need to examine and question "what they do and how, why and with whom they do it" (Walsh, 1996, p. 228). This study provided both the space and support for four teachers to embark on the journey of ideological clarity. In order to tap into the ideological orientations that informed these teachers' practice, they were asked to respond to one major question: *What are the personal and profes-sional dynamics prospective teachers negotiate in becoming teachers in an in-ternational context?* This question addresses the tensions these teachers engaged as they started on their ideological journey. These tensions fell into the following contexts: ideological, linguistic, and pedagogical.

- Ideological tensions: Interrogation of the development of ideologi-cal clarity as a means for teaching with courage, solidarity and eth-ics.
- Linguistic tensions: Interrogation of the socio-political issues of first and second language education.
- Pedagogical tensions: Interrogation of the critical knowledge base of the biliteracy teacher.

The following section defines and clarifies the theory that informed this project and the methodological processes that were developed to explore the question and tensions as they inform teacher ideology and practice.

Teachers' Journeys toward Ideological Clarity: Process

> I encourage students to reject the notion that they must choose be-tween experiences. They must believe they can inhabit comfortably two different worlds, but they must make each space one of comfort. They must creatively invent ways to cross borders. (hooks 1994, p. 182)

Qualitative approaches were used to document the development of four biliteracy teachers who were able to cross borders for the purpose of going beyond the learning experiences to develop the 'self aware-ness' necessary to begin to develop ideological and political clarity. At the core of the ITE's program theory and practice, or *praxis*, is Paulo Freire's concept of *conscientization*; the ability for teachers to take on both "exposition and explanation" as elements of critical dialogue (Freire, 1998). Through this type of engagement, teachers are able to expand their understanding of diversity, classicism, racism, sexism, spiritualism, and an ethical commitment to educational equity, a neces-sary condition in becoming an agent of change within the larger his-torical, political, cultural, linguistic, and economic structures. This teacher education framework is both comprehensive and multifaceted; both theoretical and practical; and both generalizable and more specifically relevant to particular populations (e.g., ELLs with Spanish as their native language).

In this manner, the chosen research approach was qualitative with an emphasis on critical ethnography whose goal is to engage all participants' voices and experiences to provide both the breath and depth of these teachers' ideological journeys (Alfaro, 2003).

From the twenty teachers who graduated from the International Teacher Education Program and participated in the focus groups, four teachers' journeys were developed into case studies documenting their growth and experiences. These four teachers now teach in biliteracy or dual language immersion programs in California. These teachers were selected based on three criteria: 1) they graduated from the International Teacher Preparation Program; 2) all four teach ethnolinguistically diverse students in urban settings; 3) they all had a desire to examine their teaching ideology to understand, more profoundly, how it relates to their classroom practice.

To critically examine the development of these four biliteracy teachers, I focused on the personal and professional transformation that resulted from their participation in the ITE teacher preparation program. After agreeing to participate in this study, each teacher was interviewed, classroom observations were made, and a field journal notebook was created for each teacher. I selected the case study of Carlos' journey for this chapter to provide insights into the development of ideological clarity. His journey is one that resembles those of many teachers that are presently engaged in challenging the dominant ideologies that guide our educational practices in the classroom.

Ideological Clarity: One Teacher's Journey

Carlos is bilingual; Spanish is his first language. He has a BCLAD Multiple Subject Credential and is pursuing an MA in Educational Administration. He identified himself as Chicano. He teaches in a fifth/sixth grade "newcomer" program at Santana Elementary School in Northern California. He works with predominantly Latino immigrant students that are new to California schools.

Carlos was born in Mexico and still has many relatives that live there. His parents are laborers and they don't speak English. He has six brothers and sisters. He is the first in his family to graduate from college. He came to California as a teenager and struggled as an English language learner in schools that did not offer him a program that valued his native language or culture. He was fluent in Spanish; however the

California educational system, as he puts it, "did a good job in diminishing that fluency." His personal educational and linguistic struggles and the politics existing in education were the impetus for his desire to become a biliteracy educator. He entered the teaching profession with intense passion to learn about how he could develop personally and professionally to better serve his students. He wanted to be fully prepared both pedagogically and ideologically before he took on what he considered the most important role in the world, a biliteracy teacher with a solid foundation. A foundation is needed to be a critical educator that can identify, navigate, and denounce obstacles in order to come up with strategies that shift the educational paradigm of historically subordinated groups of students.

When I invited him to dialogue with me about his teaching ideology he said he was honored. He stated he wanted to participate in this study because he felt a need for some intense dialogue, and "thinking about his thinking for his personal and professional growth." He was interested in the language of possibility with the educated hope of equalizing the unequal power relations and arbitrary attributions of low status students.

Over the last five years, his work as a biliteracy teacher has revolved around working with the Latino Immigrant community in Northern California where he grew up after leaving Mexico. He became a teacher with a definite purpose, to work with the Latino community in a large geographic area with a majority Latino population. Carlos has dedicated his efforts to becoming socially conscious in order to become socially and politically active. He is very active in his community and is committed to his students in a very profound way. Before we started with our first dialogue, Carlos said he wanted to confess that he was presently very "disenchanted" with how things were going in his school, more specifically with Latino students. In any case, he felt he needed to be very candid with me. He is presently very politically active in his school and is working closely with Latino parents. Our first dialogue covered four questions about his participation and professional development in the ITE program.

I wanted to know if as a result of participating in the ITE program, his views changed or remained the same with respect to teaching language minority and other subordinated minority student groups. Carlos stated,

> "*Pues ¿qué te dire?*... (Well what can I tell you).... since I was born in
> Mexico and raised there for a good portion of my childhood, I was

aware, first hand, of class and race issues, however, they were from a child's perspective. I knew that people of dark skin, like me *"prietito"* were considered lower class and treated as such. I came to California thinking that it was going to be great, and that I would leave that racism behind. *Que* behind *ni que nada…* (I did not leave that behind), quite the contrary. Here (in California) I was not only *"prieto"* but, I didn't speak the dominant language…I know what it is like to be from the other side."

In his response, Carlos was trying to put words to the *archaeology* of his lived experiences. As he continued, he was going through a process of better understanding his self-perception and social consciousnesses through reflection and knowing. He began to critically scaffold through his experiences as a child, adult, and educator—an *archaeology of consciousness*. According to Friere (1985) an individual must experience an "archaeology of consciousness" in order to create a natural path where consciousness emerges as the capacity for self-perception. Carlos reflected further upon his experience returning to Mexico:

"After returning to Mexico as a teacher candidate, with a focus on teaching and learning, my lens illuminated the similar inequalities and linguistic and cultural equity issues that exist across borders. However, in Mexico things are more blatant, es como es, and here in the U.S. things get sugar coated… under issues like English for the children and No Child Left Behind. As a result of participating in this program, and my experience as a classroom-teacher, I am able to see how culture, language, and socioeconomic issues are at the heart of the politics in education across borders. "

Carlos continued to reminisce about his childhood experiences; he felt that going back to Mexico as a teacher candidate helped him to view things from a different angle. He began to focus on the politics of education early on in the program. Thus, he began reflecting on his ability to identify the political, linguistic, and ideological tensions that exist and directly affect the teacher and, most importantly, the children. I then asked his opinion regarding the philosophy of the ITE program; I wanted to know if he believed it was philosophically aligned with the pedagogical needs of the students he encountered in his classroom. He responded,

"To have the opportunity to work with critical educators from Mexico, that subscribe to Freire, Chomsky, and Vygosky was intellectually and personally challenging… and philosophically right on with what we need to know as teachers. It was an additional challenge to decipher the issues that transfer over to the California classroom…not to mention that the majority of my students are from Mexico. After teaching in California classrooms for a few years, it has become clear to me."

He continued to discuss the personal turmoil he experienced when he started to critically analyze the situation both in Mexico and California. He kept mentioning how he "never thought it would hit (him) this hard." This was the beginning to Carlos' critical view of the teaching profession, or his ideological encounter:

> "I have got to stay strong in my position as a teacher and continue to fight for what is right for children…. the hard part is living out your philosophy, "*tú sabes la política*" (you know the politics)…. our California professors were also on the same philosophical page. It (the Mexico experience) highlighted the realities of the children we face in our classrooms. I truly believe that this program offers what no other campus program can attempt to duplicate! The life lessons I learned when I lived and student taught in Mexico, I utilize in my classroom today. The infrastructure of the program provided me with the opportunity to question the inequities with the goal to create change. In this program we were expected to engage in projects of change. And as far as I am concerned change is what is necessary, "*pero que batalla*" (but, what a battle)."

Carlos' journal entries reflect some incredible triumphs he had when working with the indigenous community in Oaxaca. The impact of what happened in that experience has given him the impetus to continue his work with parents and communities at large. To this end Carlos demonstrates that he is able to make pedagogical connections that put the community at the heart of the meaning making process. This led to my third question, where I asked him to share a story of one significant experience (in one of the program stages) that created a space for the development of ideological clarity.

> "*Hijole* (wow), there were so many, as you know…um…. from my reflective journal entries…one of them would definitely be…. student teaching in the Mexican public schools and seeing myself in the students that I was teaching. I worked with fourth grade students, a very mature group."

It was at this point that Carlos got very pensive, scratching his head, not knowing where to begin. His response was one that took him back to his childhood in Mexico and his experience teaching in the Mexican public schools. His reflective journal entries indicated the turmoil he experienced, it was like facing his childhood all over again, but this time with a critical teaching and reflective lens.

> "They [Mexican students] were marveled by the fact that I was from California and many wanted to know how life was over here. Similar to my thoughts as a young child in Mexico, they had visions of life being so abundant and easier across the border. I was able to turn this into a powerfulsocial studies lesson. I shared with them some <u>realities</u> and engaged them in some intense dialogues about life across the border "la frontera." We discussed socioeconomic and political reasons why Mexicanos and people from other third world countries cross the borders."

He went on to discuss his whole lesson, it was powerful! He shared this with immense passion. He infused in his unit the reality of classism and racism. He developed a color chart to illustrate the hierarchy of employment in California and had them contrast it to Mexico's reality. He brought into his classroom what Scheurich (2000) describes as a symptom of deficit ideologies of white racism:

> White people ignore racialized job patterns that are constantly before their eyes. There is a racial employment hierarchy. It is like a color chart. As you start at the bottom with those earning the least and doing the least desired work, the color is more brown and black. As you work your way up the hierarchy toward the better paid more satisfying jobs, the color slowly turns lighter, until by the time you get to the top, it is almost all white. This is not hidden. It is constantly apparent wherever you go. (p. 5)

This is a lesson that he still teaches in his present classroom, because as he said, "It is real!" On this note, he goes on to say:

> "After this powerful event, my relationship with them [Mexican students] was one that I would describe as deep in that they knew that my lessons would always deal with real world issues. At that moment I felt that I knew how to ignite their curiosity for learning in profound ways, the most amazing thing, though, was that I learned so much about teaching and learning…. through this process…. I believe I began to develop ideological clarity…it was only the beginning to my journey as a teacher with a clear purpose. "

Carlos' commitment to teaching through the use of powerful pedagogy is aligned to what Freire (1985) states:

Education must be an instrument of transforming action, a political praxis at the service of permanent human liberation. This, let us repeat, does not happen only in the consciousness of people, but presupposes a radical change of structures, in which process consciousness will itself be transformed (p. 140).

To this end, Carlos had learned to create a teaching curriculum based on the needs and interests of his students. He went on to state,

"The other very significant experience was working with the indigenous community in Oaxaca in a bilingual school. Here, I don't even know where to begin.... Um "pues" well, O.K.... because this event carried over to my classroom in California."

At this point his eyes got watery, and so did mine; I could feel his emotion and his struggle to put into words what he struggled to tell me:

"I worked with an incredible teacher, in Oaxaca, that taught me how to listen to children with my heart! I therefore, became very close to my students, my significant lesson here was to get to know your students' backgrounds in order to make learning meaningful, *¿cómo dice?* (like) Freire (says), every teacher a learner, every learner a teacher. That was incredible, but here is what is amazing...I have been dying to tell you this!"

I found myself at the edge of my seat urging Carlos to tell me what he so badly wanted to share with me; he kept choking on his words. He took a deep breath, and finally began to tell me the following:

"Last year, when I took over this newcomer class and in the middle of a chaotic first day of school, late in the afternoon a new student was brought to my classroom, and the #?>%! resource specialist, excuse my language, said to me; this is as wet as they get: straight from the jungle. I dealt with her comment later...as I was shuffling all of the paper work, *tú sabes* (you know), what the system does to domesticate us, this young man, unmatched socks, clothes that were too big for him, uncombed hair, etc... looked at me with this joy in his eyes, and said; *"Tú eras mi maestro en Oaxaca,"* ("you were my teacher in Oaxaca") he was now a few years older and more mature looking then when I last saw him. At that moment I was not able to hold back the tears."

At this point in the interview, we were both crying, it was an incredibly powerful moment, he continued:

"You asked me about a significant event, it does not get more significant than this in my book…. this program positions us in a place/space that prepares us *ideologically* for the kind of students we must become advocates for and embrace. " (italics added)

Carlos' journal entries during his work in Oaxaca were intensive and extensive. He talked about the beauty of the people and the children with whom he lived. He also talked about the spirituality that must be present in order to be all present for children. He stated:

"It is now my belief that teaching is a sacred vocation, if I expect to really reach and touch my children in a positive and powerful manner; I must do this with my heart, soul, and intellect. This cannot be separated or compromised!"

Essentially, Carlos is saying that he believes in teaching from the heart and his intellect, in order to be true to his ethical self. He has placed a priority in embracing his students' realities as a part of his personal and professional construct. Ethically speaking, his responses clearly reflect what Noddings (1984) refers to as being true to your ethical self, the fundamental caring from the inside:

When my caring is directed to living things, I must consider their natures, ways of life, needs, and desires. And, although I can never accomplish it entirely, I try to apprehend the reality of the other…to be touched, to have aroused in me something that will disturb me my own ethical reality; I must see the other's reality as a possibility for my own. (p. 14)

I finally asked Carlos, "in your opinion, what are the key dimensions in developing a clear teaching ideology?" He stated,

"First of all, to get it right, as in tenure…. I must be very well informed of all the content area standards, and the California Standards for the Teaching Profession, *porque aquí es todo lo que les importa* [because here that is all that anyone cares about]. But, you and I know that it goes way beyond the standards…. ummm…with my students and the space of freedom I have created in my teaching, I bring in their reality. I have come to see their reality as my own! Students need to know/understand *sus condiciones* (their conditions), and most importantly what they can do to change their position of low status."

Carlos is focused on developing a resilience paradigm to advocate for a shift from the "risk" paradigm to a paradigm of hope and change.

His response demonstrates his clear understanding of the politics he must deal with to stay employed. However, he continually reflects and struggles to *create a space of freedom* for his students. He is well versed on the *standards* but is conscious about delivering a powerful pedagogy that will provide his students the tools necessary for them to empower themselves. According to Freire (1989), conscientization "is not a magical charm of revolutionaries, but a basic dimension of their reflective action" (p. 89).

Following is an excerpt of our conversation in which Carlos talks about the role he understands to be undertaking as a teacher:

> Cr: Carlos, you talk about helping students understand their conditions? What about your conditions?"
>
> C: That is right, I do share my struggles with them, *ellos saben que yo tambien tengo problemas con el presente sistema* (they [students] know that I have problems with our present system). I have a core group of colleagues that I work with that help me to stay the course...O.K. but, to answer your question, I believe that to have a clear teaching ideology, I must have full knowledge of how the political educational system works and my role in it...*por ejemplo* (for example): I will not compromise what I know is good and right for my students, i.e. biliteracy instruction, meaning comprehensible input for my newcomers.
>
> I have been told that (according to district policy) I am not to use Spanish when I am teaching ELD, "it is English time" only. So I have established what we call 'Language Brokers', in this manner I assign students to help each other. I will not compromise my students' cognitive understanding to an all English ideology. So, I will not sell out my critical literacy ideology because I am afraid to lose my job. Instead, I became creative...I explain to my students the political-language dilemma (problem pose) and as a community of learners we solve it.
>
> In addition to this, I also stay on top of the latest political issues and bring them into my lessons. I revolve my lessons, no matter what content area, around social political issues. As discouraged as I may get at times, like when you first asked me to be part of this study, I felt like quitting this vocation. But, I feel that I must get more strength from my strength to help create the change necessary for better conditions for our students. (italics added)
>
> Cr: What else do you consider is important to your ideological clarity?
>
> C: It is important that I begin to take more risks, *porque* (because) I have gotten to the point where my mind gets colonized and paralyzed; consequently not allowing me to follow through with what I

know is right. I have been willing to take little risks, not big risks. I have developed strong convictions about my personal and professional values and the values of the school system that I work with, *que nuevas* (what's new) standards, tests, and English only is their value system, therefore this creates lots of tension.Reflection is another important factor, I learn so much from reflection…I have been working with my own students on the reflective process…. they are so mature when they engage in reflection. I do this through a 'Socratic Seminar,' a teaching method. I was told by my principal, is only for 'gifted' students. When she told me this, I asked her what made her think my students were not gifted. Hey, Cristina maybe that is why my principal told you I am 'too ambitious'. (italics added)

I don't mean to romanticize Carlos , but his responses gave me the chills. Here is a young Chicano in the full process of truly understanding what Dewey (1916) passionately stated; "…any education given by a group tends to socialize its member, but the equality and value of the socialization depends upon the habits and aims of the group" (p. 11). Carlos' responses indicate his continuous struggles and commitment to working towards an empowering educational context.

Classroom context/observation: When I visited Carlos' classroom he introduced me to his students as his teacher, emphasizing Freire's (1998) notion that every teacher is a learner and that every learner is a teacher. Carlos went on to tell his students that everyone has teachers. It was immediately ob vious that he had nurtured a high level of trust and authentic communication with his students. It became very apparent to me that he uses every opportunity as a teachable moment. The stu dents demonstrated their love and respect for him through their interactions of intimacy and caring. I visited with the students and observed their high quaity work. Carlos had me introduce myself and had me tell them my story. They had been taught that everyone has a story and that everyone's story must be told and juxtaposed with their own. Carlos explained to me that their classroom motto was that if anyone came into their classroom for more than two hours they became part of their community of learners. Needless to say, I felt very welcomed.

As mentioned, Carlos teaches a 5/6-combination newcomer classroom in an inner city school in Northern California. He has a total of 22 students with a variety of English Language Development levels. The majority of his students are recent immigrants from Mexico; however he also has students from China, Laos, Puerto Rico, Guatemala, and Cuba. As he states: "His class is rich with linguistic and cultural diversity." He has 10 girls and 12 boys. His bulletin board vividly displays the students' work and mirrors their culture. It is very rich in print. It is a comfortable classroom and he has set-up a cozy sofa in the library area of his room. His library reflects multicultural literature of high interest and controlled vocabulary and then some novels of varying reading levels, most importantly however, all student have authored his/her own story.

His students grow plants as part of a science/social studies project. Actually, everything Carlos teaches is under the umbrella of Social Studies. That is his way of making the content relevant to his students. He truly believes and states "my students must understand their world in order to know their role in it." I was impressed by his choice of literature, instead of using the prepackaged ELD program. Carlos rejects the prepackaged curriculum and co-creates curriculum that is meaningful and purposeful for his students. He is able to do this because, he understands that he must teach his students to read the world through the word. He has extensive knowledge of the content standards and his students' background, hence he is able to navigate and negotiate his curriculum.

In order to facilitate the learning of his second language learners, Carlos has created a classroom of "language and cultural brokers." I was able to see this in action during the ELD lesson I observed. During the time he is teaching English, he is the English language speaking model, if students don't understand something they consult with their "language broker," who has the option of explaining in English or using the primary language. He pauses during his lesson and allows students to engage in "think-pair-share" where students clarify or scaffold the lesson with a partner. This was his way around making sure his students received comprehensible input, while he "follows the school/district policy" about only speaking English during ELD time. This classroom observation was important to me, because it indicated the congruency between his ideology, his struggles and his triumphs in his practice.

In a conversation with Carlos, following my visits to his classroom, he mentioned he had been thinking about the powerful connection between his teaching and his ideology as a form of intellectual labor. He stated:

> "I am getting <u>hooked</u> on <u>critical reflection,</u> I am thankful for the opportunity to engage in dialogue, to think about my thinking and to discuss how it transfers to my classroom. " (italics added)

According to Giroux (1994), teachers as transformative intellectuals must engage in a form of *intellectual labor*, not as technicians, in order to experience schooling in a transformative way. Carlos went on to say that one of the missing ingredients in his personal and professional development was the opportunity to reflect on ideology and practice. I had gifted him a couple of my favorite Freire books; he had been struck by Freire's (1985) explanation of conscientization: "… if the type of con- sciousness that recognizes existing knowledge could not keep search- ing for new knowledge, there would be no way to explicate today's knowledge." (p. 114)

Carlos went on to say, "… they keep us so busy that we don't have time to really examine if what we are doing is really educationally sound…it is all about working up to the tests and in my particular class- room context, it is about getting my students mainstreamed, pronto [as soon as possible], into English only classrooms.

Our dialogue continued with a discussion about how society con- tinues to demean and dishearten the human resource other wise known as the teacher. He reminded me how he was feeling very disheartened when I initially contacted him. Yet, he was now engaging the language of possibility, the pedagogy of hope. He talked about connecting with some like-minded people in his school community.

In a later conversation, I asked him to reflect on his experiences during the four stages of the International Teacher Education Program. The four program stages were in the following situated learning con- texts: (Stage I) Orientation in California and Mexico; (Stage II) Teaching in Mexican Private and Public Schools, (Stage III) Teaching in an Indig- enous Community; and (Stage IV) Teaching in California Public Schools. Carlos' reflections fell into the following themes: *Values, Cultural Expe- rience of Difference, Personal Freedom Development, and Ideological Clarity.* In my observations of Carlos' development as a teacher and in his shar- ing of his reflective journal, the following documents his personal "criti- cal" examination of these four experiences.

I. Initial Program Stage: California and Mexico

Values.
With respect to my values, during the initial stages of the program, I was at a point in my life where I was rejecting what the California teacher preparation programs had to offer, you know, the standard- ization of it all. This was problematic for me because I really wanted to become a biliteracy teacher without having to compromise my lin- guistic and cultural values.

In Carlos' journal entries he describes how elated he was when he found an alternative program to teacher preparation, such as the International Teacher Education Program. He came into the program at a point in his life when he was trying to redirect his personal energy to accomplishing his goal without having to succumb to traditional—standardized teacher education program.

Cultural Experience of Difference.
In this area I thought I knew a lot more about culture and language than I really did. *Según yo* (According to me) because I was from Mexico and survived sort of speak, the American educational system I was bicultural.

Based on our conservations and his journal entries, Carlos felt that he had a solid frame of reference to effectively work with different cultures, namely Latinos and Whites. He came to the realization that he was not only physically, but also ideologically crossing culture borders. He was struggling to adapt, in a profound manner, to a form of understanding and action to equalize unequal power relations between cultures.

Personal Freedom Development.
With respect to my personal identity, I felt very certain of my radical "Chicano" identity and therefore, I was going to Mexico *para reclamar mis raíces* [to reclaim my roots]. One of my personal goals in going to Mexico was to define and redefine myself or in Hampden-Turner's terms, *self confirm*.

Carlos, was at a point in his life where he had come to identify with the Chicano Movement. He was involved in reinterpretation movements to discard the stereotypes of lazy *Mexicano* (Mexican) to replace it with the proud, historically rich Mexican American—Chicana/o, who was ready to fight for the rights of his community—all this with passion and indignation. He could not accept being colonized by a dominant culture.

Ideological Clarity.
"This is where the going gets tough…man I love Freire, but during the initial stages of the program and in retrospect, I have to say that I didn't really understand him. I guess you could say I was un poco tapado (not too swift). Then I remember you had Bartolomé and Macedo come to give us a lecture, and man it was all about Freire's letters to North American Teachers, so that motivated me to pay closer attention. That was a powerful session."

Carlos was at a point in his life where he did not yet have the language to articulate his thinking, his struggles, his needs, wants, and dreams. He made reference to a summer that Lilia Bartolomé and Donaldo Macedo came to San Diego and gave a talk that truly impacted him. Carlos already knew then that he was not a conformist; he refused to assimilate and legitimate the values of the dominant culture as his own.

II. Second Program Stage: Working in the Private and Public Schools in Mexico

Values.
As I anticipated my experience in the Mexican school system, I was feeling this sense of rejuvenation and redirection knowing that I would experience the Mexican education all over again, except this time I was in a different position or ...say..."role". You know what I mean... When I began my work in the private schools I experienced anger and a great sense of injustice, not for the students in the private schools, but for the students who could not attend this school due to their socioeconomic status. I was anxious to go work in the public schools. I found my "zone" in the public schools.

Carlos' journal entries also speak to the classicism that became so obvious to him when he did the first portion of his fieldwork in the Mexican private schools. He talks about not being fully aware of classicism or racism when he was in elementary school in Mexico, but being there, teaching in an elitist school, allowed him to recollect some experiences that, only now, made sense to him. He reflected, "as a child I thought things were the way they were, *'porque así lo quería Dios'* (because that is the way God ordained), as my mom use to say. I now realized how, through no fault of my own, I occupied a position of low status."

Once he began to work in the Mexican public schools, the system he was educated in, he felt he was where he needed to be. Carlos was not able to ignore oppression and all its implications, he was acutely struck by the blatant issues of classicism and racism, consequently feeling very unsettled, yet trying hard to direct his energies in a positive and productive manner.

Cultural Experience of Difference.
I found myself struggling to adapt to the different situations, without saying anything that would upset my host administrators and teachers at the private schools. It was also a time for some good debate

with some of my program peers. There were a couple of people in
my cohort that loved being at the private schools and even "wished"
to teach there. Anyway, got into some philosophical debates with my
colegas (colleagues).

During my conversations with Carlos as well as in his journal entries, he discussed that he knew how to comport himself (*se como
comportarme*) to communicate effectively with *los "Cremitas"* ("the elitist") and the common people. He had encountered the differences—
the different ways and logic by which people sustain and give culturally distinct meaning to their lives.

Personal Freedom Development.
During my experience in the Mexican public schools I felt that I was
ready to reveal who I was, a student that came from the same type of
social class and had gone through the same education in Mexico. I
felt ready to take some risks that would allow me to teach and learn
some lessons.

Carlos was at this point ready to deal with the social reality of his
personal syntheses. By the nature of his personal character, he was a
risk taker, he was very mindful about confronting what he considered
critical issues with what he called "kitty gloves". He was very aware
that he was a guest of the *Secretaría de Educacíon Publica de México* and
was prohibited to engage in any political movements or activities. This
was a difficult situation for him because he felt very passionate about
some of the political issues that were being addressed by the *"huelgistas"*
(protesters). This sentiment was frequently addressed in his reflective
journal. He was torn about not being able to take the risks. He fully
understood the notion that where nothing is ventured, nothing is won.
He felt that he was stifling his self-expression and disclosure, falling
into being a conformer, something he adamantly, fought against in the
states. He, however, did take some risks in the classroom with his teachings. He called these "safe risks".

III. Third Program Stage—Indigenous school in Mexico

Values.
This experience was like no other. I worked in Oaxaca in a beautiful
community …. I was treated with so much love, intimacy, and respect
that I can't even begin to explain, by this time I had taught at two different levels in the public schools. I felt well equipped to offer what

I thought was quality teaching to my new students. On the contrary, they taught me much more than I could teach them.

During our dialogical session he talked about what Freire coined as the pedagogy of the heart. He saw himself in solidarity with these indigenous students and their community; he learned how to teach from the heart.

Cultural Experience of Difference.
My cultural experience in the indigenous community allowed me to internalize my own culture—*y la diferencia* (the difference). People would tell me 'for you this experience will be a piece of cake because you are familiar with this culture since you have lived in Mexico'. But, unless you experience the difference in the culture, one can't internalize it. Just to understand the manner in which this particular indigenous community in Oaxaca creates and maintains their world view is very different from how you and I view the world.

His journal entries with respect to his work during this program, addressed his mission of "making sense" of the cross-cultural and cross-economic class lived experiences. As a researcher, this was very impressive to me, because many students have gone through this process as what Bartolomé (2000) calls "unconscious voyeurs" who view these cross-cultural and cross-economic situations through never acknowledged assimilationist and deficit ideological lenses.

Ideological Clarity.
At this time, because of the "organic" situation that I was in, I was forced to analyze my personal learning through multiple views. I didn't want this experience to be over; it was like a deep spiritual process, and I am not a religious person, so I don't mean it in that sense.

In this statement, Carlos was referring to what he had written about in his journal: "my concern has been elevated to a level of spiritual motivation and commitment to a cause, rather than just the intellectual." His found spirituality was born out of his sense of equity and social justice. According to Hall (2000), spiritual morality can activate people's sense of equity:

In secular terms, we often think of equity as synonymous with 'justice, fair-ness, and impartiality', yet spiritual morality elevates the concerns of justice, fairness, and impartiality to another level. Within the context of spiritual morality, justice includes elements of mercy, fairness takes on elements of grace, and impartiality is transformed into a compassionate consideration of multiple perspectives (p. 176).

Carlos made many dialogical entries in his journal that questioned in one form or another, the fairness of the existing social order. He shared with me that one of the indigenous teachers gifted him a book by Octavio Paz (1962), where he illuminates the concept of *"el ninguneo"* (pretend mentally that one does not exist in relationship to one's own culture and ethnicity on the outside). This was important because this community was being forced to do just that. Carlos made this connection with what is happening in California when it comes to people of color.

IV. Fourth Program Stage: California Public Schools

Values.
I would have to say that of the entire program, returning to teach in the California bilingual classroom was the most difficult stage for me. Particularly, because I had just experienced the <u>sacredness</u> of teaching in Oaxaca, I had worked with teachers that have a lot of heart! Things here in California seemed superficial. Everyone…moving around "rapidly" trying to meet the "standards" regardless of anything and everything.

Carlos now had to face his ethical courage originating from his intellectual, emotional, and spiritual commitment. His struggles were very intense. His cooperating teacher was concerned that he was taking things much too seriously. His journal entries include many dialogues that he had with his cooperating teacher about this tension. He considered her to be very bicultural, but was disturbed by her lack of ethical commitment to social justice.

"My cooperating teacher would tell me that sometimes we just 'had to roll' with the punches'. I told her I wasn't willing to play the game. She told me that that worried her, because I had the potential to be an awesome teacher. This was discouraging to me. I promised myself then, that I would not give up!"

The conversation with his teacher did not set well with Carlos. However, during his dialogical interview he said that after teaching for a few years, he now understood where she was coming from. She had been domesticated and had been beaten down and burnt out by the system.

> "Even though I was student teaching in a supposedly 'state of the art' dual language school, I couldn't help but see that the sacredness in teaching, that I had experienced, was absent from my new experience. I resented being in this position."

Carlos' reflection reminded me of my conversation with Macedo (2003), where he stated that educators will experience "tensions" when they need to protect their "middle class status" and also be true to their ideology.

Experience Culture of Difference. It is important for biliteracy teachers to recognize the nature of ideologically crossing ethnic and socioeconomic cultural borders for the purpose of understanding how some cultural groups, through no fault of their own, are marginalized by higher status groups.

In his journal, Carlos documents the dynamic nature of the marginalization of cultural groups on both sides of the border and discusses the importance of understanding this unequal playing field, particularly when it relates to teaching groups of students who occupy positions of low social status. He offers many personal anecdotes. During the interview, he discussed his commitment to implementing a culturally and linguistically relevant pedagogy to both ensure and enhance the achievement success of his students. Carlos states that his student teaching situations both in Mexico and California were exclusively with Latino children.

> "Nothing wrong with that, but in my present teaching situation, I have other children of color that come from different ethnic backgrounds. So my new lens includes a multicultural perspective, a stretch from my bicultural view."

Personal Freedom Development.
Under this area, I felt, personally challenged when I returned to California…. I was having trouble getting reoriented to being here; the program calls this 're-entry culture shock'. I guess that in some ways it is that. I felt very much in conflict with all that I had learned about myself and my need to live out my newly acquired view of life and, more importantly, my role as a teacher.

Carlos returned to California struggling to understand through a dialectical process that seeks to reconcile apparent opposites. In his present teaching position he is struggling to continue true to his "ethical self" by continuing what Hampden-Turner (1970) coined as "self suspension" and "risk taking". Carlos realizes that this is not an easy process, but continues to state: "I will not sell out my ideological stance, because that would be selling out my students, that to me would be a bigger burden to carry."

> *Ideological Clarity.*
> I have lost sleep over trying to honestly examine where I am ideologi-
> cally. I struggle to make my classroom a democratic space where chil-
> dren can experience the principles of equality and justice. You know,
> where else will they have a chance? My ideological clarity is neces-
> sary for the success of my students.

Carlos stated this with much emotion—his voice shook as his eyes penetrated mine. Freire (1998) stresses that teaching requires love for the very act of teaching. Through this love the act of teaching can become transformative and liberating. Carlos was experiencing the "archaeology of consciousness" that Freire (1985) discusses as a natural path where consciousness emerges as the capacity of self-perception. Carlos is very clear about his self-perception and his level of confidence in the classroom has helped him to obtain what Freire (1970) terms "praxis". He has demonstrated a high level of commitment and solidarity with his students and his students' communities. He is passionate about practicing a transformative pedagogy where he expects his students to take ownership and risks in applying new knowledge.

Implications for Becoming a Transformative Teacher

The pedagogical and social/political journey taken by Carlos, first in his pre-service program and in his five years as a practicing teacher, documents his tensions and growth towards ideological clarity. Such growth can be summarized through the following reflections and perceived tensions in his life around the issues of ideology, language, and pedagogy. These issues are summarized through the followings observations:

Ideological tensions. Carlos had the predisposition to developing an ideological clarity to sustain his vocation. He indicated a desire to develop a transformative teaching ideology that is based on values, cultural experience of difference, personal freedom, and ideological clarity. He recognized for example, that his ideological beliefs are connected to his classroom practice. The tensions included the personal and professional dynamics that dealt with his experience of dissonance and risk taking in challenging school practices that worked against the development   of students' biliteracy. Carlos was capable of engaging in risk taking as part of his ideology.

Linguistic Tensions. The linguistic tensions experienced by Carlos were based on his engagement in context reduced and context embedded situations in formal and informal settings. With Carlos the fact that he was Mexican and did not speak the "formal" Spanish caused him to be criticized by the Mexican natives. Additionally, he experienced, in Mexico as well as in California, the cross-cultural and cross-economic devaluing of the indigenous languages and cultures. Carlos continues to struggle with the present political tension of equity and social justice policy and practices that seek to assimilate English language learners as quickly as possible to the dominant language without concern for their academic (cognitive) development or biliteracy. Carlos continues to maintain solidarity with the linguistically diverse communities he proudly serves.

Pedagogical tensions. Carlos engaged in dialogue and reflection about his ideological orientation and practices. This is a tension that crosses geographical borders, in that he has experienced this conflict in classrooms in both Mexico and the United States. Carlos continues to struggle with the pedagogical tension of standardization of education that has replaced the *intimacy* and *sacredness* of teaching and learning that he internalized when teaching in the indigenous schools in Oaxaca, Mexico. Carlos has gained the capacity and commitment to begin *anew*, a concept introduced by Freire (1993), that fervently calls for the

> Capacity to always begin anew, to make, to reconstruct, and to not spoil, to refuse to bureaucratize the mind, to understand and to live as a process--live to become—is something that always accompanied me throughout life. This is an indispensable quality of a good teacher. (p. 98)

Given this capacity to begin anew has enabled Carlos to internalize the oppression of teachers by confronting political oppression perpetrated by the standardization of teacher preparation/ professional development and schooling in general. The lessons learned by Carlos' experiences suggest that teachers must be willing to reflect on their own teaching and learning. Beginning anew has equipped Carlos with *courage, solidarity,* and *ethics* necessary to stay the course.

Given this, I hold the greatest respect and admiration for teachers and their commitment to the intellectual labor in daring to become teachers as cultural workers. Documented in Carlos' journey is his commitment to culturally responsible education for his students. Teachers need to respond to the task of becoming "transformative intellectual teachers" through the process of developing ideological clarity within an intense socio-political climate, a climate that creates daily tensions and struggles for teachers in search of providing educational spaces that promote practices that equalize unequal power relations for low status students.

Uncovered in Carlos' journey is an insight into how teachers perceive their social and political reality within the school system. He unveils a yearning to have a voice, to be treated with respect and dignity (as an intellectual and social being), to have his struggles and desires brought to the center, and to be considered capable of participating in co-creating the curriculum with his students through the implementation of culturally engaged pedagogy. As the themes unfolded, a need to revamp pedagogical approaches is forever present. Deeply ingrained in the voice of Carlos is a firm belief that teachers need an explicit space to develop ideological clarity for teaching with *courage, solidarity* and *ethics*. Foremost to the teachers' voices is a *desire* to legitimize their pedagogical struggles within the classroom and the communities they serve. A move in such a direction would contribute to the notion of teachers as transformative intellectuals and would eradicate the domestication of teachers reducing them to the level of technicians.

The passion, courage, struggles, pain, fear, and levels of dissonance uncovered through this dialogical process is extremely significant in light of our present political climate. Teachers' stories clearly illuminate areas that need to be considered in teacher preparation and professional development. Also, they reveal ways in which pedagogy and unequal power relations in education need to change in order to provide an atmosphere in which teachers will be given the space and encouragement to develop ideological clarity as a means to empower themselves. As such, teachers' voices reinforce the belief that teachers are intellectual social beings that need to be included as an integral part of the educational paradigm shift.

Conclusion

This case study suggests the urgency for both prospective and practicing teachers to develop an ideological and political clarity that will sustain and guide them in denouncing inhumane and discriminatory practices in the classroom, while seeking to transform the pedagogy of schooling to be culturally democratic and inclusive. Teacher education at the pre-and in-service levels can be informed through the findings of this teacher's journey. Teacher education programs need to develop the voices of prospective teachers to have the courage, solidarity, and ethics to defend the linguistic and academic development of ethnically and linguistically diverse students. Teachers must have the ideological clarity that perceives every student as a competent and capable individual that has the power to create culture, language and voice as active participants in our democracy.

Like Carlos, the teacher in this study, Freire reminds us of how critical it is to identify the obstacles in order to create clear and realistic strategies to negotiate, navigate, and overcome them. Carlos' struggles towards ideological clarity illustrate the multiple issues imbedded in the epistemological journey of becoming a bilingual-biliterate teacher with courage, solidarity, and ethics. Noddings (1984) passionately states; [...] to be touched, to have aroused in me something that will disturb my own ethical reality, I must see the other's reality as a possibility for my own. (p. 14).

To this end, teacher preparation should never be reduced to a form of training. Freire (1998a, 1998b), argues that besides technical skills, teachers must be equipped with the knowledge of what it means to teach with courage. Freire challenges us to denounce the inequities that oppress historically subordinated student populations by teaching with courage, solidarity, and ethics. Teacher preparation should go beyond the technical preparation of teachers and be rooted in the *ethical* formation of both selves and history, and towards the development and practice of cultural democracy.

References

Alfaro, C. (2003). <u>Transforming Teacher Education: Developing Ideological Clarity As A Means For Teaching With Courage, Solidarity and Ethics.</u> Unpublished doctoral dissertation, Claremont Graduate University & San Diego State University.

Bartolomé, L. (2002). Democratizing bilingualism: The role of the critical teacher Education. In Z. F. Beykont (Ed.), <u>Lifting every voice: Pedagogy and politics of bilingualism</u> (pp. 167-185). Boston: Harvard Education Publishing Group.

Bell, E. D. & Munn, G. C. (1999-2000). Can We Create Dreamkeepers For Diverse Classrooms? <u>National FORUM of Teacher Education Journal</u> (Online Journal). Volume 11E, 3. Retrieved on May 24, 2003 from <u>http://www.nationalforum.com/ BELLte8e3.html</u>

Bennett, M. (1986). Towards ethnorelativism: A developmental model of intercultural sensitivity. In M. Paige (Ed.), Education for the intercultural experience. Yarmouth, ME: Intercultural Press.

Brisk, M. (1998). Bilingual education: From compensatory to quality schooling. Mahwah, NJ: Lawrence Erlbaum.

Darder, A. (1991). Culture and power in the classroom: A critical foundation for bicultural education. Westport, CN: Bergin & Garvey.

Delpit, L. (1995). Other people's children: Cultural conflict in the classroom. New York: The New Press.

Dewey, J. (1938). Experience and education. New York: Collier Books.

Friere, P. (1970). Adult literacy processes as cultural action for freedom. Harvard Educational Review, 40, 205-225.

Freire, P. (1985). The Politics of Education: Culture, Power, and Liberation. South Hadley, MA: Bergin & Garvey.

Freire, P. (1993). Pedagogy of the oppressed. New York: Continuum Publishing.

Freire, P. (1997). Pedagogy of the heart. New York: Continuum Press.

Freire, P. (1998a). Pedagogy of freedom: Ethics, democracy and civic discourse. New York: Rowan & Littlefield Publishers.

Friere, P. (1998b). Teachers as cultural workers: Letters to those who dare to teach. Boulder, CO: Westview.

Giroux, H. (1994). Disturbing pleasures. New York: Routledge.

Hall, (1993). Introduction. In Park, P. (Eds.) Voices of change. Participatory research in the United States and Canada. Westport. CT: Bergin & Garvey.

Hampden-Turner, C. (1971). Radical man. New York: Schenkman.

hooks, b. (1994). Teaching to transgress: Education as the practice to freedom. New York: Routledge.

Kuhlman, N., Alfaro, C., Attinasi, J., Driesbach, M., Merino, R., (2003). Mextesol. Winter & Spring 2003. vol. 26, no. 3 & 4. Transforming California Teachers: A Biliteracy Program in Mexico.

Ladson-Billings, G. (1995). Toward a theory of culturally relevant pedagogy. American Education Research Journal, 35, 465-491.

Macedo, D. (2003). Literacy for stupidification. Workshop paper presented at the National Council of Teachers of English Assembly for Research Mid-Winter Conference, February 21-23, 2003. The College of Education & Human Development, University of Minnesota.

Noddings, N. (1984). Caring: A feminine approach to ethics & moral education. Berkeley, CA: University of California Press.

Ochoa, A. (2002). Latino Summit: Biliteracy Development. San Diego County Office of Education.

Smith, R. & Zantiotis, A. (1989). Practical teacher education and the Avant-Garde. In H.A. Giroux & P. McLaren, (Eds.), Critical pedagogy, the state, and the cultural struggle (pp. 105-124). Albany: State University of New York.

Troyna, B., & Rizvi, F. (1997). Racialization of differences and the cultural politics of teaching. In B. J. Biddle, T. L. Good, & I. F. Goodson (Eds.), International handbook of teachers and teaching (pp. 237-266). Boston: Kluwer Academic Publishers

Walsh, C. E. (1996). Making a difference: Social vision, pedagogy, and real life. In C. Walsh (Ed.), Education reform and social change: Multicultural voices, struggles, and visions (pp. 223-239). Mahwah, NJ: Lawrence Erlbaum Associates.

Chapter 4
Racism and Language Minority Students: A Critical Race Theory Approach to Explore Oppositional Acts by Latina/o Educators Working with Spanish-speaking Students
by Yvette V. Lapayese, Ph.D.
Loyola Marymount University

Abstract

The racist climate in California sets the stage for the chapter's exploration of the experiences of Latina/o teachers working with Spanish-speaking students. In-depth interviews of 7 Latina/o teachers working in K-5 classrooms comprised of predominantly Spanish-speaking students provided alternative knowledge on efforts of resistance aimed at transforming the conditions that oppress Spanish-speaking students. The chapter discloses that Latina/o teachers are critically aware of racial discrimination, racial segregation, and racial inequities that systematically disadvantage Spanish-speaking students and engage in oppositional acts that can serve as transformational instances of resistance. By resisting English only policies, segregation and racial microaggressions, and the marginalization of Latina/o families, Latina/o teachers are engaged in counteracts which oppose racial inequities. As such, their insurgent knowledge base contests white understandings of the schooling experiences of Spanish-speaking students. These oppositional acts provide concrete strategies for other Latina/o teachers and critical educators interested in challenging the structures of oppression that govern our schools. Lastly, in light of Latina/o teachers' experiences and perspectives, the chapter also suggests changes in teacher preparation programs to better meet the needs of Latina/o educators invested in transformational resistance.

The mis-education of Spanish-speaking students can be traced to white supremacy and its persistent manifestation in educational policy, notably in the English only movement. Indeed, education scholars concur that language minority students have been traditionally schooled with the intent of deculturalization (Macedo, 2000; Gutierriez, Asato, Pacheco, Moll, Olson, Horng, Ruiz, Garcia, and McCarty, 2002). Be it in segregated or integrated classrooms, such intentions are largely based on notions of Anglo and English superiority and the alleged inferiority of language minority students. In California and other English-only states, federal and state policies have ensured that teachers remain un-equipped and unsupported to meet the linguistic, cultural, and aca-demic needs of Spanish-speaking students.

In California, Proposition 227 reaffirmed English as the superior and sole language to be learned in school. Putting an end to bilingual education reasserts monoculturalism and monolingualism as central principles governing school instruction. Gutierrez, Asato, Santos, and Gotanda (2002) argue that this political backlash is rooted in white dis-content over recent trends in California, notably the "increasing politi-cal influence and social presence of people of color, particularly immi-grant Latina/os and Asians coupled with a perceived loss of entitle-ment, and in particular a perceived decrease in access to elite educa-tional institutions and to the marketplace" (p. 338). Ultimately, monoculturalism and monolingualism uphold white privilege by si-lencing multiple voices and perspectives, reinstating the learning of English as the primary vehicle for assimilation.

The socio-political climate in California sets the stage for the chapter's exploration of the experiences of Latina/o teachers working with Spanish-speaking students. As an assistant professor in a teacher education program in Los Angeles and as a former elementary school teacher working in a Structured English Immersion classroom, I wit-ness the strategic ways Latina/o teachers resist racism in our schools. Nonetheless, Latina/o teacher resistance is overlooked in educational research. It is imperative that educators understand how teachers of color engage in resistance strategies that counteract racist educational practices in an antibilingual climate that threatens the education of Span-ish-speaking students.

In this chapter, I contextualize the work experiences of Latina/o educators within the frameworks of critical race theory and transfor-mational resistance. Critical race theory and transformational resistance comprise an agenda that involves a critique of oppression, in this case, racism, coupled with a struggle for change. Latina/o teachers are criti-cally aware of racial discrimination, racial segregation, and racial ineq-uities that systematically disadvantage Spanish-speaking students and engage in oppositional acts that can serve as transformational instances of resistance. These oppositional acts provide concrete strategies for other Latina/o teachers and critical educators interested in challenging the structures of oppression that govern our schools. Lastly, in light of Latina/o teachers' experiences and perspectives, the chapter also suggests changes in teacher preparation programs to better meet the needs of Latina/o educators invested in transformational resistance.

Approach and Process of Engagement

This chapter underscores the epistemological knowledge that Latina/o teachers share in understanding their efforts of resistance aimed at transforming the conditions that oppress Spanish-speaking students. Although teachers of color represent a small percentage of the teaching population, I contend that their perspectives and insights are critical in understanding racial dynamics in schools serving Spanish-speaking students. I prioritize the narratives of Latina/o teachers by using a critical race methodology to ground my analysis in the distinctive experiences of people of color. One of the defining tenets of critical race theory is the centrality of experiential knowledge (Solórzano, 1998). Educational research grounded in critical race theory views the life experiences of People of Color, in this case Latina/o teachers, as valid and acknowledges both the individuality and connectivity of those experiences through methods like counterstories, narratives, *testimonios*, and oral histories (Dillard, 2000). This "call to context" insists that the social/experiential context of racial oppression is crucial for understanding racial dynamics (Solórzano and Yosso, 2002; Villenas and Deyhle, 1999; Pizarro, 1998).

The arguments found in this chapter are the result of a 12- month qualitative study focused on two school districts in Southern California made up of predominantly white administrators and teaching teams. Data were obtained through in-depth interviews of seven Latina/o teachers working in K-5 classrooms comprised of predominantly Spanish-speaking students. My active involvement in these districts has enabled me to observe first hand the education of Spanish-speaking students. Drawing on colleagues working in the two districts, participants for the study were strategically selected to represent all K-5 grade levels, have at least three years of teaching experience working with Spanish-speaking students, and possess a track record of advocating for the needs of second language learners.

Interviews and observations took place at the school sites. I also conducted a focus group interview comprised of six Latina/o educators. Gaining a sense of the participant's point of view was crucial to the success of the research. Thus, it was necessary to establish trust and maintain it throughout the course of the study. I made sure to talk about my own experiences in the beginning, to let the educators know the many ways I struggled with several of the same issues they face. My own experiences as a Latina elementary school teacher working in a Structured English Immersion classroom facilitated my building a trusting and open rapport with the teachers involved. In many of the interviews, there was frequent code-switching by both the participants and myself. My previous knowledge of racism and schools and my own personal and professional experiences with these themes allowed for a more in-depth and open discussion of racism and language minority students. This relates to a concept called theoretical sensitivity (Strauss and Corbin, 1990; Delgado Bernal, 1998) in which the researcher embodies a personal quality that makes one more sensitive or aware of the subtleties of meaning.

All of the interviews and observations were coded for analysis. Through this process, recurrent patterns throughout the interviews were discovered and grouped into major themes that form the assertions of this chapter. The experiences of the Latina/o educators along these themes are presented through direct quotations and vignettes, and tied together through interpretive analysis (Emerson et al., 1995; Erickson, 1986).

Oppositional Acts, Transformational Resistance, and Latina/o Educators

Critical race theory and transformational resistance provide appropriate lenses for researching the experiences of Latina/o teachers working with Spanish-speaking students. Critical race theory places race at the center of critical analysis to explore how educational structures sustain white supremacy and uphold similar hierarchies within gender, class, and sexual orientation (Crenshaw, 1995; Matsuda, 1995).

One of the defining tenets of critical race theory is a commitment to social justice (Solórzano & Yosso, 2002). In this chapter, commitment to social justice is understood as the commitment to engage in a process of transformational resistance which comprises both a critique of oppression and opportunities for struggle in the interest of social emancipation. Critical education scholars are using the theoretical frameworks of critical race theory and transformational resistance to document and explore oppositional acts by People of Color (Solórzano & Bernal, 2001; Covarrubias & Revilla, 2003; Yosso, 2000). For instance, Delgado Bernal's reexamination of the 1968 East Los Angeles Blowouts illuminates the transformational potential of resistance. Building on Giroux's description of resistance, Delgado Bernal re-articulates the characteristics of oppositional behavior and suggests four various types of oppositional behavior: reactionary behavior, self-defeating resistance, conformist resistance, and transformational resistance. Although oppositional acts by Latina/o educators fall within various categories of oppositional behavior, the purpose of this chapter is to document instances of transformational resistance which "offers the greatest possibility for social change" because it combines both a deeper level of understanding and a commitment to change (Solorzano & Bernal, 2001, p. 319).

Building on the work of Solórzano and Delgado Bernal, I concur that transformational resistance within the framework of critical race theory allows one to look at resistance among teachers of color that is "political, collective, conscious, and motivated by a sense that individual and social change are possible" (p. 320). This chapter incorporates a model of transformational resistance that comprises the dialectic between structure and agency in examining the oppositional behaviors of Latina/o teachers working with historically marginalized students. This dimension of transformational resistance highlights the actions of People of Color that demonstrate a commitment to social justice. Below I present some strategies Latina/o teachers use in the struggle to create a less oppressive learning environment for their Spanish-speaking students.

Resisting English Only Policies and Safeguarding the Spanish Language

Schools discourage the use of Spanish and require English with minimal support. School policies and activities emphasize the learning of English, often accompanied with the perception that the use of Spanish takes away from the learning of English. Despite school policies that discourage the use of Spanish in the classroom, all the teachers rely on their students' primary language in their teaching. The educators admit that they resist the demands of administrators to silence the use of Spanish in the classroom. As one teacher declares,

> "I mean there are times that they tell me you cannot teach math in Spanish, it has to be taught in English only, let the aide take care of the previewing and reviewing or whatever. But there are times that I say I am closing my doors, I'm going to teach my kids the math in Spanish. They need to learn these concepts, these terms."

Although the oppositional act of reinstating bilingualism in classroom instruction remains behind closed doors, the teachers argue that the classroom space is transformed. The students feel safe and accepted knowing that the knowledge they have, in this case Spanish, is valid and worthy. As one teacher puts it, "At least they know that in these four walls, this is their space, their home." I was able to observe that the students do not hesitate to address their teachers in Spanish. The students consistently express their critical ideas about the story they are reading or the history project they are working on in their primary language. One teacher allows her students to complete homework and book report projects in Spanish. Another teacher has the students translate their English spelling words to Spanish as part of her curriculum.

The teachers also make sure to highlight the political significance of bilingualism in their teaching as a means to safeguard and preserve the home language. One teacher expounds,

> "I don't want to say to my students that the only reason they are allowed to use Spanish in my classroom is because it will help them learn English. No, no. Knowing Spanish in and of itself is important. It's part of who they are and their cultural identity. Whether or not it helps in the learning of English is secondary."

The teachers argue that the message being sent to their students is that learning English is more important than being bilingual. During one observational visit, I attended an awards ceremony at a school experiencing a significant increase in the number of language minority students. The teacher informed me that "the principal was going overdrive to make sure that these students mastered English because their test scores were apparently hurt by the increasing bilingual population." To reward the learning of English, the students were retested in the weeks prior to the ceremony, and during the awards ceremony, a "Learning English" certificate was issued to the student who advanced the most levels in language acquisition.

By using Spanish in the classroom, the teachers send a counter message to their students. "I want my kids to feel very proud of the language they speak at home. I don't want them to be embarrassed or to start thinking that Spanish isn't as good as English. That's why I speak Spanish a lot in the classroom. It shows them that I am very proud of that!"

Resisting English only policies occurs outside the classroom as well. Teachers are actively engaged in changing the attitudes that fuel an antibilingual climate at their school sites. For the Latina/o teachers, this means speaking up at faculty meetings and advocating for the rights of their students in preserving their home language. One 5th grade teacher recounts,

> "There was actual talk about a no Spanish policy, that teachers and students could not speak Spanish in the class or outside. What was really scary was that most of the teachers didn't object to that idea. One teacher thought it was a good idea because it would help the kids learn English faster, and that's probably what their parents wanted anyway...well, it ended up being that we didn't do it. I fought hard for this policy to not happen...but what was interesting was the argument that won them over. We didn't do it not because the school thought it would hurt the kids more than help them, but because we couldn't figure out an effective way to enforce the policy."

Another teacher resisted the grading policy imposed upon her Spanish-speaking students. In fact, all the teachers argued that grading policies towards Spanish-speaking students are problematic in that they penalize students who are simply learning a new language. Case in point, none of their students made it to the honor roll this year despite the fact that some of their students perform above grade level in terms of content. One teacher recounts,

> "I remember when I first started in my 4th grade classroom, my kids were mostly from Mexico and Central America. These immigrant students were fluent in Spanish, some of them were above grade level. And because I was bilingual, I could assess that, I could assess that they got the concepts I was teaching, even though they were still learning English. So when report card time came around, I was giving A's & B's to low level ELD students. And I remember turning in my report cards and getting them back with a note saying that ELD students could not get A's & B's. That if they're at a certain level, the highest grade they can get is a C because they have to have a certain level of proficiency in English...I started thinking, isn't this another way to send a message to Latina/o students saying you're still not good enough. Like if I'm the teacher, and I can honestly say that they are A students in terms of content, they get it, but now the school is telling me that I can only give them a C, then isn't that another way of keeping them down, penalizing them for being at a certain level in their language development...So what I did was give out two sets of report cards. I explained to the parents that the official report card was completed according to the school guidelines, which only took into consideration their language level...but that my report cards, although not official, showed them where their kids were in terms of understanding the content."

Oppositional acts by Latina/o teachers change the impact of English only policies on their students. One second grade teacher advocated for PTA and school newsletters to be written in Spanish in an attempt to create a more inclusive environment for Spanish speaking parents. Another teacher arranged for the school to pay one of her mother volunteers to conduct translations at the school site so that parents could have access to school information. One 4th grade educator makes sure that books in Spanish are available at the annual book fair. Again, the teachers continually engage in counteracts to preserve the importance of bilingualism for their students.

Resisting racial microaggressions in a segregated milieu and promoting cross-cultural understanding and communication

Schools continue to marginalize and academically separate newly arrived immigrants. Separating students according to linguistic background creates racially and linguistically segregated spaces which limit the possibilities for cross-cultural understanding and communication. One teacher, who works in an exceptionally segregated school, adds,

> "Just go out to the playground and you can see the division. Even when the lunch times overlap for 10 minutes, the kids don't play with each other. So many times during recess duty I have kids who tattle and refer to each other by their race, like that Mexican kid hit me, or the white kids over there..."

Some of the teachers argue that segregation affords a comfortable set-up for white administrators and teachers. A common observation among some of the teachers was the hesitation of white teachers to work with Spanish-speaking students. One teacher adds,

> "I've heard white teachers refer to Latina/o kids as Mexican without really knowing if they are Mexican. There's kind of this attitude with some of the white teachers that because they don't speak Spanish they can't work with ELD students. In my school we do divide the students by their language level...I remember this one teacher saying that it's better that way because if she had recess duty with these kids, she wouldn't be able to understand them, especially in an emergency."

Meaningful interaction among students from a variety of racial and linguistic backgrounds is immobilized. The lack of cultural exchange and communication reifies the "us versus them" dynamic, giving rise to otherness and marginality. One teacher articulates, "I'm so tired of my class being seen as the low class with the low kids." In an effort to oppose this marginalization, some of the teachers integrate their classrooms. One teacher, for example, co-teaches Science with an English-only classroom so that his students are exposed to a more diverse stu-dent body. Another teacher collaborates with an English-only teacher for Language Arts. The students pair up to teach each other both Spanish and English. These efforts provide a multicultural space for students to develop an understanding of diversity. One teacher states, "How do you expect students to get to know other cultures if you keep them away from each other."

Segregation also provides fertile ground for the prevalence of racial microaggressions towards Spanish speakers at these school sites. Racial microaggressions, rarely investigated in educational settings, can impact the educational experiences of students of color (Solórzano, Ceja & Yosso, 2000; Steele and Aronson, 1995). Yosso (2002) defines racial microaggressions as "subtle (verbal, nonverbal, visual) insults of People of Color, often done automatically or unconsciously." Microaggressions can comprise complex affronts that mix together identifiers like race, culture, language, immigration status, and phenotype, ultimately privileging whites to the detriment of People of Color.

Although the teachers could easily cite instances of overt racist comments, like "It's amazing what those little brown kids can do in your class," most of the descriptors towards Spanish speakers consisted of more subtle innuendos, like "I don't understand you, speak better," or "I don't know why those parents just never show up." These innocuous forms of racist behavior constitute racial microaggressions and are much more insidious (Davis, 1989). Racial microaggressions, as covert and subtle as they are, become much more difficult to contest and resist. One teacher notes,

> "It's kind of like you hear something about your students that just doesn't sit right and so I'm usually pretty good at asking people, 'what do you mean by that?' Immediately you get this reaction like once again I'm making a big deal out of nothing or I'm too sensitive about race, it's not all about race. It's so easy to turn it on me again."

During the focus group interview, a common theme that emerged was the fact that racist language was often coded under language ability. Deficit thinking attitudes permeated faculty lounge conversations, faculty meeting discussions, and school policies. "You always hear 'what can we do about those kids?' They're seen as a problem and we need to fix them...So you have people who feel that they're better. They don't refer to them as poor immigrant people, they just say English language learners, but it's the same." Most of the educators concurred that the label 'English language learner' could easily be replaced with poor immigrant, Mexican, et cetera, in the minds of some of their white colleagues. Simply put, labels referring to language and ability, act as a smokescreen for the larger category of race – clearly, "redefining the categories of difference makes it easier to identify and subsequently normalize and socialize the so-called deviant population" (Gutierrez, et al, 2002). In addition, these deficit explanations on the part of administrators and teachers are patterns connected to white strategies of assimilation, a strategic way of privileging the normalcy of white middle-class norms (Villenas and Deyhle, 1999).

The teachers admit that racial microaggressions are insidious and difficult to resist. All of the teachers commented that they are psychologically drained from the negative racial climate at their schools and that this carries over into their performance in the classroom. The teachers talked about feeling more tired and overburdened with the responsibility of making sure the students succeed in the face of so many obstacles. One teacher states, "Some days I'm really tired of it. I hate to admit this but I do think of quitting. It can get to be too much...If I didn't have other teachers and parents who give me the emotional support, I don't think I would still be here."

Overall, the teachers talked about how subtle racist comments are constant reminders that there is much work to done. They walk into their classrooms with the commitment to provide optimal educational experiences. One teacher declares, "It just makes me fight harder. Yeah I know what you think of what my students can do, but I'm going to prove you wrong. I'm going to make sure that in spite of all the odds, my students can succeed."

For Latina/o educators, resisting racial microaggressions involves open and critical discussions of race and language both inside and outside the classroom. Inside the classroom, the teachers implement several activities to develop student understanding of discrimination and prejudice. These opportunities to explore race and racism transform the classroom into a political space where students delve into topics that enhance their critical consciousness of the world around them and how racism affects their lives. Most of the teachers begin discussions of racism by relying on historical events, like the Holocaust, Japanese internment camps of World War II, or the California missions. One teacher explains, "It's definitely not an easy thing for students to see or hear, but I think it's more dangerous if they go through life without knowing what's happened."

The teachers also highlight the need to ground discussions of racism in the lives of their students. Thus, the students develop an understanding of racism on both a global and local level. But personal dis-cussions of race and racism are challenging for some students. One teacher argues, "I mean some of my kids aren't even aware that what they have gone through or the TV show that they watch can be seen as racist. But the important thing with these talks is not that they feel hopeless, like wow the world is working against me because of where I come from, but that this awareness makes them stronger and more determined to work and fight harder."

Outside the classroom, the teachers struggle with administrators and speak up at faculty meetings to make sure that the school is meeting their students' interests. This may mean requesting assemblies that are more culturally in tune with students' backgrounds or advocating for more language resources to equalize the playing field. For one teacher, transformational resistance involved a protest to the traditional California Mission activity carried out in all 4th grade classrooms. She states, "I refused to have my students spend money and time creating these Missions without really understanding what went on there. My job is to make sure these kids are exposed to more perspectives than the one they get in a Social Studies book. If you're going to talk about the Missions then you have to talk about racism...so my students wrote a class letter protesting the Mission project and sent them out to all the classrooms. Some of the teachers agreed, but some of them thought I was being too radical and rebellious."

The lack of critical discussions of racism and how it impacts language minority students, which are necessary in creating an antiracist and democratic educational environment, protects white educators and reifies marginality and otherness. By limiting cross-cultural communication and understanding, Spanish speaking students remain in a segregated milieu impacted by racial microaggressions. Moving towards integration and open dialogue on matters of race can transform schools by naming the oppressive conditions that continue to impact the learning experiences of language minority students, and ultimately changing those structures set in place.

Resisting the marginalization of Latina/o families and forming alliances

Culture and language around the home do not become barriers unless specific school practices and policies make them so. Schools overestimate the literacy skills, knowledge of the working of the school system, and other resources Latina/o families have to assist their child academically (Romo & Falbo, 1995). The teachers concur that schools tend to be less responsive to the needs of Spanish speaking parents. The teachers reported that after talking with parents over the years, they learned that their parents were often unaware of their child's academic progress, they felt intimidated when approaching teachers and administrators to discuss their child, and due to language barriers, they could not rely on phone calls home to discuss issues.

For these teachers, establishing a meaningful relationship with parents is the first step toward transforming the relationship between Latina/o families and schools. The ability for these Latina/o teachers to establish meaningful bonds with their parents is often based on cultural and linguistic similarities. For one teacher, Open House night sets the tone. He explains,

> "First of all I make sure the parents know they can bring their kids… babysitting is not an option for some of my parents. I also tell my kids I want anyone who is involved in taking care of them to come, like older brothers or sisters or grandma…I am very honest with my parents. I let them know the high standards I have for their children…and I tell them about how I grew up, about having two parents who worked all day, who couldn't help me with my homework, and stuff like that. I talk to them in a way that maybe some other teachers can't."

Another teacher expounds, "As a Latina/o educator I know I am valued because I can relate to my students… I think that counts for so much. Just the fact that a kid can walk in and tell me they can't complete the science project because their parents don't get paid until next Friday, makes sense to me. I get it. I know what that's like."

The educators also argued that being able to communicate with the parents greatly impacts the learning experience for their students. One teacher comments,

> "I know for a fact my parents value me. When they drop off their kids they stick around in the classroom, and after school too. They feel comfortable here because they can talk to me. I ask them what they did over the weekend, or they tell me things that maybe I would not have known otherwise. Like for example, one of my girls was really out of it in class for the last couple of days. Her dad told me they were separating. This conversation didn't happen during a formal parent conference. It was right outside my door, minutes before class started. But he felt comfortable telling me, and that was the only time he could do it. It's those little pieces of information that just make all the difference in the world with my teaching."

By establishing a proactive relationship with parents, the teachers are able to form alliances, often through cultural intuition, to create change. Forming alliances is seen as an oppositional act in that Latina/o parents are often beset with stereotypes, and as a result, untapped as resources. The teachers talked about how there is this mentality that Latina/o parents do not care about the education of their children or that they are submissive and passive and will simply "go with the flow." In contrast to these stereotypes, the teachers argue that their parents are very motivated and committed to advocating for their children. In fact, research points to the reality that supportive relationships are more important than the student's family composition, income level or intelligence scores, and that successful Latina/o students are more likely to have a teacher, coach or other person in the school that is willing to take action (Hernandez, 1997).

A teacher-parent alliance allows parents to access information about the education of their language learners. For instance, the teachers inform parents about their rights when it comes to school procedures like IEPs and ELD testing. Also, the teachers make sure that their administrators are aware of their parental support, especially when it comes to negotiating resources for their students. For one teacher, accessing extra funds for a field trip to a museum would not have been possible without the support of classroom parents.

The teachers also make sure to include parents and other family members in the everyday running of the classroom. Spanish speaking parents, especially mothers, volunteer on a regular basis. Grandparents and older brothers and sisters are invited for classroom functions. By resisting the marginalization of Latina/o families, these teachers transform the relationship between families and schools. As one teacher affirms, "I know for a fact that my parents are more involved than they have ever been. You just have to make them feel that they have a place here even if they don't speak English and that we have something to learn from them. I learn a lot from my parents…I especially learn about their kids in a deeper way, like I learn about what works and doesn't work in terms of learning styles."

As a result of these alliances, the teachers argue that their students are more successful in the classroom. In fact, during the focus group interview, the teachers talked about how surprised and shocked administrators and colleagues are at the success of their students. "My principal questions my success with my students. She's suspicious because she can't believe that these students can do well, that they can think in a sophisticated way…Instead of being a cause for celebration, it's more like okay are you sure these students are taking the tests the way they should be." Other teachers pointed out that fellow-teachers are curious about why so many Spanish speaking parents show up for Open House and Parent Conferences.

The previous three themes do not constitute an exhaustive list of oppositional acts aimed at changing the schooling experiences for Spanish-speaking students. In addition, these examples are not limited to certain groups. Instead, the chapter's discussion of oppositional acts points to some forms of transformational resistance that some Latina/o teachers engage in. This description serves as a starting point as we start to think about supporting Latina/o teachers who are committed to making available a more socially just learning environment for Spanish-speaking students.

Supporting Latina/o Educators Engaged in Transformational Resistance

The voices of Latina/o educators allow us to understand the racialized learning experiences of language minority students from a different perspective. As this chapter demonstrates, their insights on the pervasiveness of racism in schools serving Spanish-speakers force us to rethink language issues in light of transformational resistance. By resisting English only policies, segregation and racial microaggressions, and the marginalization of Latina/o families, Latina/o teachers are engaged in counteracts which oppose racial inequities. As such, their insurgent knowledge base contests white understandings of the schooling experiences of Spanish-speaking students.

Despite the prevalence of racism in our schools, teacher education programs do not require a serious study of race relations as preparation for teaching in our multilingual and racially divided society. And when race and racism are discussed, those conversations cater to the interests of monolingual white teachers. In teacher education courses, I often notice that discussions of racism continue to center around the experiences of white people and their struggle with coming to terms with their own whiteness or their frustrations in working with language minority students. In fact, part of white privilege is the placement of white people at the center of inquiry, and that even discussions specifically designated for members of a non-privileged group are often hijacked by white students accustomed to the expectation of occupying center stage (Grillo & Wildman, 1997). As a result, in-depth discussions of race and racism are missed, leaving teacher candidates of color with the role of defending the argument that racism is real.

Clearly, U.S. schools continue to be learning spaces where an increasingly homogeneous teaching population will come into contact with an increasingly heterogeneous student population in an anti-immigrant and anti-multilingual social climate. Accordingly, most of the literature on antiracist education focuses on the manner in which new teachers, and thus white teachers, are prepared to effectively educate today's diverse student population. Missing are discussions on how to reframe our courses to better meet the needs of teachers of color invested in transformational resistance vis-à-vis racist schooling practices. Thus, I argue that to better serve the needs of Latina/o teachers, we must reconceptualize our courses so that teachers of color and other critical educators can explore acts of resistance aimed at creating a more socially just learning environment for Spanish speaking students and other historically marginalized students. The following are two main suggestions for beginning this transformation.

1. Putting into practice subjugated epistemologies

We must revisit the epistemological bases of our teacher preparation courses. Offering courses from the racial epistemologies, or ways of knowing, of People of Color decenters Eurocentric ways of seeing and understanding issues in education, particularly issues impacting historically marginalized students. Critical race theory aims to decenter Eurocentric epistemology by recognizing that the "experiential knowledge of Women and Men of Color is legitimate, appropriate, and critical to understanding, analyzing, practicing, and teaching about…racial subordination (Solórzano, 1997, p. 7). Critical race theory not only aims to expose the centrality of racism in our schools, but it also aims to provide a powerful voice that envisions social discourse in new ways.

Subjugated epistemologies offer unique ways of knowing and understanding the world based on the various raced experiences of People of Color. By organizing our curricula around the subjugated knowledge of People of Color, we recognize there is more than one way to look at the world and thus, open up possibilities for understanding the schooling experiences of Spanish-speakers, for example, in new and different ways. These margin perspectives can take the form of counterstories. Counterstories are narratives that challenge the dominant version of reality and lead to the development and acceptance of epistemologies that recognize that People of Color make sense of the world in ways that differ from the dominant white view (Delgado, 1989).

Including counterstories in our syllabi and curricula allows Latina/o teachers to connect to outside literature that may speak to their experiences and interests and allows them to build upon their lived experiences and insights in regard to race and education. Using the knowledge base of People of Color provides a starting point for in-depth dialogues about the multiple ways in which racism functions in schools on an everyday basis and how racism intersects with other oppressions, like sexism, classism, and ableism. In addition, counterstories expose more relevant topics of investigation for teachers of color, such as sexism within communities of color, inter-ethnic discrimination, and internalized racism.

2. Developing oppositional consciousness and activism

Teachers are at the mercy of a system in which their teaching has become increasingly prescribed and monitored by external agencies. Accordingly, teachers are ill-prepared to contest the conservative and oppressive attitudes and policies that permeate schools. We know that educators who conscientiously practice empowering and autonomous teaching practices are often marginalized. Critical and responsible teachers too often find themselves treated as pariahs, outsiders who risk banishment with their "bad attitudes" and their reluctance to become "team players." Resistance is viewed negatively, and so the work of many critical educators remains unsupported in our teacher education programs.

Teacher preparation programs must support teachers in developing an oppositional consciousness aimed at transformational resistance. Developing and supporting oppositional consciousness prepares teachers to undermine, reform, or overthrow racist policies impacting language minority students. Courses should provide reflective and collaborative spaces for students to explore oppression and resistance and to develop concrete strategies for creating change. It is critical, then, for teachers of color to build alliances with other educators who resist and change what often seems a hegemonic system of power relations. For instance, instructors and students could explore examples of organized or everyday resistance to racism and make contacts with individuals and organizations committed to eliminating racism in our schools. Ultimately, tapping into oppositional consciousness and activism enforces the idea of teachers as political agents of change.

If we are committed to addressing racism, equity, and social justice in a substantive way, then we must explore acts of transformational resistance aimed at creating a more equitable and antiracist learning environment for marginalized students. Documenting the political acts of Latina/o teachers begins the dialogue of how change can take place.

I hope that through their voices and perspectives, the reader has learned something about the possibilities of teacher insurgency.

References

Carter, R. (2000). Reimagining Race in Education: A New Paradigm from Psychology. *Teachers College Record 102*, 864-897.

Covarrubias, A. & Revilla, A. (2003). Agencies of transformational resistance. *Florida Law Review 55*, 459-477.

Crawford, J. (1992). *Hold your tongue: Bilingualism and the politics of English only*. Redding, MA: Addison-Wesley.

Crenshaw, K. (1995). Introduction. In K. Crenshaw, N. Gotanda, G. Peller, & K. Thomas (Eds.) *Critical race theory: The key writings that formed the movement*. New York: New Press

Davis, P. (1989). Law as microaggression. *Time Yale Law Journal, 98*, 1559-77.

Delgado, R., & Stefancic, J. (2000). *Critical race theory: The cutting edge*. Philadelphia: Temple University Press.

Delgado Bernal, D. (2002). Critical race theory, Latino critical theory, and critical race-gendered epistemologies. *Qualitative Inquiry*, 8, 105-125

Delgado Bernal, D. (1998). Using a Chicana feminist epistemology in educational research. *Harvard Education Review*, 68(4), 555-582

Dillard, C. (2000). The substance of things hoped for, the evidence of things not seen: Examining an endarkened feminist ideology in culturally engaged research. *International Journal of Qualitative Studies in Education, 13*, 661-681.

Emerson, R., Fretz, R., & Shaw, L. (1995). *Writing ethnographic fieldnotes*. Chicago: University of Chicago Press.

Erickson, F. (1986). Qualitative methods in research on teaching. In M. Wittrock (ed.) *Handbook of research on teaching*. New York: MacMillan.

Goodman, J. (1992). Elementary schooling for critical democracy. Albany, NY: State University of New York Press.

Grillo & Wildman (1997). Obscuring the importance of race. In R. Delgado & J. Stefancic (Eds.), *Critical white studies: Looking behind the mirror* (pp. 619-626). Philadelphia: Temple University Press.

Gutierrez, K., Asato, J., Santos, M., & Gotanda, N. (2002). Backlash pedagogy: lan guage and culture and the politics of reform. *The Review of Education, Pedagogy, and Cultural Studies, 24*, 335-351.

Gutierrez, K., Asato, J., Pacheco, M., Moll, L., Olson, K., Horng, E., Ruiz, R., Garcia, E., & McCarty, T. L. (2002). Sounding American: The consequences of new reforms on English language learners. *Reading Research Quarterly, 37*(3), 328-343.

Hernandez, L. (1997). Families and schools together. Harvard Family Research Project.

Ladson-Billings & Tate (1995). Toward a critical race theory of education. *Teachers College Record, 97*, 47-68.

Macedo, D. (2000). The colonialism of the English only movement. *Educational researcher, 29*(3), 15-24.

Martinez, R. (2001). A crisis in the profession: Minority role models in critically short supply. *Vocational Education Journal , 66*(4), 24-46.

Matsuda (1995). Looking to the bottom: Critical legal studies and reparations. In K. Crenshaw, N. Gotanda, G. Peller, & K. Thomas (Eds.) *Critical race theory: The key writings that formed the movement*. New York: New Press

McLaren, P. and Munoz, J. (2000). Contesting whiteness: Critical perspectives on the struggle for social justice. In C. Ovando and P. McLaren, *The politics of multiculturalism and bilingual education*. Boston: McGraw Hill.

Mohanty, C. (1991). Under Western eyes: Feminist scholarship and colonial discourses. In C. Mohanty, A. Russo, and L. Torres, *Third world women and the politics of feminism*. Bloomington: Indiana University Press.

Monzo, L. & Rueda, R. (2001). *Sociocultural factors in social relationships: Examining Latino teachers' and paraeducators' interactions with Latino students*, Research Report 9. Center for Research on Education, Diversity & Excellence: Santa Cruz, CA and Washington, D.C.

Parker, L., Deyhle, D., and Villenas, S. (eds). 1999. *Race is—Race Isn't: Critical Race Theory and Qualitative Studies in Education*. Boulder, Colo.: Westview Press.

Pizarro, M. (1998). "Chicana/o power!" Epistemology and methodology for social justice and empowerment in chicana/o communities. *Qualitative Studies in Education, 11*(1), 57-80.

Solórzano, D. & Yosso, T. (2002). Critical race methodology: Counterstorytelling as an analytical framework for education research. *Qualitative Inquiry, 8*, 23-44.

Solórzano, D. & Delgado Bernal, D. (2001). Examining transformational resistance through a critical race and LatCrit theory framework: Chicana and Chicano students in an urban context. *Urban Education 36*, 308-342.

Solórzano, D., Ceja, M. & Yosso, T. (2000). Critical race theory, racial microaggressions and campus racial climate: The experiences of African American college students. *Journal of Negro Education, 69*, 60-73.

Steele, C. M., & Aronson, J. (1995). Stereotype threat and the intellectual test performance of African-Americans. *Journal of Personality and Social Psychology, 69*, 797-811.

Strauss, A. & Corbin, J. (1990). *Basics of qualitative research: Grounded theory procedures and techniques*. Newbury Park: Sage.

Villenas, S. & Deyhle, D. (1999). Critical race theory and ethnographies challenging the stereotypes: Latino families, schooling, resilience and resistance. *Curriculum Inquiry, 29*, 413-445.

Yosso, T. (2002). Critical race media literacy: Challenging deficit discourse about Chicanas/os. *Journal of Popular Film and Television*.

Yosso, T. (2000). A critical race and LatCrit approach to media literacy: Chicana/o resistance to visual microaggressions. Unpublished doctoral dissertation, University of California, Los Angeles.

Chapter 5
Teachers' Self-knowledge of their Personal and Professional Epistemologies as Seen Through the Teaching of Writing
by Antonella Cortese, Ph.D.

Abstract

This case study examines how teachers' personal and professional ideological beliefs of literacy are connected to their instructional practice. Taking a critical participatory action research perspective, the goal of this study was to provide a space for teachers to reflect on the "contact zones" they navigate and negotiate; where the historical, political and social of their personal and professional "selves" collude (Pratt, 1990; Ellsworth, 1997).

The research process included interviews and classroom observations analyzed through the lens of Cultural-Historical Activity Theory which posits that in order to have a clear sense of the origin of anything, one must have understanding of the pro-cess of development and change undergone as understood by the individual self and others (Vygotsky, 1962/1978 adapted by Engeström, 1999). Through this dialogical process teachers were articulate in "best practices" but not as comfortable in identifying their beliefs related to their practice. This, ultimately, was reflected in their awareness of instructional processes and ambivalence of their own positioning—a product of local school and district culture.

How the teaching of writing, or any subject matter, is characterized is not as simple as a teacher *objectively* following an instructional method. As Purves (1990) states, when it comes to learning to become a "scribe [r]ather than consider the child that enters the system, one can begin by thinking of the adult who emerges from it. Once one knows the destination, then one can consider the path." (italics added) (p. 89)

In this manner, what teachers bring *in*to their classroom practice— their personal political, social, cultural, and linguistic perspective(s) fundamentally impacts their students at the academic level. That is, it is more than the knowledge that an individual teacher brings to the endeavor, in this case writing instruction, but also the knowledge(s) he/she presents and represents on a personal *and* thus, professional level.

Much research addressing teachers and their classroom practice characterizes teachers according to the features or indicators performed, reducing the notion of teaching to a simple list of descriptors. Teaching has become, in many cases, the search for "the answer out there somewhere"; the knowing of *exactly* which actions, what content knowledge(s), and/or which part of ourselves is needed or correct to attain the results desired—students who can achieve their highest potential academically and personally (Ellsworth, 1997). It assumes that the teacher undertakes an objectively driven process exclusive of his or her own personal and professional development, and *reflective* engagement in the area of teaching:

> We rarely talk with each other about teaching at any depth—and why should we when we have nothing more than "tips, tricks, and techniques" to discuss? (…) [I]f we want to grow as teachers—we must do something alien to academic culture: we must talk to each other about our inner lives—risky stuff in a profession that fears the personal and seeks safety in the technical, the distant, the abstract. (Palmer, 1998, pp. 11-12)

The principle driving question is: What is the relationship between teachers' everyday practice and teachers' self-knowledge of their everyday practice of writing?

In order to begin to address this question it is important to be cognizant of the fact that a key piece to the answer lies in what teachers bring to the table, to —*their* history as a student, their lived realities as individuals in various spaces (i.e., their family, neighborhood, and surrounding community), and as teachers, those individuals with whom 'knowledge' resides. All of this is imperative to understand, to go beyond the one-dimensional, professional ahistorical reality from only the classroom context so as to not be "reduced to the ghostly status of the general, the abstract or the ideal—or the unreal" (Kemmis & Wilkinson, 1998, p. 25).

The goal of this chapter is not to evaluate the effectiveness of any specific writing program or teacher practitioner. Rather, its purpose is to illuminate why and how teachers make the choices they do by providing a space for teachers to dialogue and reflect upon their practice in writing instruction from a multi-faceted perspective—social, political, cultural, and pedagogical; to both *see* and *look* at how their prevailing ideologies on a personal level and their resulting pedagogical epistemologies are expressed and illustrated through views on the literacy process and teaching of writing. In this chapter I will illustrate the process I undertook through the stories of two teachers specifically and the activities in which they participated. The chapter begins with the framework used to investigate two teachers' historical context from a personal and professional perspective, the theoretical perspective adapted, and the larger study within which these teachers and study are framed.

Cultural Historical Activity Theory as a Lens *In*

I chose to utilize Engeström's (1999) expanded Cultural-History Activity Theory (CHAT)1 (Figure 1) framework based on the work of Vygotsky and Leonte'v (1978). The idea, as Engeström (1999) postulates, is that Vygotsky perceived human control of behavior a consequence of the *outside* influence of society and the culture driving it, *not* a basis of biological urges. In the case of teachers, their activities are implicitly and explicitly affected by a "culture of teaching" via a process of socialization within which individuals engage and are engaged (Ríos, 1996). To illustrate the interactions that give rise to the culture of teaching, Figure 1, "Framework for Examining Teacher Practice in the area of Writing Activity Development," exemplifies the relational components within the context of teacher practice in the teaching of writing. The figure illustrates the relationship of actions from multiple directions and how the understanding of artifacts (tools) used in actual activities (object, outcome, rules, division of labor), in genuine settings (community), are an integral facet of human cognitive functioning and cultural evolution (Wartofsky, 1979). In this way, the CHAT paradigm brings into focus the interconnectedness and multiple dimensions of classroom teaching—from the individual teacher and students to community within which the school is located—all of which impact the course of daily life in the classroom.

Figure 1: Framework for Examing Teacher Practice in the area of Writing Activity Development

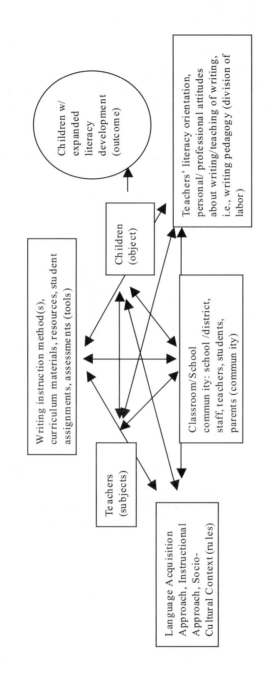

Navigating the "Contact Zones" –Participatory Action Research

Kemmis and Wilkinson's (1998) critical participatory action research approach (PAR)[2] is the foundation to the research process of listening to the voices of teachers. It is employed to engage participants' voices and experiences, and provide each participant the "space" to engage in dialogue on their own conditions, in their own terminology and language(s). In fact, the teachers participating in this study welcomed the opportunity to engage in an honest dialogue about their teaching practices in an "era of standards" in the area of writing. In this manner, I created and employed a series of tools in order to permit teachers to reflect upon issues of literacy, teaching, and writing in general, on a personal and professional level and in light of their own practice. These tools are described in the sub-section below:

Research Journal: I recorded notes following each informal meeting with each teacher into a research journal that I kept during the entire research study process. It served as a space for me to reflect upon and note down moods (my own as well as others), personal reactions, and random thoughts and questions that would later help recapture details seemingly unimportant in the moment.

First Interview and Graphic Organizer: The goal of this research study was to learn why and how teachers make the choices they do; to voice their beliefs about writing instruction in their classrooms; and to see how their beliefs connect or do not connect to their practice. The initial interview I conducted with each teacher participant followed a standardized open-ended question format. As well, each question was linked with its respective part of the CHAT framework. For example, one question, linked to the CHAT framework components *"outcomes," "object,"* and *"rules"* was: "In the area of writing, what do you expect your students to accomplish by the end of the year?"

To facilitate the initial interview, a word web graphic organizer (Figure 2), similar to Cadiero-Kaplan's (2004), was created and given to each teacher prior to the scheduled interview. The web was developed based on topics that were derived from both research literature and interview questions regarding the definition, instructional strategies, curriculum, assessment and the process of writing which is in the center of the web. The twelve outlying concepts including personal experience, definition of literacy, student experiences, teaching strategies, instructional goals, and curriculum resources, are reflected in the research literature as areas that shape and affect the teaching of writing.

Figure 2: Word Web Graphic Organizer for First Interview

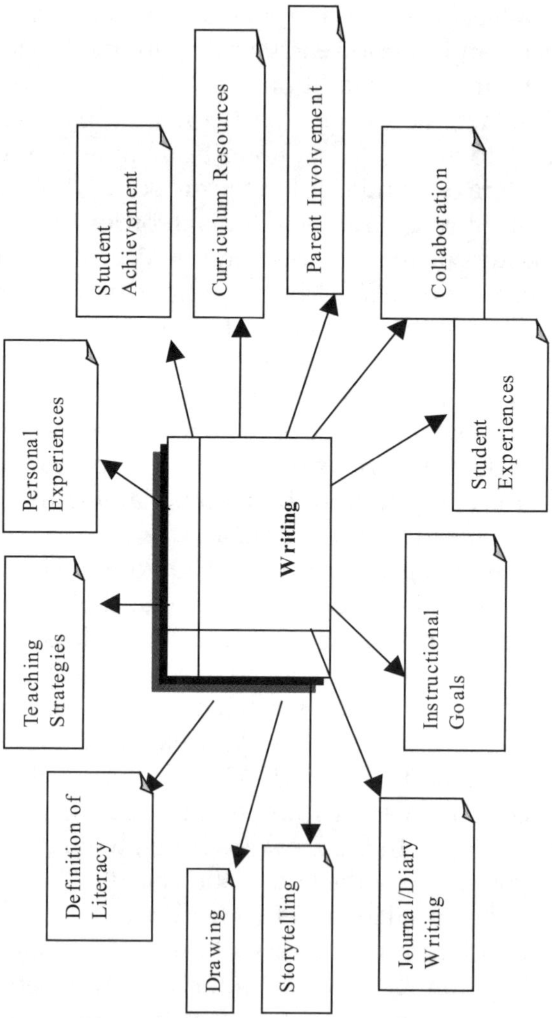

Classroom Observation and Second Interview: The second interview took place after the conclusion of classroom observations. The format of the second interview was in the form of an informal conversational interview (Quinn-Patton, 1990). This approach provided the opportunity to pursue the unique issues raised by each teacher participant in the first interview and to learn further what teachers' intentions were when engaged in their teaching. I also recorded reflections on tensions I encountered in working with the teachers. These notes informed my final analysis of the data regarding my own conflicts with regard to theory and practice (and are discussed in the final section of this chapter).

Each teacher participant was informed of my focus for the classroom observations and each one introduced me to her class as either a "teacher and researcher" or "teacher doing a project for school" interested in seeing what their classroom looked like. I was a partial participant within the classroom context and present in each classroom community. I answered questions that students would ask me during classroom free time, or provided assistance to a teacher if needed. My goal was to not interfere with teacher practice, nor influence it.

My purpose was to be able to chronicle the accounts of individuals' behaviors in detail. Part of this included collecting students' writing assignments and teaching curricula. The collection of these artifacts provided further evidence for the questions addressed in this study as they are the tools with which teacher participants interacted; how they planned their daily lessons, how they evaluated their students, how they put into practice their own ideas, personal and professional, about the teaching of writing. On the whole, teachers spend personal time and money to make tangible and openly visible *their* philosophy of teaching and learning in their classroom by their selection of wall hangings, classroom seating arrangements, work/study centers, classroom library, and by those things not so visible: textbooks, lesson plans, teaching aides, curriculum guides, and homework assignments. As a result, both the visible and the invisible artifacts, together, that it is—the personal more subjective self and the professional, more so-called objective self—create the classroom culture from which students will take their first cues as to what it is to learn and to *become* a learner (Ellsworth, 1997). In considering this, I adopted a categorical structure for my observations, each of which was aligned to the CHAT paradigm:

- *Program Setting* (Rules/Community/Outcome)—illustrated via a "classroom map" which describes the physical environment, including student seating chart, bookcases and file cabinets, learning centers, wall hangings (Jones & Prescott, 1984);

- *Human/Social Environment* (Subject/Community/Rules)—patterns of interaction as illustrated in diverse classroom activities/settings, grouping during activities, human reactions to in class or outside events;
- *Classroom Activity* (Tools/Rules/Outcome)—sequence of informal and formal events and activity, introduction and implementation of formal activities, materials used, duration, the "who, what, where, when, and how" of the activities observed;
- *Language of the Program* (Rules/Subject/Community)—this includes routinized procedures and non-verbal communication.

Drawing upon the view of the PAR perspective, that of "helping people understand themselves as the agents, as well as products, of history," (Kemmis, 1993, p. 3) teachers also were asked to read and reflect upon the interview transcript data and classroom observation notes. Teachers were asked to speak to those scenes or spaces within the data where they saw and heard tensions in their practice or ideology. The purpose of such a process was to provide a space for teachers to reflect upon those personal and professional contact zones they navigate and negotiate inside and outside the institution of school, where the historical, cultural and political collude (Pratt, 1990). This approach permitted teachers to *read* their own history and to dialectically engage their ideologies (personal and professional) in relationship to the instructional space they occupy and work within. In this way, they were able to work toward coming to terms with the "socio-political construct that contributes to what individuals, as students, understand and live as knowledge and meaning" (Friere & Macedo, 1987, pp. 14-15).

Anne and Mary[1]: Performers Suspended Between the Self and the Other

As Ellsworth (1997) states, "pedagogy is a performance that is suspended in between the self and other" (p. 17). As such, to not include the personal is to negate the self. In this fashion, this section summarizes the personal and professional profiles of Anne and Mary based on the initial interview and interview following classroom observations.

1.   Anne is bilingual in Spanish, which is her second language. She learned Spanish in college and credits her work experience at a country club with native-Spanish speakers to her ability to being able to prac-

tice Spanish in order to use it to learn it. She is a native English speaker and holds a Bilingual/CLAD credential. She started her teaching career in Oakland, California where she taught primarily in what she calls a mixed class; the student population was mostly African-American and native Spanish speakers. She defined her instructional practice in Oakland as split, that is between English reading in the morning and then Spanish in the afternoon. She also mentioned that her previous principal had a "top-down" administration style and didn't express interest in teacher feedback. She has been at Tri-City Elementary for two years and has only taught 3rd grade. She also recently received her tenure at the district.

In talking about her class, she mentioned that in comparison to last year, she is teaching a Structured English Immersion[3] (SEI) class with 26 students in which she also has students who are native English speakers whose English language arts skills are very low. Of her initial group, she commented that there was a "huge transience this year. I don't think half the kids I had when we had our class picture taken are here." For the number of students that have left, since the beginning of the school year—anywhere from seven to nine students—as many have come in to "fill those empty desks." She noted that two students in her classroom came in about 2 months before the classroom observation time began in her classroom. She noted that these students are native Spanish speakers with no previous English language experience.

When the conversation moved to a more personal level and Anne's "literacy autobiography," she quickly remarked she came from a very "literate family, a family that really valued education." Her father would take her to the Anaheim Public Library "every Friday night from 1966 to 1972. It was our Friday night ritual and he would peel off to the adult section and I would go to the kids' section and we would meet back when we were done."

She also recounted the story her mother told her about when she was four or five and she wanted a library card of her own. She tells of how the librarian told her she could have her own library card when she was able to print her name. She practiced until she got it just right. She remembers loving reading, as she still does. Growing up, she also remembers having kept diaries, doing well on school writing assignments, but when it came to writing, described it as "a really painful process for me, although I am very good at it." And though she has been told that she is a good writer, she does not pursue it in light of the time it would take and the direction in which to focus.

2. Mary, is a bilingual speaker, her second language is Spanish. She

has lived in Southern California all of her life and has been a teacher for 27 years. She has taught mostly in Southern California and has been teaching at Tri-City Elementary for well over 10 years. She has an M.A. in Bilingual Education, has a lifetime B/CLAD K-12 credential and has been teaching 3rd grade for six years at Tri-City Elementary. She is currently teaching a 3rd grade Bridge[4] class with 20 students. She defines her class as a group consisting of "mainstream English speakers with low skills, Mexican born students who do not speak Spanish and a couple of students who are designated as English language learners." She highlighted that this was her first year teaching a Bridge class. In past years, she has taught the SEI classes in which the students are designated as Beginning to Early Intermediate per district test score results. Her Bridge students are designated as Early Intermediate to Intermediate level. One thing, she states, that has not changed in teaching a new class is the fact that, as has been in most cases, she isn't sure what her students' literacy level is, be it if their native language is or isn't English, as their academic records are sketchy. That is, as she states, "(…) because many of the students that come into our school are either just coming into the country, coming in from another school [from another state] let alone the district, I don't always know where they're at."

She remarked about her bilingual students in particular and spoke quite succinctly stating that she doesn't teach bilingual education, but rather ESL[5] as her school district adopted to implement Proposition 227. Her feelings about this are expressed in the following manner: "I mean, if the kids are of normal intelligence and have the required ESL time, I feel that they can transition into a mainstream English class within the three years as stipulated by the district."

Our conversation then moved on to her own literacy autobiography in which she talked about her experiences in becoming bilingual (she studied in Mexico during her time studying for her teaching credential) and as an adult goes to her "real house and life in Mexico" most weekends, every summer and holidays. Like Anne, Mary fondly remembers going to the library with one of her parents. In Mary's case, it was with her father who was working on his Master's degree at the University of Southern California (USC). She recalled and spoke about reading <u>Heidi</u> by streetlight as well as having read <u>Black Beauty</u> and all the *Nancy Drew* mysteries. She remarked that she read a lot as a child and still does. In her words, she could "let the house burn while reading" and that she has "burnt many a dinner" losing herself in reading. To this, she added that although she reads a lot, she isn't a good speller and in all, doesn't like to write. She does write a few letters and uses electronic mail, but she says, "those are sent back corrected." In closing about her own literacy autobiography, speaking about her writing, she comments:

> I write like I speak, I mean, rambling, changing subjects and not think-
> ing ahead. I don't understand grammar, I mean, I know how to say
> things correctly, but I don't know the rules for it for writing. I learned
> more about English by learning Spanish in school.

Each of these teachers comes to the endeavor of teaching in a specific school district, with different academic and professional experiences, and as a result, most importantly of all of this, with differing attitudes as to how they "see" their own students as "selves." According to Pajares (1992), "beliefs are the best indicators of the decisions individuals make throughout their lives" (p. 307). The profiles provided an initial context from which to begin the dialogue process and influenced the engagement of the interactions within the interview portions of this study and classroom observations, both of which helped shed more light onto the what and resulting why and how of individual histories which are brought to the classroom everyday. The next section outlines the trends and shared traits across both teachers, Anne and Mary, as they expressed and discussed their attitudes and beliefs in their everyday teaching of writing in their classrooms, in their school and school district.

The Human Heart: The Source of Good Teaching

> In our rush to reform education, we have forgotten a simple truth:
> reform will never be achieved by renewing appropriateness, restruc-
> turing schools, rewriting curricula, and revising texts if we continue
> to demean and dishearten the human resource called the teacher on
> whom so much depends. (...) [N]one of that will transform education
> if we fail to cherish-and challenge-the human heart that is the source
> of good teaching. (Palmer, 1998, p. 3)

Deborah Hicks (1996) wrote of the relationship between teaching and learning that, it "occurs as a co-construction (or re-construction) of social meanings within the parameters of emergent, socially negotiated, and discursive activity" (p. 136). The teachers participating in this research study held the best interests of their students, maintaining high expectations for them and their educational success. This is a critical point, for upon further examination of their teaching strategies and processes, each one limited student achievement with regard to writing instruction in differing ways. That is, although the teachers in this study maintained an altruistic and empathetic notion as to how their individual students' lived realities impact their classroom learning, they all expressed their ideas and beliefs, in *deficit* terms. This was pointed out and expressed by the teachers in how they selected the types of writing homework to give their students and how they perceive students' success rate in doing such work at home. Their concerns ranged from students not having an appropriate English language skills role model to parents' unavailability or absence in the home or even their lack of interest in their child's education.

Ideological Beliefs and Pedagogical Approaches toward the Teaching of Writing

Overall, Anne and Mary were ideologically progressive in their beliefs about literacy. They expressed a desire to encourage their students' ability to communicate via writing as well as to engage them in writing as a medium to express their knowledge, on both a personal and academic level. In defining "Literacy" in their own words, it became an avenue by which each one of them identified themselves and their practice. Below are Anne's and Mary's definitions:

> *Anne*: "Well... the most pedestrian definition is just ability to read and write. For me it would be the...the ability to traverse the world of language...to make sense out of it...to access information through it...to be able to express yourself through it, to get enjoyment out of it."
>
> *Mary*: "Geez. I'm not sure. The ability to listen, speak, read and write. But I've met many people that cannot read and they have a wisdom that is so special, like my gardener, his children, for example. He is so knowledgeable about so many things and his children too, they know so much."

During their separate interviews, in defining their notions about what literacy is as a reflection of their individual selves, they also responded to this question with regard to their role as teacher to their students and those individual forces that make up the "institution" of educational practice—their local school and district administration. In one manner or another, they expressed that the curriculum they are required to use is unbalanced and does not address students' needs linguistically or academically in the area of writing. This came through when I asked each of them about how she felt she puts into practice her own ideas about literacy:

Anne: "(…in terms of writing, that's always a tricky area for me because…the tension between what I am charged with teaching them in terms of writing, what the third grade standards are, and what I believe about teaching writing and using a Writer's Workshop[6] approach are so diametrically opposed. You know? It's like trying to move in two different directions at the same time (…)."

Mary: "I'm just not sure. In teaching the kids I try to hook it all together. So, like I try to do themes. Like now, we are doing careers, so I try to find literature to read to them that is about someone, like Amelia Earhardt. Then we're going to do a word web about what they want to do when they grow up so they can do a paragraph writing. But, really, I am not sure how successful I am. I don't know how to teach writing well at all."

Mary, throughout the study, spoke candidly regarding her own feelings about writing and her personal opinion about her own writing ability as a function of both her attitude towards teaching writing and her ability to teach it. In this way, Mary concentrated on using more functionally-based activities and processes in her teaching, only using more progressive processes when they were precisely defined and able to be employed with little to no extra instructional input on her part, again, expressing uncertainty in her own ability to manipulate curriculum materials for her students' individual needs:

"Well, I think it [teaching of writing program] is partly due to the fact that I
don't like to write much at all. I would much rather read. Plus, I don't feel that there is a lot of writing in the Wilda Storm[7] program either, not as much as there was in this other program, I can't remember what it was called."

Anne engaged her progressive ideology to the greatest degree. She used progressive strategies throughout most of her teaching of writing to engage the learning of "functional" knowledge important to their continued learning of more complex concepts and language structures:

"I try to expose them [the students] to as many different kinds of print and text as I can…and model for them…scaffold…it's the gradual release of responsibility. Where it's I'm doing the work, then we do it together, then they do it and I watch 'em. I mean, every week we learn a new song, a new poem, and a new idiom…and, (…) you know, it's like, (…) that's like our shared experience…that's something we all have to refer to."

Along this same vein, Anne continued to explain more specifically that in a class like hers, where the students are designated as having very low to no English language experience, she engages all the different forms of literacy in order to create as many avenues for learning for all her students. In this regard, Anne, more so than Mary, was more proactive in her teaching, engaging issues— ranging from students' language levels to transiency— and those representative of her local school and district administration:

> "One is, we've gotten all sorts of new curriculum, again, and not necessarily at the beginning of the year (...). I'm only feeling like the year's really getting started [laughs]...we have two months left to go and I'm like 'hey, I'm in a groove now!' That, and I've had like huge, huge transience this year. I don't think half the kids I had when we had our (...) class picture taken are here. I've had seven, eight, nine kids come and just as many leave. And every time it happens, you know, (...) we lose our momentum, (...). I got two kids, in the last month or so that don't have any English, and I've been like scaffolding their English, you know, weaning them off of the Spanish in class."

Though they did not state it in theoretical terms, both believed there exists a hidden agenda that impedes their practice, and thus, the success of their students. This was articulated consistently in their reflections on the use of "mandated district curriculum" and standardization of instruction based on that curriculum, and classroom assignment of students based on results of a reading-based standardized measure. For Mary and Anne the result of these concerns revolved around the issue of time to teach writing. Along these lines, Anne spoke to the tension to teach in the manner best for her students, and at the same time, to fit in everything that is required according to the dictates of their district and school administration:

> *Anne:* (...) half-hour, forty-five minutes to do English as a second language... to do the <u>Into English!</u>[8], (...). *I have to put it in there,* (...), the matrix for the report card uses various things that I don't have time to put in my day. So, how am I supposed to assess them in this area when you only have so many minutes in the day? And you were there in the classroom, you saw how chopped up it was. Twenty minutes? Okay, now we're going to do something else. Alright everybody, hitting your stride? 'cause sorry, I've gotta change it again because it's time, ya' know? (italics added)

As Anne continues, it is below, in this last excerpt, in which she situates herself in a more critical ideological space; she reflects on her values and what she knows to be the best method for teaching writing while struggling with teaching within a "prescribed" and functional model, one which is more closely aligned with the types of assessments mandated by her district:

> "[T]he standards have to do more with the product. Teaching writing is more process. I want to put more emphasis on process and the standards want to put more emphasis on the product. (…), it's easier to assess a product. It's a time crunch. (…) there's not much of a writing component in <u>Into English</u>. There are worksheets that go with each unit. It's not really writing as far as I'm concerned. I mean, I'm sure Hampton/Brown will say, 'We have a writing component' (…). I sacrifice Hampton Brown time. If writing is going really well on a particular day, I don't want to give it up, and then I'm like, I've gotta cover Unit 1 this month. It kills me, you know, we've just gotta cover it. You know, because the district has adopted that as our ESL program and I need to use it."

The excerpt above came towards the end of our interview time, and gives the most insight to Anne's commitment towards her students' learning, along with the frustration she has regarding how she is being directed to teach them. As most of the excerpts of our discussions together demonstrate, she is struggling to work within a system that doesn't match her intentions of what teaching writing should entail, supporting more progressive and critical views versus those of a more functional basic skills orientation.

In listening to Mary speak to the issue of how time impacts her practice, she expresses, from a critical point of view, that it is her local school and district administration that determine the role that writing plays in the overall learning process of her students by virtue of the time "delineated" for it:

> *Mary (M):* "(…) it's really difficult to even think about how to do the writing when we have to do 45 minutes of phonics, 45 minutes of ESL, half-hour of calendar, reading and writing, and handwriting and fluency."

> *Antonella:* "So, reading and writing are set up as separate?"

> *M:* "Well, you know, the reading is easier to do. With the phonics and ESL and all. But you know, we don't do a lot of writing. I mean, we do, in my class I am trying to do more and I have to sit in some of my colleagues classes who do Writer's Workshop. I don't know how they fit it in."

In listening to her speak consistently on this issue, that of how time impacts teachers' practice, I chose to pursue this and ask her about how she negotiates the tension she feels with regard to time to teach writing:

> "I mean, as it is we're asked to do so much with such a time constraint. (…). Wilda Storm really made me think. I really enjoyed her. Some of the things were okay, but (…) I'm not a centers type of person, and it takes a lot of time. And I just don't know, or understand, where she[9] has the time. I mean, I know some teachers just skip the ESL part. It's not right to not teach it, if they need it and you know, if it is done right, they will learn English. "

As I listened to Mary speak, and again listened to this portion of the recorded transcript, I realize that it is here in which she refers back to her opinion of bilingual education versus teaching under Proposition 227. And though she is not a solid proponent of the measure passed, she feels there is value in teaching children in English if done correctly and consistently. With this said, Mary's comments above place her within a more "cultural-progressive" framework when speaking of English language learners. That is, she values the need to use a student's native language in order to promote early learning of the second language, but at the same time sees the value in teaching in English if the method is done developmentally appropriately. To this, she added with regard to writing, specifically that:

> "(…) the program we are using isn't meeting the kids' needs. I mean, it's too systematic. It expects everyone to be at the same level. I just don't think it is meeting their needs."

In the excerpt above, although Mary expresses a more critical orientation toward the current writing program she is being asked to use, she is unable to articulate any more beyond this. Upon further questioning, it became clear that Mary is only able to express her beliefs in relation to those espoused by her local school administration and district which both emphasize a more product-based and assessment driven instruction, a distinct banking model to teaching approach and functional orientation toward literacy learning on the whole.

The degree to which Anne and Mary were able or chose to adhere to their own literacy ideology via instruction was clearly a consequence of teaching emphasis in light of classroom population and manner in which each one worked with her own students, and how the district influenced each of them. As result, each teacher reacted to differing degrees, each one experiencing different levels of resistance, from Anne being more proactive in her teaching while Mary maintained a more complacent behavior as seen in her instruction.

Orientation Toward Writing Instruction as a Process to Learning

By investigating teachers' ideological orientations toward literacy, the concern lay in how teachers' overall approach toward writing instruction is influenced. This was reflected in how each teacher perceived writing as a mechanism of students' overall literacy learning and consequently how they 'taught' writing. The trends found suggest the following characteristics in understanding how teachers view writing as part of the literacy learning process:

- Orientation towards Writing: Teachers' ideological orientation was inconsistent overall. Both teachers maintained having a progressive perspective, yet operated from an oppositional teaching process when confronted with her local and district administration;
- Curriculum and Evaluation Processes: Overall, there is a strong basic skills emphasis. Teachers engaged students in writing that would best serve academic achievement based on standardized assessments; and
- Intervening Variables: Overall, both teachers are impacted by a top-down mandated curriculum, supported by their local school administration and dictated by their school district. But each teacher is impacted differently according to her own perception of how they engage their local school and district administration.

Examining all the data, Anne and Mary were congruent in their beliefs as it related to their practice. More specifically, Anne employed a more consistent progressive approach in her teaching as well as use of curriculum. She was critical in how the curriculum was structured and thus would re-orient activities so that they would be more culturally relevant to her students on a real-world plane. For example, she negotiated the 'order' in which required writing activities for assessments would be done according to how, based on the time of year, students' lives and experiences lending themselves better to encourage writing:

(....) [Y]ou want kids to write about what they know about, you know? (....) So, you start off with journal writing so, (...) everybody's fairly comfortable writing on a regular basis. I do narrative writing first

> because October (…). Halloween is just, you know, chock-full of char-
> acters. I use a graphic organizer for them. The first box they decide
> the character, setting, problem and solution. Just 'cause if they don't
> [have it], they're off into the ether, you know? (…) the other three box-
> es are for (…) the beginning of the story, the middle, and the end of
> the story. They don't write it, they draw it, so they aren't hindered by
> (…) the lack of vocabulary or whatever. Then they talk about it. (…).
> And then they write. I think it's really useful and helpful to them to
> have graphic organizers. I recognize that they also have the ability to
> limit kids sometimes, but I think for the population that I'm teaching
> it gives them a little bit like, training wheels. You know?

Anne engaged in teaching processes that were more student-centered and constructivist in nature. However, at the same time, as was
observed in her writing activities, she communicated within a
constructivist approach those functional skills to ensure students had
access to language and grammatical formalisms necessary for achiev-
ing success on the required standardized assessments as used by her
grade level and school.

Socio-Cultural Context: Are We How We Were Taught?

What each teacher communicated over and over again was their
desire and commitment to the best teaching they can in order for their
students to be both able to write and be writers, and to remember as
part of the experience that "writing is fun" and to remember one writing activity "they really loved." This commitment was illustrated by
Anne's and Mary's participation in this study which involved their
willingness, on a professional and personal level, to reflect on their practice in the area of writing instruction. As the introduction to this research study implied, the driving principle in undertaking this research
came from the question, "who is the self that teaches?" As Ellsworth
(1997) states, as teachers, we are in a "position in which we have no
knowledge or certainty about what consequences our actions as teachers will have on our students" (p. 19). To this end, it was imperative to
include who Mary and Anne are as people, individuals with a vocation
often reduced to technique, yet driven by what Palmer (1998) defines
as *integrity*, that which forms and reforms the pattern of one's life, and
identity, that which includes all the forces that constitute one's life.

In telling each of their stories of how they came to literacy and thus
their feelings about writing, the one commonality Anne and Mary presented was the disconnect between their literacy experiences and their
academic experiences. Neither named a teacher who inspired or challenged them in the area of literacy. Rather, their most vivid memories

were enveloped in family photographs of going to the library, writing to aunts, or writing in a diary. Even more to the point was when memories did turn to their coming to their academic experience, specifically, their recounting was negative. Anne spoke to more negative recollections of writing. Growing up, she remembers doing well on school writing assignments, but also remembers her "harsh in-deck editor", nurtured by her own school teachers during her experience as a student herself:

> "[It's] really hard to get the ideas out while that voice is going 'oh that really sounds like crap you know (...).'"

Mary, on the other hand, expressed more of a self-evaluation of her writing skills resulting in her attitude toward writing for herself—that she "can't and doesn't like to", and how she doesn't teach writing as much and "maybe communicates that dislike" to her students:

> "Well, I think it is partly due to the fact that I don't like to write much at all. I would much rather read. (...) Well, you know, the reading is easier to do. (...) [W]e don't do a lot of writing. I mean, we do, in my class I am trying to do more (...)."

As Palmer (1998) states, good teaching requires self-knowledge: "it is a secret hidden in plain sight" (p. 3). Each of these teachers, to some degree, has been influenced by their own experiences as students, but also by their own individual lived realities. Anne, who spoke the most openly in this regard, made the following statement as to how she negotiates her own personal feelings about writing and her charge in teaching her students:

> "I'm better at (...) making a big deal out of their writing, (...) than modeling my own stuff for them. (...) So, you know, (...) we publish our books and they do "Author's Chair", so they get a sense of importance, they see their stuff up and around the room, so they also get a sense of that it's important to me, for me enough to put it up there."

Each teacher, as she discussed her "coming to literacy," also reflected on how it impacted her teaching of her students. Both expressed attitudes about being "taught how to write" and "needing to write" resulting in current attitudes toward their instruction ranging from making sure students know what it is they are being asked to do, to not concentrating as much on writing because she doesn't like it.

The ideas expressed are by no means intended as value judgments upon each of these teachers, rather, validation of their experiences and how they have effected their own development, much like how their students' experiences will be influenced. It must be said that all these teachers engaged this process of inquiry openly and honestly. Such courage to unveil oneself is commendable—they are teachers who have good days and bad days, and "whose bad days bring suffering that comes only from something one loves" (Palmer, 1998, p. 1).

Socio-Political Context: Are We Who We Teach?
As was highlighted by their profiles, Anne and Mary are the demographic "norm" when it comes to "who" teaches in US schools and "who" is taught in most urban schools. A second commonality is that they teach in a school district which supports a *Standards-Based approach* in the education of all its students in classrooms consisting of bilingual Spanish speakers and monolingual English speakers of US (White and African American) and Mexican descent. Though each one valued their students' ethnolinguistic and cultural diversity and expressed a strong desire to see all their students' progress to their highest potentials, they were not critical role models in engaging students' diversity. And although, they both utilized students' linguistic and cultural knowledge background to encourage and motivate learning overall and more specifically, the learning of writing, the goal is always clear; multiple voices are *heard*, but not necessarily *listened* to. This was reflected as they employed more progressive approaches to teaching. They never truly engaged in critical interrogation of how the curriculum itself plays out in their practice:

> *Anne:* I don't do a lot of writing homework because they don't, their parents can't help 'em write in English. (...) if I were teaching a bilingual class the parents could be a lot more involved because they wouldn't have the language barrier. So, any writing homework is gonna have to be something they know really, really well. Like after we have stopped, after we had moved on from letter writing and moved into paragraph writing, that's when I'll put a writ-ing, like the letter in the homework packet. I can't depend on there being somebody there at home that can help them with it, which is not to say that the parents are not supportive. I mean, I have parents that are wonderful support. They value education and they transmit that to their children, and they, you know, are on their kids to get their homework done. (...) primarily the contributions that I think my students' parents' make is being literacy models, their kids seeing them use text functionally, seeing them use text for enjoyment teaches my students

a whole lot. So, they're tremendously supportive. (...) you can support your children in their learning without being able to read the
same language they are, you communicate how important that is to
you. And I can see what student's have support at home and which
ones don't.

Mary: [P]arents are so important, even those that didn't get a formal
education. They're educated in other ways that are important. If the
kids see their parents, grandparents, aunts, uncles care about education and what and how they are doing, they will do better.

Both embraced students' cultural and linguistic diversity as a source
from which students could access knowledge(s) in order to achieve the
goal of learning to write. And though neither Anne nor Mary explicitly commented negatively with regard to students' linguistic or cultural diversity, each one expressed great concern as to how the fact of
being "low" in English, negatively impacted not only student learning, but in some cases, each of their own ability to undertake writing
instruction with the desired results reflected in district mandated standardized curriculum and assessments. This concern was expressed as
each teacher spoke to students' socio-economic status as they reflected
upon the activities they assign students. Such comments made per-
tained to "life situations" and as such, impacted teachers' decision-
making as to what type of activities to have students do at home, so as
to not need help if no one is present, or in the case of educational level
of family members, that it be doable for students.

Both teachers have pursued education beyond their credentials and
participating in continued professional development through district
workshops and conferences. However, even with such a commitment
to fostering their own mastery in the field in order to provide their students a quality education model, they are not consciously aware, or
choose not to be aware of the disconnect between their ideological beliefs and the methods and processes they employ in teaching their students. Both, continuously, in thoughtful reflection, reacted to the processes dictated by their district and local school administration in the
area of writing instruction. Yet, neither further examined this beyond
her feeling of frustration and instructional "rejection" by implementing more varied teaching strategies at different junctures of their day-
to-day work with their students, in their own classrooms.

Concluding Remarks

The analysis and reflections of the four areas that illustrate the practice of teachers in the area of writing, namely, ideological beliefs, orientation towards writing instruction, socio-cultural context and socio-political context point to tensions and incongruencies between teachers' role and the ideologies within which they work and their personal ideologies that inform their role as a teacher. Each one of these teachers, to some degree, is being invalidated and thus is invalidating student knowledge due to the fact that they themselves either have not had the opportunity to truly interrogate the curriculum they teach and associated processes or been positioned in a space rendering them ill-equipped to unveil the hidden hegemonic structures effecting their teaching of writing, and teaching overall. However, by virtue of participating in this process, Anne and Mary have ensued on their own journey to critically examine their own role within the space they occupy and how it effects their ability to teach according to the dictates of their personal selves ideologically.

Anne and Mary want the best for their students on a personal and academic level. This is evident with each hug they gave, each smile they reciprocated, each achievement they acknowledged. The critical issue was not that they didn't care, or didn't value their students, or didn't aspire to high standards for themselves and their students. On the contrary, they participated in this study to engage in honest dialogue about their teaching practices in an era of standards in the area of writing with a desire to have the opportunity to share and therefore learn more about themselves as teachers. To this end, this project was successful, as they each drew from it what they could at this point in time. By this, I mean, depending on the level they were able to honestly reflect on their beliefs and practice, they grew in awareness. It is true that these teachers were not completely changed as to how they engage the teaching of writing, as this was not the goal of this research study. Rather, the goal was to begin to open a space within which conversations can occur around the teaching of writing and how and what decisions are made and why. In the case of these teachers, their decision making processes are tightly woven within the fabric of the state's standards based movement adopted by their school and their district. As such, each of these teachers are constantly negotiating not only how to teach writing, but whether to teach it at all.

Each teacher valued the process as they "finally got the chance to vent", in some cases, but more importantly, they were able to speak frankly and not sugar coat how they see their teaching of writing as effective or not, as a form of literacy they like to teach, or not. It is important to note that they were not always comfortable with the use of dialogue to engage the research questions. As a result, I based my desire to engage in this process not to change how teachers teach, but rather, beginning the dismantlement of the mechanism that dictates their pedagogy from a professional and personal locale. This mechanism is exemplified in the current rhetoric of teaching effectiveness in which teacher practice has become objectified as a series of movements and acts with no dialogical processes that listen to teachers' or students' voices.

Endnotes

[1] The component parts that make up the CHAT framework are defined below:
- The *object* is the most elemental constituent of the activity system from the subject's point of view. It is the *goal* of the activity, the person, procedure, or concept upon which the subject's actions are focused.
- The *tools*, as Vygotsky (1978) defines, are *mediating artifacts*, indicative and present within the individual culture through which the subject is able to communicate, realize, and transform the object.
- The *outcome* is the purpose of the activity. From the perspective of the subject, it is the result of his/her involvement in an academic or personal endeavor; a more developed background and/or greater awareness of the global contexts the subject may inhabit.
- The *rules* represent what may be construed as the socio-cultural, political, religious, economic, and/or linguistic contexts of the activity *(object)* in question. These rules are not those driving only the individual(s) within the activity, but the *community, tools,* as well as the *outcome* ascertained. In other words, the rules may be a constant of the immediate activity system in question (i.e., the microsystem; a classroom) or embedded in some larger context (i.e., the macrosystem; the school district).
- The *community* refers to the population or cooperative group of individuals comprised of their collaborating, socio-historical, and cultural norms. This aspect of the system impacts the activity in light of everyone and every*thing* involved, as a whole.
- The *division* of labor may be interpreted as the articulation of the activity under analysis; the *community* to be studied, how the *learner(s)*and/or *(subject(s)* may distribute roles, how the *rules* impact roles, how the *tools* (mediating artifacts) may be utilized/transformed according to learner (s') role(s), rules, *outcome* desired, and how such may be impacted at the micro and/or micro level of the whole system.

[2] This perspective has a number of distinctive features as defined by Kemmis and Wilkinson (1998, pp. 23-22):

- It is a *social activity* in that it "deliberately explores the relationship between realms of the individual and the social, recognizing that no individuation is possible without socialization, and no socialization is possible with individuation" (Habermas, 1992, p. 26);
- It is *participatory* in that it "engages people in examining their knowledge (understandings, skills and values) and interpretive categories (the ways they interpret themselves and their action in the social and material world). It is a process in which each individual in a group tries to get a handle on the ways their knowledge shapes their identity and agency, and to reflect critically on how their present knowledge frames and constrains their action;
- It is *practical and collaborative* in that it engages people in examining the acts that link them with others in social interaction. It is a process in which people explore their acts of communication, production and social organization, and try to reconstruct their interactions by reconstructing the acts that constitute them;
- It is *emancipatory* in that it is a process in which people explore the ways in which their practices are shaped and constrained by a wider social (cultural, political, and economic) structures, and consider whether they can intervene to release themselves from these constraints—or, if they can't release themselves from these constraints, how to best work within and around them to minimize the extent to which they contribute to irrationality, unproductivity (inefficiency), injustice, and dissatisfaction as people whose work and lives contribute to the structuring of a shared social life;
- It is *critical* in that it is a process in which people deliberately set out to contest and reconstitute irrational, unproductive (or inefficient), unjust, and/or unsatisfactory (or alienating) ways of interpreting, describing their world (language/discourse), ways of working (practice), and ways of relating to others (power); and
- It is *dialectal* in that it aims to help people to investigate reality in order to change it (Fals Borda, 1979), and to change reality in order to investigate it.

[3] Structured English Immersion (SEI): Defined as part of the passage of Proposition 227 (California's 1998 ballot decision to eliminate bilingual education), it is a one-year program in which English is used "overwhelmingly" for instruction with a curriculum designed for English language learners

[4] A "Bridge" class is one in which students are placed who have had two years of SEI. It is similar in concept and practice to an Early Transitional Bilingual class. In the case of Merside Unified School District (where Tri-City Elementary is located), English is exclusively used to teach children in Bridge classes.

[5] ESL: English as a Second Language. Classes that teach English to non-English speaking students.

[6] The Writer's Workshop approach is the creation of a writing environment in the classroom that helps students want to write and to assume responsibility for their writing development. Indicative of this approach are writing conferences, various methods to responding to students' writing, different types of writing exposure and experiences.

[7] 3rd grade teachers at Tri-City participated in a Writing Workshop In-Service with Wilda Storm and were introduced to the writing program that was implemented during the school year.

8   Into English! (1997) is published by Hampton/Brown Publishers. It is currently being used in Merside Unified School District for ELD/ESL instruction.

9   In using the pronoun "she", Mary referred to a specific teacher within the entire transcript when speaking to the issue highlighted in this portion of the data analysis. The researcher has chosen to not include her name.

10 For the complete research study, please contact the author directly via electronic mail: acortese@mac.com

References

Cadiero-Kaplan, K. (2004. The Literacy Curriculum & Bilingual Education: A Critical Examination. New York: Peter Lang.

Ellsworth, E. (1997). Teaching positions: Difference, pedagogy, and the power of address. New York: Teachers College Press.

Engeström, Y. (1999). Activity theory and individual and social transformation. In Y. Engeström, R. Miettinen, & R-L. Punamäki (Eds.), Perspectives on activity theory (pp. 19-38). Cambridge, UK: Cambridge University Press.

Friere, P. & Macedo, D. (1987). Literacy: Reading the word and the world. Westport, CT: Bergin & Garvey.

Hicks, D. (1996). Contextual inquiries: A discourse oriented study of classroom learning. In D. Hicks (Ed.). Discourse, Schooling and Learning (pp. 104-141). New York: Cambridge University Press.

Jones, E. & Prescott, E. (1984). Dimensions of teaching-learning environments. Pasadena, CA: Pacific Oaks College.

Kemmis, S. (1993). Action research and social movement: A challenge for policy research. Education Policy Analysis Archives, 1(1), 1-7.

Kemmis, S. & Wilkinson, M. (1998). Participatory action research and the study of practice. In B. Atweh, S. Kemmis, & P. Weeks (Eds.), Action research in practice: partnership for social justice (pp. 21-36). London, England: Routledge.

Pajares, M. F. (1992). Teachers' beliefs and educational research: Cleaning up a messy construct. Review of Educational Research, 62, 307-332.

Palmer, P. J. (1998). The courage to teach: Exploring the inner landscape of a teacher's life. San Francisco: Jossey-Bass Publishers.

Pratt, M.L. (1990). Arts of the contact zone. Profession 91, 33-40.

Purves, A. C. (1990). The scribal society: An essay on literacy and schooling in the information age. New York: Longman.

Quinn-Patton, M. (1990). Qualitative evaluation and research methods (2nd edition). Newbury Park, CA: Sage Publications.

Ríos, F. A. (1996). Teachers' principles of practice in multicultural classrooms. In F. A. Rios (Ed.), Teacher thinking in cultural contexts, (129-150). Albany, NY: State University of New York Press.

Vygotsky, L. S. (1978). Mind in Society: The development of higher psychological processes, ed. M. Cole, V. John-Steiner, S. Scribner, & E. Souberman. Cambridge, MA: Harvard University Press.

Wartofsky, M. (1979). Models: Representation and scientific understanding. Dordrecht, Germany: Reidel.

Chapter 6

**Taiwanese Student Teachers'
and Teachers' Views on Efficacy of
English Preparation Programs**
Shu-ching (Michele) Chu
Wenzao College of Foreign Languages
in Taiwan

Abstract

This study investigated the perceptions of student teachers and classroom teachers toward teacher preparation programs for elementary school
English teachers in Taiwan, a non-English-speaking country in terms of
pedagogical practices, resources, and support. This study also examined
the extent to which student and classroom teachers share or have different perceptions about teacher preparation for English instructors. The
results of this study provide insights on how Taiwan's teacher education programs can provide more practical and effective training while
they improve the quality of English education for children whose primary
language is not English. The findings of this international study parallel the concerns of pedagogical relevance and practice in the United States.

Introduction

Historical Background

In the past decade it has become increasingly clear that English acquisition is of vital importance to the Taiwanese children of the 21st
century. This concern is also prevalent in the United States as thousands of English Learners enter schools on a yearly basis and are given
a year to develop their English proficiency. In the case of Taiwan, oral
proficiency and comprehension of English will open doors internation-
ally and allow Taiwanese children to compete and be at ease in a world
market and culture. Prior to 2001, English instruction began in seventh grade, and the primary focus of the instruction was on reading
and writing. Therefore, the Ministry of Education (MOE) in Taiwan
launched a reform to extend English instruction to the fifth and sixth
grade with a focus on oral proficiency , and the instruction will be further extended to the third grade by 2005 (MOE,1998).

The quality of English teachers will determine the success of the new English curriculum in elementary schools. Therefore, the MOE authorized numerous universities to establish teacher preparation programs and called upon these institutions not only to produce English teachers in quantity, but also in quality (MOE, 1999). While Taiwan leading educators, S. Shih (1998), Y. Shi and H. Chu (1999), and F. Su (1999) applaud this new decision by MOE, they express a deep concern about the quality of training currently available for the teachers of elementary school English curriculum.

To aid in the process of developing English instruction criteria, the MOE defined goals for the elementary English curriculum; however, it did not provide specific guidelines and standards for elementary school English teachers and teacher preparation programs. The teacher preparation institutions were left to self-determine the curriculum and practices adequate for the development of teachers (Huang, S.L., 1999). In a previous study, Chu (2001) found that the quality of teacher education does affect prospective teachers and influence what they do in the classroom. Taiwan teacher educators are still attempting to determine standards for quality preparation programs. In comparison, the United States has already created such standards for teacher preparation programs for English language teachers (NCATE, 2002), and these standards may be a resource for Taiwan. Hence, this study was designed to investigate how student teachers and experienced classroom teachers perceived teacher preparation programs. This study addresses the concerns expressed by practitioners in the United States and Taiwan. Namely, the importance of having the necessary training, learning resources, and personnel support systems that contribute to the understanding and improvement of teacher education programs in Taiwan and in similar English teaching contexts throughout the world.

Models Of Teacher Preparation

Inadequate teacher preparation often results in poor teaching practices that have a negative impact on student motivation and performance. "The lack of preparation manifests itself in poor instruction and low academic performance among students" (Smylie & Kahne, 1997, p. 355). The National Commission on Teaching and America's Future (NCTAF, 2002) recommends re-examining the role of teacher education and improving teacher education programs to provide quality teachers for every classroom. Stewart-Wells's study (1999) also reveals a pressing need to understand the expectations and perceptions of prospective teachers. Not only do student teachers need to learn about teaching, but teacher educators need to learn about teachers' learning processes and their needs. Therefore, it is critical to conduct studies to examine the needs of teachers, the preparations made to address them, and to help teachers face the challenges they will encounter in the classroom.

Based on scholarly findings, effective teacher training programs should have a balance between theory and practice, provide authentic teaching experiences and support systems, as well as establish a good relationship with the community. Furthermore, teacher-training programs tend to present theoretical knowledge in isolation and provide practical knowledge without connection to theory (Freiberg & Waxman, 1990; Goodlad, 1990; Grimmest & MacKinnon, 1992). Theories presented to prospective teachers as an intellectual exercise without any connection to classroom experience will rarely become an integral part of their teaching practice. Research and practice indicate that the best way to learn to teach is through teaching (Lanier & Little, 1986; Guyton & McIntyre, 1999). Unfortunately, it is still the case across national borders that most student teachers do not have the opportunity to practice real teaching until their one-semester teaching practicum or, even worse, when they enter the classroom (Johnson, 1996). Field experiences do not have to wait until the end stage of training. It is imperative that teacher preparation programs establish a close relationship with local schools and create abundant opportunities for early field experiences (Rigden, 1997).

In addition to presenting future teachers with the necessary knowledge, sufficient support systems are crucial for success in teacher preparation. Fisher (2001) found that what is most often lacking in training situations is the availability of sufficient support and resources. Therefore, if the majority of models for teacher training reflect a disconnect between theory and practice, late or short field experiences, and little contact with real teaching and learning, ESOL teachers will be left isolated and thwarted in their professional development (Bowman, et all, 2000). In addition, the absence of support adds to the amount of pressure teachers endure during their first years of teaching. Teaching requires a degree of dedication that is both physically and emotionally draining and to be successful it is imperative that programs have continuous training and support for continued development (Eisenman & Holly, 1999). Various ways to provide this support include frequent scheduled meetings, telementoring, and email as well as on-site mentors and study groups.

Teacher Education For Taiwan: Processes Of Inquiry

Given that in Taiwan there are no specific guidelines for preparing teachers of English, and given the absence of teachers' voices in shaping teacher education, the intent of this study was to investigate the existing teacher-education programs in Taiwan for the purpose of identifying areas of need in order to improve the teacher preparation programs.

Three questions served to examine the needs for training:

- How do student teachers and experienced classroom teachers perceive pedagogical practices in the preparation of teachers to teach English?
- How do student teachers and experienced classroom teachers perceive the availability and adequacy of the resources needed for teacher preparation and classroom teaching?
- How do student teachers and experienced classroom teachers perceive availability and adequacy of the support systems needed for teacher preparation and classroom teaching?

The answers to these questions provide insights into the needs of teachers and point to the most effective changes for enhancing and improving teacher preparation programs. This study, while conducted in Taiwan, includes methods and approaches that can be taken up in U.S. contexts, as the questions and results reach across nternational borders.

Method of Inquiry

Instruments

The study incorporated both quantitative and qualitative methodologies. The quantitative methodology utilized a 44-item survey with a five-point Likert scale to disclose the perceptions of student teachers and experienced teachers of English concerning the adequacy of their teacher preparation programs (TPP) and identifying the training practices, support and resources that are essential during training. The items regarding the resources and support were adapted from Fisher's (2001) survey study on teachers' perceptions of support and resources need. The survey was pilot-tested in Taiwan. The internal consistency was a = .76. For face validity (Anastasi & Urbina, 1997; Brown, 1990), three language educators and three English teachers reviewed the survey and agreed that this survey appears to measure what this study is intended to measure.

The survey was written in English and accompanied by a translation in the native language of the research participants to clarify meanings in case participants were not sure of some terms in English. The qualitative methodology was accomplished through face-to-face interviews. Because surveys limit the type of information elicited from the participants, the interviews helped to clarify the survey study. The purpose of the interviews was twofold. First, they served as a survey reliability check. Second, the interview was used to elicit more insight from participants regarding English teacher education standards. Field notes and tape recordings were utilized. The interviews were conducted in Mandarin Chinese, the language in which the interviewees felt most comfortable. The findings of this study, however, based on the survey and the interview information from the student teachers and experienced teacher participants in urban areas in Taiwan, may be limited in their generalizability.

Data Sources

The survey part of this study had two participating groups. The first group consisted of 90 student teachers (ST) taking teacher training courses in English teacher preparation programs at universities in Taiwan. There were 76 female and 14 male participants in this group. The second group consisted of 162 Taiwan public elementary school English teachers (CT). In this group, there were 143 females and 19 males. The survey for student teachers was administrated at the institution sites during November 2002. In the same time period, the survey was mailed to English teachers at elementary schools in two major cities in Taiwan. Those who responded were asked if they would be interested in participating in the second phase of the study, the follow up interview. Sixteen student teachers and ten elementary school English teachers participated in the interviews. The interviews were conducted individually and face-to-face.

Teacher and Student Perceptions of their Experiences

To answer the question, *"How do novice teachers and experienced classroom teachers perceive pedagogical practices in the preparation of teachers to teach English?"* a survey was given to experienced teachers and student teachers, with the goal of learning their views towards the pedagogical practice of various teacher preparation programs. To measure their responses, a Likert scale of five values was used. Number 1 meant "strongly disagree"; 2 indicated "disagree"; 3, "not sure"; 4, "agree"; and 5, "strongly agree. Twenty-eight items addressed specifically pedagogical practices of teacher preparation programs such as courses, skills and activities, research, culture, resources, and overall influence. The data results reported here will highlight student teacher (ST) and classroom teacher (CT) responses to questions in the areas of:

- courses offered in teacher preparation, type and relatedness to other course work;
- types of training activities that STs and CTs participate in;
- exposure to methods and practice in conducting classroom research training processes for developing cross-cultural awareness and knowledge
- resources available for English development and STs and CTs overall attitude towards training for teaching English in elementary settings

Responses were compared between student teachers who recently completed or were in the process of completing their programs, and classroom teachers presently teaching in schools.

In terms of the *variety of courses* offered in teacher preparation programs, the student teacher group showed more positive responses than did the teachers towards these courses. Most of the classroom teachers didn't think that a sufficient variety of courses was offered in the Teacher Preparation Program (TPP) they attended and felt restricted in that they couldn't take courses based on their own interests, but rather only those courses required. In regard to the connections between courses, or their relatedness to each other, more classroom teachers understood the structure and the interconnection of the courses than the student teachers.

In terms of *training activities*, many more student teachers thought the program had a balance of theory and practice than did the classroom teachers. Most of the classroom teachers indicated that the training the student teachers received did not reflect the reality of daily class situations and that trainers (teacher educators) did not model methodologies sufficiently for student teachers to implement with confidence.

As for *research models*, the results showed that the training the classroom teachers received did not provide them with sufficient tools for doing research, additionally the student teachers were unsure whether they could ask to participate in faculty research projects. In the area of *culture*, neither group felt they had sufficient information or models related to different aspects of local and English speaking cultures or teaching processes for multi-cultural education.

In the opinion of most classroom teachers, neither the department library nor the school library in the TPP had sufficient English teaching resources (i.e., books, tapes, films) at the time they attended their program. Even though some students thought their school or department had resources, many of them expressed uncertainty as to where they were located or how they could access them.

The opinions of both groups showed that sharing teaching experience with their peers and having classroom teachers as mentors were extremely helpful. The results indicated that the teacher preparation program did motivate both the CTs and the STs to teach English and that their education did have an influence on them, but their responses differed as to the degree this influenced preparation. That is, STs felt the teacher preparation program had a much greater influence on their attitudes toward methodologies of teaching English than did the experienced classroom teachers. A second intent of the survey was to discover the perceptions of classroom and student teachers toward the resources and the support systems available to them which they require in teacher preparation. The classroom teacher group was also asked about the resources and support that were available in their prior teacher training and the connection to their current work situations. A Likert scale of five values was utilized to compare the responses of these two groups. Number 1 meant "I *don't* have it and it's *not* needed"; 2, indicated "I have it and it's *not* needed"; 3 meant, "not sure"; 4 indicated, "I *don't* have it and it's needed"; and 5 meant, "I have it and it's needed." The percentage of their responses from value 4 and 5 were summed up to identify the needs of the student teachers and classroom teachers. And the percentages of their responses from value 2 and 5 were summed up to determine the availability of resources and support to the participants. Thus, the second part of the survey answered the second research question, *"How do student teachers and classroom teachers perceive the availability and adequacy of the resources needed for teacher preparation and classroom teaching?"* Table 1.1 – 1.3 identify the differences between the participants' need for resources and the access which they had to them.

When asked about the resources in their prior teacher training (Table 1.1), the classroom teachers perceived English teaching training as extremely needed followed by opportunities to attend conferences or workshops, teaching materials and supplies, and professional journals. Many teachers felt desperate for training and the related teaching materials and supplies. The highest discrepancy between resources they needed and those that were available to them were items such as teaching materials and supplies, professional journals, as well as research tools. Many CTs disagreed that the school and department library in the training institutions had sufficient resources.

Table 1.1 Classroom Teachers' Perceptions toward Needs and Availability In Resources in **Prior Training**

Questions	Needed (%)	Available (%)	Difference (%)
Q29 Access to Eng. teaching training	83.9	61.7	22.2
Q30 Opportunities to attend conferences/workshops	71.6	44.5	27.1
Q31 University's training courses	61.1	37.6	23.5
Q32 Private language school's training courses	58.1	45.1	13.0
Q33 Access to professional journals	68.5	32.1	36.4
Q36 Research tools	63.0	28.4	34.6
Q37 Access to teaching materials & supplies	70.4	42.6	27.8

When asked about the resources in their current work situation (Table 1.2) at the elementary schools, what they needed the most were teaching materials and supplies and opportunities to attend conferences or workshops followed by access to training in English language teaching and to professional journals. However, of those things needed in their present teaching and of those available to them, the highest discrepancy was in professional journals and teaching materials and supplies.

Table 1.2 Classroom Teachers' Perceptions toward Needs and Availability in Resources in **Current Work Situation**

Questions	Needed (%)	Available (%)	Difference (%)
Q29 Access to Eng. teaching training	79.6	62.3	17.3
Q30 Opportunities to attend conferences/workshops	81.5	58.0	23.5
Q31 University's training courses	58.1	32.8	25.3
Q32 Private language school's training courses	58.7	45.7	13.0
Q33 Access to professional journals	74.1	27.1	47.0
Q36 Research tools	71.7	27.2	44.5
Q37 Access to teaching materials & supplies	82.7	49.4	33.3

What the student teachers needed the most (Table 1.3) were teaching materials and supplies followed by more access to training in English teaching and to professional journals. The resources that showed the greatest gap between needs and availability for the student teachers were opportunities to attend conferences or workshops and access to professional journals as well as teaching materials and supplies.

Table 1.3 Student Teachers' Perceptions toward Needs and Availability in Resources in **Teacher Preparation**

Questions	Needed (%)	Available (%)	Difference (%)
Q29 Access to Eng. teaching training	83.3	72.2	11.1
Q30 Opportunities to attend conferences/workshops	75.6	3⊦.1	44.5
Q31 University's training courses	76.7	58.9	17.8
Q32 Private language school's training courses	48.9	21.1	27.8
Q33 Access to professional journals	83.3	51.1	32.2
Q36 Research tools	80.0	56.1	23.9
Q37 Access to teaching materials & supplies	88.9	60.0	28.9

The third part of the survey provided findings for the third research question, *"How do student teachers and experienced classroom teachers perceive the availability and adequacy of the support systems needed for teacher preparation and classroom teaching?"* From the two groups, there were numerous reports of support systems not available but needed, including informational and personnel support. Table 2.1- 2.3 identify the range of resources for which the participants felt a need and the limited extent to which that access was available.

During their prior training (Table 2.1), the support that classroom teachers needed most was from teacher educators, English teachers, and their peers. They also indicated a great need for information on how to teach cultures and how to adapt lessons. But the difference was very high between their need and the availability of information in the two areas.

*Table 2.1 Classroom Teachers' Perceptions toward Needs and Availability in Support in **Prior Training***

Questions	Needed (%)	Available (%)	Difference (%)
Q34 Information on how to adapt lessons	66.1	34.0	32.1
Q35 Information on teaching cultures	71.0	35.8	35.2
Q38 Support from peers	64.2	48.1	16.1
Q39 Support from English teachers	67.2	35.8	31.4
Q40 Support from teacher educators	67.3	33.9	33.4
Q41 Support from other elementary school teachers	54.3	27.1	27.2
Q42 Contact with children support personnel	37.7	16.7	21.0
Q43 Meeting with teacher educators	59.3	23.5	35.8
Q44 Time allowed for meetings	49.3	21.6	27.7

Table 2.2 Teachers' Perceptions toward Needs and Availability in Support in
Current Work Situation

Questions	Needed (%)	Available (%)	Difference (%)
Q34 Information on how to adapt lessons	75.9	36.4	39.5
Q35 Information on teaching cultures	75.3	35.2	40.1
Q38 Support from peers	70.4	43.2	27.2
Q39 Support from English teachers	72.3	38.9	33.4
Q40 Support from teacher educators	67.9	25.9	42.0
Q41 Support from other elementary school teachers	64.2	35.8	28.4
Q42 Contact with children support personnel	40.8	17.3	23.5
Q43 Meeting with teacher educators	64.8	22.2	42.6
Q44 Time allowed for meetings	56.2	25.3	30.9

In their current teaching (Table 2.2), the classroom teachers ranked the need for information on teaching cultures and adapting of lessons to learning levels as *extremely high*. CTs also expressed their need for support from other personnel, including English teachers, their class peers, teacher educators, and other elementary school teachers. However, the most critical reported difference between a needed support and its availability to classroom teachers was support from teacher educators and time to meet with them. They also felt very much in need of support from other English teachers. The student teachers perceived support from the elementary school teachers (Table 2.3) as something that was missing from their experience, that is the STs expressed greater need for support from English teachers, their peers, and teacher educators. They also felt the need for more information on adapting lessons and curriculum for different class situations and for teaching different cultures.

Table 2.3 Student Teachers' Perceptions toward Needs and Availability in Support in **Teacher Preparation**

Questions	Needed (%)	Available (%)	Difference (%)
Q34 Information on how to adapt lessons	78.9	35.5	43.4
Q35 Information on teaching cultures	78.9	25.5	53.4
Q38 Support from peers	82.2	66.6	15.6
Q39 Support from English teachers	82.3	45.6	36.7
Q40 Support from teacher educators	80.0	46.7	33.3
Q41 Support from other elementary school teachers	83.4	47.8	35.6
Q42 Contact with children support personnel	66.6	7.7	58.9
Q43 Meeting with teacher educators	67.8	20.0	47.8
Q44 Time allowed for meetings	50.0	20.0	30.0

Prospective Teachers' and Classroom Teachers' Voices

The survey results, reviewed in the previous section, indicate that classroom teachers and student teachers gave similar responses on existing pedagogical practice in the development of micro skills. They also agreed on the effectiveness of training techniques and activities such as teacher educator's demonstrations of methodology, real class teaching practices, classroom observation and the need for more resources and support to help them develop teaching skills. However, the results also revealed that student teachers held more positive views on teacher preparation programs than did the classroom teachers. To gain further insight into the views these two groups held, follow-up interviews with student teachers and classroom teachers were conducted. The interviews consisted of four questions.

- In your opinion, what should be the components of effective teacher preparation programs for elementary school English teachers?

- (To prospective teachers) What kinds of resources and support do you need from the teacher preparation program to assist you in becoming an effective teacher of English? (To experienced class-room teachers) What kinds of resources and support do you need to teach English effectively at elementary schools?

- In what ways do you feel unprepared?

- What do you expect from teacher preparation programs?

The data from the interviews positively correlate with the survey results. Results from the survey indicate that classroom teachers and student teachers gave similar responses on existing pedagogical prac-tice in the development of micro skills. They also agreed on the effec-tiveness of training techniques and activities such as teacher educator's demonstrations of methodology, real class teaching practices, classroom observation and the need for more resources and support to help them develop teaching skills. However, the survey results also revealed that student teachers held more positive views on teacher preparation pro-grams than did the classroom teachers. The interview results indicated that the student teachers believed the primary components of teacher preparation programs needed to include the following: teaching meth-odology courses, real classroom experiences, and teaching demonstra-tion. Classroom teachers also held a similar view in this area.

Teaching methodology courses.
All teacher interviewees agreed that teaching methodology courses were a central component of an adequate program. When asked about teaching methodology courses, most interviewees named teaching techniques as more important than teaching theories.

> CT02: Teachers need to attain mastery of teaching methodologies, skills, lesson planning, and classroom management.

> ST06: Teaching methodology is really important, I suppose. If teach-ers use inappropriate methodology, it will affect how children feel about English.

Real classroom experiences.
Teaching skills. From the interview, both of the student teacher and experienced teacher groups perceived teaching practices and class ob-servations as very important. However, many more student teachers thought it important to have teaching demonstrations than did the ex-

perienced classroom teachers. Classroom teachers are teaching in their own classrooms and perhaps have found that the best way to learn to teach is by experiencing the real situation. In the interview, STs identified student teaching as an important component of the program. According to these interviews, a great majority of classroom teachers (90%) and student teachers (87.5%) were clear that actual classroom teaching practice was vital. The results also indicated the importance of doing classroom observation so that student teachers can better understand what teaching requires of them. About 75% of student teachers felt the need for classroom observation and 68% of teachers agreed. Also, a high percentage of the prospective teachers thought classroom observation was necessary, and 60% of class teachers agreed.

> CT04: The first hand class observation or student teaching is very effective.

> CT08: Teacher trainees need to constantly do student teaching in the elementary schools, do teaching practices, and have opportunities to get to know children.

> ST08: When we do teaching demonstration, our peers pretend to be the students. We do not exactly know how children would respond to our teaching. Teaching actual children must be different. There is a gap between an imaginary situation and reality. It is better to do teaching practice at elementary schools. It's more realistic.

The student teachers' views were congruent with those of the experienced teachers on the importance of actual teaching experience, class observation, skills to create a learning environment and manage classes, and sufficient resources. However, they had very low congruency on assessment methods, teaching demonstrations as well as teacher educator's experience.

Creating a good learning environment.

Learners were one of the major concerns of both classroom teachers and prospective teachers. A majority of the teachers (70%) agreed with the student teachers (68.8%) on the development of skills in creating a good learning environment for students. To better understand children, many interviewees talked about the need to be familiar with child psychology, child language acquisition, and children's characteristics.

They also named decorating the classroom, using games and songs to increase children's interest in learning.

> CT02: Taiwan has little English environment, so it's important to create a good learning environment for students.

> CT01: We [English teachers] need to be aware of students' differences.

> ST05: Elementary students are mostly forced to learn English, so it's important to have an enjoyable learning environment.

Classroom management training.

A majority of the classroom teachers (70%) thought developing classroom management skills was crucial; but not as many novice teachers thought the same. Of 16 student teachers, 9 of them (56.3%) mentioned classroom management. In terms of classroom management skills, more teachers from northern Taiwan noted its importance than did teachers in the southern region. Classroom management was not as high a concern to prospective teachers as it was to classroom teachers who had to face the every day class situation.

> CT01: Classroom management is the key to the success of instruction. Learning how to manage a class is very important. It does not work to teach through the use of excessive authority.

> CT07: When we did teaching practice at the elementary school, usually two or three novice teachers were in charge of one class, which was very different from handling a class by oneself.

> CT03: Currently, teacher preparation lacks training on classroom management. Many English teachers with excellent language skills cannot handle the class well. They often have to spend more than half of the class time dealing with students.

> ST14: Classroom management is the first and teaching is actually second. Based on my interview with an elementary school English teacher, learning how to deal with students is by far the more important skill.

Language proficiency training.

There seems to be a consensus on the requirement of language proficiency of elementary English teachers and student teachers especially in regard to pronunciation. Many classroom teachers agreed with the student teachers that teacher preparation programs need to include language training.

Quality of teacher educators.

Many of the prospective teachers also mentioned the quality of teacher educators as one key element. As one student teacher said, teacher educators are as important as training courses. The qualifications of teacher trainers should include teaching experience, keeping current with teaching, and professional knowledge. Seven teachers out of ten (70%) indicated that teacher educators need to have sufficient teaching experience, especially teaching at the elementary school level; half of student teacher interviewees also mentioned that. To the trainees, it is crucial that the teacher educators have sufficient teaching experience and most importantly, experience in teaching children.

> CT01: Most teacher educators are too idealized, and they are not aware of the reality of the classroom. Even the teachers from the teaching counselling groups do not understand the exact problems and frustrations elementary school teachers are dealing with everyday in the classroom, problems such as the extreme discrepancy of students' levels and individual differences and how to balance teaching accordingly.

> CT10: University trainers ought to have experience teaching in the elementary school. They do not understand how to teach children. Some of their ideas cannot be applied to the classroom.

To prospective teachers, the attitudes of teacher educators made a difference. They need to have good teaching attitudes such as patience and a passion for teaching, encouraging students, making eye contact with students, and being able to apply what they teach.

> ST12: Teachers are important. They need to have incredible patience and passion for teaching, and sufficient professional knowledge.

> ST08: Teacher educators need to have attitudes just as they require

it from the trainees because these trainees will become educators in the future.

And last but not least, being up to date with current teaching trends is necessary. Quite a few teacher interviewees felt that trainers are not familiar with English instruction at elementary schools. A couple of student teachers felt the same. Three of the classroom teachers agreed with the student teachers that teacher educators should be up to date with current trends and believed that teacher educators have to continue learning.

CT01: Teacher educators should do more research to understand elementary school English teaching.

CT04: The quality of teacher education varies. Some university teacher trainers have high academic degree, but they are not aware of elementary school teaching situations and culture. They don't know how to teach children.

CT06: Teacher trainers should find out how teachers teach English at bushibans (private language schools).

ST02: Teacher educators have to continue learning, studying new teaching concepts, the newest theories. It is important to understand the current Taiwan teaching environment and not to completely apply western theories to the teaching situations in Taiwan.

Resources.

The interview results showed that in terms of physical resources, trainees expected teacher preparation programs to be equipped with adequate facilities such as audio equipment and visual as well as aural materials in language learning and teaching. Access to resources was a major concern for most student teachers. Several student teachers complained that they could not check out the resources.

ST07: The school should allow students to use the computers in the special children's English room since they are not in use after class…. Only teachers have access to most resources. The school should let students use teaching materials and aids. Resources like flashcards and tapes are limited to use in the resource centre only. We have to rely on ourselves to obtain materials. The most difficulty we have during training is not being able to check out materials. For example, we would like to make a recording using the double deck tape player, but we cannot use it after class.

ST04: There are some foreign films. But [the supply of] teaching materials and teaching aids is quite insufficient. English teaching requires a great deal of materials and props. So far, a lot of materials are from professors' personal collections. We often have to purchase or create them ourselves. It's better if the school can provide those.

When the experienced teacher interviewees were asked about what resources they needed for teaching at the elementary schools, almost all teachers (90%) found special English instruction classrooms with sufficient teaching resources such as audio and printed materials were absolutely necessary. Among them, 70 percent of the teachers said that schools should have children's English readers and electronic equipment but pointed out that proper funding is crucial for required resources.

CT07: It would be nice if schools provided special English classrooms. We could decorate the learning environment and it is easier to set up audio equipment.

CT08: Schools lack proper facility and resources. Many teachers feel the same way I do. Lack of facility and resources posts as a desperate problem.

CT08: Facility is very important for teachers. ...I used to have to run around different classrooms. Every time, I need students to help out with equipment. That's not good. English learning is kind of like computer learning. It requires a special facility. Children need English learning environment. If there is no special English classroom, students can be doing home economics or writing calligraphy in the previous class, and when the English class starts, there is still a mess all over the room. And it may be confusing for children. It makes it extra hard for instructors to create theme based learning if there's no designated room for English. Children should feel free in the learning environment but not feel restricted to be in one classroom learning all different subjects.
CT05: English is a curriculum like other subjects. It is not a subsid-

iary curriculum. It requires resources and funding for teaching aids, posters. Sometimes there are no sufficient funds. Our funds vary every year. For example, the school provided NT$700 (about US$20) for a Halloween activity. There is not much we could do with that amount of money.

Support systems.

The results of the survey indicated that the student teachers need most support from peers, teacher educators, and other English teachers. However, there is also a big discrepancy between the availability of support and the needs of student teachers for support from classroom teachers, other English teachers, and teacher educators. In the interviews, the student teachers identified a great need for the support of elementary school English teachers. They really hope the teacher preparation institutions can provide contact information or establish contact with elementary school teachers for them. They also would like their institutions to invite experienced teachers to share their experience and expertise with them. The information they would like to obtain from teachers was mainly concerned with classroom management and real classroom teaching situations.

> ST05: We would really hope to have the chance to talk to English teachers with real elementary school teaching experience, would really like to talk to elementary school teachers asking them how to manage a class and how to deal with children and observing their classes to have a better understanding of how to do our school assignment. We don't really have connection with elementary school teachers because no one can provide us information for how to contact them. We interviewed one elementary school teacher for a school assignment last semester, but it was because of my friend's connection. To find elementary school teachers is really difficult. We hope the teacher preparation institution can help out.

Student teachers also expressed the needs to have more time with their teacher educators. Many trainees had a concern about professional opportunities. The information they need the most includes requirements and availability of jobs and graduate schools.

According to the survey, the highest needs of classroom teachers in the elementary school setting were support from teacher educators, other English teachers, and other school teachers. Findings from the interviews were similar. A majority of the elementary school teachers (80%)

who were interviewed thought peer sharing and cooperation was necessary. They would like the chance and time to discuss teaching with their colleagues and share their experiences.

> CT01: It would very helpful if there were discussion panel and support groups among our colleagues so that we could discuss teaching and bring us to the same level. It would make teaching much more effective.... We don't just need experts and scholars. Most importantly, among our peers, teachers, across areas, if there were seminars and cooperative learning groups, there wouldn't be such a big discrepancy in instructors like too theoretical, too worn out.

Besides their colleagues, classroom English teachers continued needing support from the educators even after leaving the training program.

> CT03: It would be nice if there were a connection between teacher educators.... There should be more specific cooperation projects, for example, bringing students into [elementary school] to do student teaching

In terms of personnel support, the survey did not include administrators; however, 60 percent of the interviewees talked about the important role administrator could play in the promotion of English. Besides administration, support from other school teachers is also required for the success of implementation. However, not every school agrees on the importance of English learning.

> CT05: We need support from other teachers and school administration. So far teachers are quite cooperative. It will also depend on schools' policies. If schools pay more attention to English instruction, there will be more support.

> CT02: The support English teachers need the most is from the school administration office to promote or carry out English related activities. The other teachers I met in workshops have the common problem that head teachers do not really cooperate. If administrators send out formal memos, they will help out eventually. In other words, we need support and promotion of English for successful implementation. The administration office needs to support and be mediators between teachers.
> According to the interviews, in addition to support from school and

teacher training institutions, there is a lot that parents and the community could offer in both teaching and supplies.

> CT03: English teachers also need parental support especially those who have good language skills. And I hope that parents give more encouragement than criticism.

> CT04: Teachers can ask parents to help out with teaching aids or any other helps according to their expertise. The school can organize activities with parents. We can hold drama or music performance. Teachers can invite their foreign friends to school to mingle and chat with students.

In the areas where trainees felt unprepared, the interviews showed little congruence between the class teachers and student teachers. Teachers felt under-prepared and in need of enhanced training in regard to teaching different academic levels. Of the teacher group, 60% of interviewees expressed a sense of inadequacy in that area, whereas only 31.3% of the student teachers felt the same. Classroom teachers appeared to have a more pressing need in dealing with students in different levels because they have faced learners and have been confronted with that challenge while student teachers were more concerned with how to manage a class. Other areas in which student teachers felt inadequately prepared included actual teaching and administration. According to the interviews, the teacher training institutions neither provide them with sufficient real classroom experience nor prepare them for handling administrative work.

> CT01: Teachers often find themselves in the bottle neck. Teachers find it hard to adjust teaching for different levels. If the teacher teaches to the higher level, the rest of students suffer, and the teacher suffers too since the majority of the students will not meet the high standards. On the other hand, if the teacher teaches students in a lower level, students with better language skills will lose attention and cause a disturbance in the class. And a lot of parents complain that what teachers teach is too easy.

> ST04: The school did not really develop our ability to communicate with administrators and students. Mostly they taught us how to teach. They could open a class on interpersonal communication skills.

Based on the interview results, teacher preparation programs in Taiwan seem to lack variety, availability and interconnection of the training courses, and there was a major discrepancy between their need for additional training and its availability.

Discussion

The results from the surveys and interviews revealed that the two groups of teachers while sharing some similar needs hold different perceptions about teacher education. Student teachers entertain a more idealized understanding about training and teaching than do the classroom teachers. Classroom teachers tend to be more critical toward teacher training because they are in the front line of teaching. They are well aware of the diversity of situations and challenges in the everyday classroom. As they gain empirical experience, classroom teachers realize that teacher preparation programs do not reflect the reality of classroom teaching. Experienced classroom teachers found that the training programs present isolated skills without connection to other skills or content. The results support Pennycook (1989) who found that the training teachers receive often does not reflect what is happening in the classroom. Vann (1999) likewise acknowledges that the academic world teacher educators' experience is quite different from the environment pubic school teachers' experience. Both student teachers and experienced teachers expressed a preference for practical knowledge over theory. The results support the need for the presentation of theories and methods in a way that can be transferred into classroom practice. The training provided for teachers should go beyond technical training and transmission of knowledge (Harrington, 1994); otherwise trainees will not be able to connect it with actual teaching.

The findings also suggest that sufficient resources are a primary concern. Both student teachers and classroom teachers pleaded for more teaching materials and supplies. Audio equipment as well as aural and visual materials are among the basic resources with which teacher preparation programs should be equipped. Although training institutions offer material resources, they are inadequate. There is a critical need for a full range of children's English readers on multiple levels; this is most urgent, a first priority that is closely followed by the need for videos, cassette tapes, CDs, and computer software in both English teaching and language skills.

Another problem student teachers addressed is accessibility. Perhaps understandably, faculty members have much easier access to school resources than student teachers. Many student teacher interviewees complained about their restricted access to the resources. According to student teachers, they can use the resources in class or in the resource center; however, they are as a rule prevented from taking them outside of the center or the classroom, thus making it extremely difficult for them to prepare and produce teaching materials. Also, the library resources are not organized efficiently, thus it is hard for trainees to locate books they need. Most elementary schools have very few English teaching materials and children's readers. Classroom teachers stated in the interviews that they had to be self- reliant in acquiring the resources they need, which could be a daunting challenge in regard to time and money. These findings resemble the results of Fisher's study (2001) in which he found that resources available to teachers in their classrooms are generally insufficient. As a whole, Taiwan schools do not offer an environment that supports the speaking of English. Therefore, teachers express the need for a classroom dedicated to the teaching of English, in which all materials displayed and used would provide students with an experience of English. The results of the study suggest elementary schools should not only provide more materials and professional journals related to English teaching but also to give the teachers more opportunities to receive more training.

In addition to physical resources, personnel support systems are critical to the process of teacher development. The study revealed that student teachers and elementary school teachers require different support systems. For student teachers, the most important support they need is from elementary school teachers who have what the novices lack — classroom experience. Student teachers also desire more opportunities to observe classrooms taught by an experienced teacher; however, many find contacting elementary school teachers to be an intimidating challenge. If the institutions or the teacher educators could make the initial contact, it would help trainees get their foot in the door. A good relationship will not happen without conscious effort (Millar, 1995). Teacher educators are another important source of support for student teachers. Student teachers require other kinds of assistance, including information and advice on teaching careers and the process used in the recruitment of English teachers.

Based on the interviews, the support elementary school English teachers need the most is from other English teachers and teacher educators. Crookes and Arakaki's study identified the need for "inter-teacher communication." (p.18). The data of this research study points to a similar finding. Classroom teachers perceive the sharing of teaching and learning experience to be critical. Teachers want to exchange ideas with colleagues and to support one another, especially in regard to English which is a new element in the curriculum. Teachers would also like to have more opportunity to discuss teaching with teacher educators.

Conclusion

This study intended to discover the perceptions of student teachers and experienced classroom teachers about pedagogical practices, resources, and professional development support needed for English teacher preparation programs. This study indicates that the current teacher preparation programs in Taiwan that are designed to prepare English teachers do not fully reflect the needs of student teachers and classroom teachers. While student teachers and experienced classroom teachers shared similar perceptions about their teacher preparation, they had different perceptions particularly in curricular training and the support systems. However, the disparity between the student teachers and experienced classroom teachers found in this study is often not addressed in the teacher preparation programs.

The findings from the study suggest that administrators and teacher educators associated with training institutions must acknowledge the importance of the voices of student teachers and classroom teachers in addition to addressing their concerns. As Poplin (1992) suggests, before the needs of the teaching population can be met, instructional leaders need to understand who their teachers are so that true teaching expertise can be developed. It is through this awareness of what teachers know and what they need to know, that those in charge of teacher training can design, develop, and conduct high-quality training programs.

This study echoes the concerns of relevance, practice and support in learning a second language in the United States. This study and the research on the development of a second language call for placing attention to three modes of language acquisition. The three modes in learning a second language that need to be emphasized are: the interpersonal mode that involves two-way communication; the interpretive mode that calls for the understanding of spoken or written language; and the presentational mode that focuses on creating spoken or written communication. Lastly, the findings also suggest that as we work for biliteracy in our global society, the development of a second language requires that we gain knowledge of other cultures; connect with other academic subjects; develop insights into the

nature of language and culture through lived experiences, and participate in multilingual communities at home and around the world.

References

English References:

Anastasi, A & Urbina, S. (1997). Psychological testing. Upper Saddle River, New Jersey: Prentice Hall.

Bowman, et all. (2000). Connecting Teachers across Continents through On-Line Reflection and Sharing. TESOL Journal, 9 (3), 15-18.

Brown, J. D. (1990). Understanding research in second language learning: A teacher's guide to statistics and research design. Cambridge: Cambridge University Press.

Chu, S. (2001). Elementary school teachers' attitudes toward English teaching methodologies. Selected papers from the tenth international symposium on English teaching, Taipei, Taiwan, 367-379.

Crookes, G, & Arakaki, L. (1999). Teaching idea sources and work conditions in an ESL program. TESOL Journal, 8 (1), 15-19.

Eisenman, G., & Holly, T. (1998). Telementoring: Helping new teachers through the first year. THE Journal, 26 (9), 79-82.

Fisher, D. (2001). Teachers' perceptions of supports and resources needed to prepare English language learners for the future. The CATESOL Journal, 13 (1), 7-22.

Freiberg, H., & Waxman, H. (Eds.). (1990). Changing teacher education. New York: Macmillan.

Goodlad, J. (1990). Teachers for our nation's school. San Francisco: Jossey-Bass.

Grimmest, P., & MacKinnon, A. (1992). Craft knowledge and the education of teachers. Washington, D.C.: American Educational Research Association.

Guyton, E., & McIntyre, D. (1999). Student teaching and school experiences. New York: Macmillan.

Johnson, K. (1996). The vision versus the reality: the tensions of the TESOL practicum. In Donald Freeman, & Jack Richards (Eds.), Teacher learning in language Teaching. New York: Cambridge University Press.

Lanier, J., & Little, J. (1986). Research on teaching education. New York: Macmillan.

Millar, J. (1995). Effective public relations with schools. In G. A. Slick (Ed.), Preparing new teachers, (pp. 47-69). Thousand Oaks, CA: Corwin Press, Inc.

National Council for Accreditation of Teacher Education (NCATE). (2002 October 9). ESL standards for P-12 teacher education programs. Retrieved October 9, 2002 from hTPP://www.ncate.org/standard/programstds

Pennycook, A. (1989). The concept of method, interested knowledge, and the politics of language teaching. TESOL Quarterly, 23 (4), 589-618.

Poplin, M. (1992). The leader's new role: Looking to the growth of Teachers. Educational Leadership, 49 (5) 10-11.

Reilly, D. H. (1989). A knowledge base for education: cognitive science. Journal of Teacher Education, 9-13.

Rigden, D. W. (1997). What teachers think of teacher education. Education Digest, 63 (1), 51-54.

Thiessen, D. (2000). Developing knowledge for preparing teachers: Redefining the role of schools of education. Educational Policy 14 (1), 129-145.

Smylie, M, & Kahne, J. (1997). Why what works doesn't in teacher education. <u>Education and Urban Society, 29</u> (3), 355-363.

Stewart-Wells, G. (1999). An investigation of student teacher and teacher educators perceptions of their teacher education programs and the role classroom management plays or should play in pre-service education (Doctoral dissertation, Claremont Graduate University and San Diego State University, 1999).

Vann, A. S. (1999). Four steps to improve teacher quality. <u>Educational Horizons, 77</u> (2), 59-60.

Chinese References:

The following references are available in Chinese. Please contact the author for more information.

Chang, G. H. (2003, January 8). ____ 1000___¨ [Elementary and secondary English standards: announcement of 1000-word essential vocabulary]. United Daily News. Retrieved January 8, 2003 from htpp://udn.com/NEWS/NATIONAL/NATS7/1166989.shtml

Huang, S. L. (1999). [Critique and analysis of Laws regarding Teacher Training]. In Teacher Development Organization (Ed), <u>Evaluation of Teacher Development.</u> Wunan Publisher.

The Ministry of Education (MOE). (1998). ____ [Ministry of Education announcement], 286. Taipei.

The Ministry of Education (MOE). (1999). ____ [Ministry of Education announcement], 290. Taipei.

Shih, S. G. (1998). [From elementary school English education to teacher education in teacher colleges and applications]. <u>Educational Information and Research, 24, 11-14.</u>

Shih, Y. H. & Chu, H. M. (1999). [The mission and characteristics of elementary English curriculum]. <u>Educational Information and Research, 7</u> (2), 1-8.

Su, S. F. (1999). [Discussion of problems in applying English to elementary school curriculum]. <u>English Teaching and Learning, 23</u> (3), 22-37.

Chapter 7
Multiple Perspectives and Multiple Positions: Post-Proposition 227 Language Policies in a California School– 1998-2004

by Tamara Collins-Parks
San Diego State University

Abstract

This is a micro-political case study of the district level dynamics surrounding the implementation of Proposition 227. In 1998, Proposition 227 mandated Structured English Immersion as the automatic placement for English Language Learners unless they submitted a yearly waiver petition. The context of the study was the implementation of Proposition 227 in a majority Latino district. The district denied almost all waiver petitions and implemented an English-only instructional policy.

The stakeholders included were parents, community members, teachers and administrators. Within each group, participants were selected to illustrate the variety of perspectives, including support, opposition and neutrality. The study used interview data to analyze the dynamics among the participants, particularly their perspective on the implementation of Proposition 227 in the district and awareness of both the implementation and the perspective of other stakeholders.

The study contributes to a greater understanding of the dynamics of communication, conflict and cooperation surrounding the implementation of new policy impacting ethnolinguisticly diverse students. The study indicated a need for better communication with the impacted community, inclusion of stakeholders, and democratic implementation of policy.

Californians of European ancestry—"whites"—became a minority near the end of the 1980s . . . . Our political leaders should [reaffirm] America's traditional support for immigration, but couple that with a return to the assimilative policies which America has emphasized in the past. (Unz, 1999, Summary)

The United States is in the midst of a demographic shift towards a more ethnically balanced population (U.S. Census, 2000). The English-Only movement has been attempting to maintain the privileged position of English in the face of this shift (Macedo, 2000). In California, where the demographic shift is more advanced than in the nation as a whole, English-only advocates helped pass Proposition 227, an initiative seeking to eliminate or reduce bilingual education and make instruction in English the standard policy for English Learners (i.e. students who speak other languages and are in the process of learning English) in California's public schools. The programs implemented under the new policy were termed Structured English Immersion (SEI) and roughly defined as specialized instruction for English Learners given overwhelmingly in English and not normally meant to exceed one year. This policy reinforced the privileged position of English within our school system and limited the choices available to meet the linguistic and academic needs of students who spoke other languages. After it was interpreted and written into law by the California Department of Education, districts across the state created their own interpretations as they decided how to implement it within their schools. This chapter examines the implementation of Proposition 227 in one such school district as it is variously supported and contested by the main adult stakeholders: teachers, administrators, parents, and active community members.

California's Proposition 227 passed in June of 1998 with 61% of the vote. One-Nation, an organization promoting English–Only policies, proclaimed it "The End of Bilingual Education" (One Nation web site, 1998). While bilingual education was not completely eliminated, it did disappear in some districts. Enrollment in bilingual programs fell from about 33% of English Learners in 1998 to 11% in 2002 (Yettick, 2002). In keeping with the emphasis in Proposition 227 on quick transition into mainstream classrooms, both bilingual and SEI (Structured English Immersion) programs tended to reduce the *proposed* time-span of special programs for English Learners — although the *actual* time span, as measured by the reclassification rate, rarely changed (Grissom, 2004).

Prior to 1998, schools had leeway to use any program for English Learners that had been proven effective. Some schools had bilingual programs; others had English only programs for English Learners. After Proposition 227 passed, the default program was SEI. Proposition 227 included a provision that parents could request waivers for bilingual education after a month of SEI. Both before and after Proposition 227, parents had the right to opt out of the specialized programs and place their child in mainstream education.

In "Case" *Unified (the district examined in this chapter) bilingual programs were eliminated after Proposition 227 and parent waiver requests to waive SEI in favor of bilingual education were broadly denied. Case Unified garnered national media attention in 2000 as an exemplar of English-Only instruction (i.e., providing both language and academic instruction via the medium of English irrespective of the students' level of English proficiency). Articles portraying Case Unified as a success story appeared in *The New York Times, The Arizona Republic, the Omaha World Herald, the U.S. News and World Report, and* other major newspapers. The media reports on Case Unified centered on test scores, anecdotes, and opinions. Beyond the fact that they were using English in the classroom, details on the implementation of Proposition 227 in Case Unified, and the positions and actions of those directly involved were notably absent. Academic studies such as that by Rossell (2002) contained more details but did not take into account the various stakeholders involved.

A little over six years has passed between the passage of Proposition 227 and the writing of this article. During this time, those involved in its implementation not only have enacted the policy, but also created, re-created, and resisted it (Alschuler, 1980; Freire & Macedo 1987). As the rest of the nation undergoes the same demographic shift and similar "instruction in English" policies are implemented in other states, a critical examination of California's experience is crucial to understanding the dynamics at work. This chapter offers a snapshot of that experience from the point of view of the stakeholders in a key district.

Policy Implementation

Although traditional policy analysis focuses on policy formation (Parsons, 1995), writing policy into law or the educational code is only the first step. The policy is then filtered through organizations and put into practice (Palumbo & Calista, 1990). Ball and Bowe (1991) iden-

*a pseudonym

tify two types of policy: intended policy vs. policy in use. Intended policy consists of the written often legislated guidelines and goals for organizations to follow. Ambiguities, contradictions, and omissions in intended policy provide opportunities for interpretation. Even without these openings, however, the culture of the institution and the beliefs of those working under the policy act to mediate the policy design (Yanow, 1987). The result is "policy in use." While policy in use is influenced by intended policy, it does not always follow it. Figure 1: Intended Policy and Policy in Use illustrates these relationships.

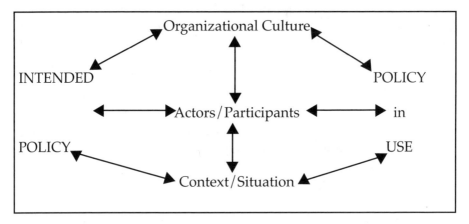

Figure 1: Intended Policy and Policy in Use

In Figure 1, the intended policy is filtered through the organizational culture, the actors/participants, and the context/situation to become the policy in use. The arrows, indicating the use of political agency are two sided to indicate that the process is not a sequential model but rather continuous and mutually influencing. The intended policy also changes as institutions demand clarification, actors/participants provide input or feedback and the context/situation changes.

Methodology

This research was a process-oriented case study. Berends, Nataraj Kirby, Naftel, and McKelvey (2001) assert "We need to incorporate the perspectives of a variety of actors throughout the system," (p. 15). Consequently, the 16 study participants represent the four groups of adult stakeholders within the district: parents, community members, teachers, and district staff. The core data came from semi-structured interviews (Patton, 1990). These interviews served a dual purpose: (1) to gather background information on the situation, and (2) to elicit narratives, opinions, and justifications.

The interviews were analyzed using a process similar to thematic analysis (Tashakkori & Teddlie, 1997). Instead of emerging themes, however, the units of analysis were the participant's perspectives on the implementation of Proposition 227 within the district, and their awareness of both the implementation itself and the perspectives of other stakeholders.

Background Information

Setting. Case is a coastal city of moderate size (pop. 173,307 projected from Census 2000). The population is mainly White non-Latino (53.6%) and Latinos (30.2%), but with significant Asian and Black populations (10% each). Within the schools, Latinos are the majority (47.8% Latino vs. 31.9% White non-Latino, per California Department of Education, 2002). Because of this population differential, as well as the White concentration of political power and representation, Whites have a disproportionate influence on the education of Latino children in this district.

With a median income of $46,145, Case is slightly lower on the socioeconomic scale than the surrounding towns (US Census, 2000). During the time of this study, about half of the students at Case Unified were on free or reduced lunch — (data from Case Unified's website). Most (95.8%) of the English Learners in Case Unified are Spanish speaking (California Department of Education, 1999) and are concentrated in the lower grades.

Subjects. The majority of participants were female, as is typical in education, particularly in the early grades. The Superintendent and one other administrator, one teacher and one community member were the only males. The majority of the participants identified themselves as either Hispanic or Latino. Most of those were either from Mexico or born in the United States with Mexican ancestry. One administrator and two teachers were the only non-Latinos. The parents appeared to have the lowest income level (three of the four parents rented apartments rather than owning houses). The administrative and teacher stakeholders were well educated by definition, as degrees and credentials are criteria for their employment. The educational level of the parent and community stakeholders varied.

The criteria for participation in interviews were as follows: All participants lived or worked in the district under Proposition 227. School personnel worked with or made decisions affecting English Learners. Parents/Guardians had students who were classified as English Learners. Community members actively supported or opposed the district's interpretation of Proposition 227.

Table One: Participants by Ideology shows the positions of the participants, broken down by stakeholder category. Although an attempt was made to illustrate both the pro English-only instruction and pro-bilingual perspectives, several participants did not fit easily into either category. In addition, some of the participants fit more than one stakeholder category. Although these other experiences informed their positions (e.g. the administrators had been teachers), participants responded primarily from the perspective of their assigned category.

Table 1: Participants by Ideology

	Pro district's 227 interpretation	Pro Bilingual (in general)	Other Positions
Administrators & District Staff	-Superintendent -Program specialist		-Principal -Former district level resource T
Teachers	-T advocate for SEI program.	2 Ts supportive of waivers.	-T was pro-SEI, now pro bilingual
Parents	-P supports district's SEI program.	2 Ps applied to waive SEI for bilingual.	-P opted out of bilingual & SEI.
Community members	-Sch Board member. -Director of a community center.	-Founder of waiver support group. -Legal advocate.	

Key: T= teacher, P = parent, Sch = school

Implementation of Proposition 227 in Case Unified. Prior to Proposition 227, provisions for English Learners in Case Unified varied by school site. "Every school was different. Some had bilingual programs, some didn't," (Admin3 Interview, 2004). Schools with lower English Learner populations had programs with little to no native language support. Schools with high Spanish speaking English Learner populations usually had some form of transitional bilingual program but they were not always consistent. The degree of support for English Learners was determined by English Learner enrollment and school personnel (Teach5, interview, 2000). "Bilingual" programs in Case Unified included varying amounts of Spanish and English, and all were transitional. According to research, however, the most effective bilingual programs are long term (5-7 years) and take an additive approach aimed at acquiring English while maintaining the primary language (Baker, 2001; Collier & Thomas, 2002).

As specified in Proposition 227, the district had to develop the new policy and programs over the summer, and implement them immediately the following September. The intended policy in Case Unified was that instruction and all materials should be in English (Case Unified English Learner Master Plan, 8/12/2003). Some teachers understood this as a ban on Spanish although the district's Master Plan stated that teachers could use Spanish under limited circumstances such as in emergencies, to communicate with parents or for classroom management and discipline. In the first year of implementation, in accordance with the district policy of English-only instruction, Spanish language materials were removed from the classrooms. Despite this, the "policy in use" in some classrooms included some reading, homework, instructions, and explanations in Spanish.

When the new policy was implemented in the Fall of 1998, a few parents attempted to find out about obtaining waivers for an alternative bilingual program as provided for under Proposition 227. Administrators discouraged teachers from discussing programs with parents. In January 1999 the district released waiver guidelines. With help from a community group that had formed to support parents who wanted to waive SEI in favor of bilingual education, 144 waiver applications were eventually filed. Of those 144, the district granted seven (Local Newspaper, 10/24/00), well short of the 20 at one grade level in one school that triggers a mandate to provide a waiver program. The bilingual waiver support group protested and went on to file complaints with the State Department of Education and the Office of Civil Rights. The State Department of Education put the district under a review process known as comité and was still monitoring the district at the time this article was written. The number of waiver petitions decreased markedly in the next years and continued to be denied by the district.

Data and Analysis

Administrative Stakeholders

The participants in the administrative stakeholders group consisted of Case Unified, district level employees who had worked for the district since before Proposition 227 passed. Two of the participants currently worked at the Case district offices (the superintendent and Admin2). Two had moved on to administrative jobs outside of the Case district office. (Admin3 and Admin4).

Implementation from the administrative perspective. For the administrative participants, implementation largely consisted of working out the mechanics of the new policy. They supported English-only instruction for various reasons. The superintendent originally supported bilingual education but determined to implement the law when Proposition 227 passed. He described himself as a convert to SEI based on the results he saw in the classroom (Superintendent interview, 3/04/04). Admin2, a former bilingual teacher, decided to stay and support the SEI program primarily because of what she saw as the level of commitment.

> Admin2: [E]verybody from the superintendent to the site administrator really meant what they were talking about and implementing as far as making an adoption (interview, 2/18/4).

The positions of Admin3 (the district level resource teacher) and Admin4 (the program coordinator) were unclear. They mainly seemed to be carrying out their jobs. Both stated that they actively avoided conversations about bilingual education. By following a "don't ask/don't tell" policy, they were able to preserve their relationships with stakeholders on all sides of the issue.

Awareness. All of the administrative participants were aware of the programs offered and of the positions of other stakeholders. The superintendent in particular was highly aware of who was involved on both sides of the issue and what they were doing. Admin2 denied that there was any conflict.

> Admin2: I really . . . I don't necessarily feel that teachers have a conflict with this program, rather [it was a case of] teachers coming together and saying, "OK, this is what we're doing; how can we do it better?" (interview, 2/18/4).

Teacher Stakeholders

All of the teacher participants were currently working for Case Unified. Two identified themselves as Hispanic and all were either bi- or tri-lingual. Most were experienced teachers with bilingual credentials and had been English Learners themselves.

Implementation from the Teacher Perspective. For the teacher participants, the district's new policy created uncertainty. It was created without their input and they were unsure as to the exact provisions, particularly regarding language. In my background sample of eight teachers representing six schools, every one reported that teachers at their site felt confused and overwhelmed.

> Teach4: There was an atmosphere of fear at the school, that if the teacher was heard speaking in Spanish to her students or reading a book in Spanish, that the risked losing her job, (interview, 12/1/3).

A strong theme in the interviews was the desire for more control of their teaching situation and more input in the decisions that were made.

Through the first year of implementation, some bilingual teachers found the environment too hostile and/or had moral qualms about the policy of English-only instruction. This showed up in teacher interviews and administrators mentioned it as well.

> Admin4: There was a lot of anxiety between teachers too. Some of the English mainstream teachers felt that they could go up to SEI teachers who were using Spanish and tell them "You're not allowed to do that anymore." (interview, 01/06/04).

A few left (Teach6 and Teach7). Most bilingual teachers stayed. Reactions to the new policy varied from implementation (Teach1) to non-implementation (Teach2) to direct opposition (Teach 3 and Teach4). Teach1 stated that her strategies were those of SEI even before Proposition 227 passed. Teach2 did not directly oppose the district policies, she remained quiet at meetings and did not speak to parents about waivers. This did not mean that she agreed with the policy. Teach2 found the ban on Spanish impractical and did not follow it in her classroom.

> Teach2: The principal says you're not allowed to speak Spanish unless it's an emergency but I do. . . . If I give [homework] in English, I'm not going to get any back . . . .Something or nothing — what would you take? (interview, 8/31/2).

On the other hand, Teach3 and Teach4 expressed their opposition directly by testifying to the investigative group from Comité and helping the waiver support group.

Awareness. Like the administrative participants, the teacher participants tended to be very aware of the programs offered. Regardless of whether or not they supported the district policy, all showed a critical awareness of the problems the district faced. They had conversations with administrators, other teachers, and parents. Although the district had a policy that questions about programs were to be directed to the appropriate administrator, three of the teachers reported that they talked about programs with parents. These conversations were held or phrased circumspectly in order to avoid the appearance of overt oppositions to administrative policies. Despite communicating with a variety of stakeholders, teachers mainly mentioned cooperating with other teachers. All were aware of the positions of other stakeholders.

Parent Stakeholders

All of the parent stakeholders were Latinas of Mexican origin, Spanish dominant, and active in the district. Parent1 and Parent2 were fluently bilingual and chose to interview in English. They had both waived the district's SEI program in favor of mainstream education for their children and supported English-only instruction. Parent3 and Parent4 were most comfortable in Spanish and chose to interview in that language. They had unsuccessfully petitioned to waive the district's SEI program in favor of bilingual education and were active with the group supporting such petitions. They strongly believed not only in the value of bilingualism but also the schools' responsibility to nurture it.

Implementation from the Parent Perspective. The parent participants had no voice in the implementation of Proposition 227. As English Learners, their children were automatically placed in SEI. In order to challenge that placement, they had to inform themselves of the options and purposefully travel to the school to request an alternative.

For those waiving in favor of mainstream, the process was a case of asserting their choice. If they were sufficiently assertive, their child would be placed in mainstream classes. For those petitioning to waive in favor of an alternative bilingual program, the process was more formal. It involved a trip to the school to find out about the program options, a two page petition explaining their child's needs, individual reviews of each case by a school/district team, and a final decision by the Superintendent. The outcome was doubtful. Most petitions were denied. The few waivers that were approved did not meet the 20 students per grade level cut-off for implementing an alternative bilingual program.

A major theme in the interview with the two parents who petitioned for bilingual education was fear and the lack of involvement by other parents. Parent3 stated that she was not going to ask for a waiver again.

> Parent3: ¿Qué vale si es nada más nosotros [dos] pidiendo? (interview, 02/02/04) [*What is it worth if it is only us asking?*]

Parent4 felt fear herself and recognized it in others. Parent3 had a bolder approach.

> Parent3: No somos muy unidos. No debemos tener miedo. [Pedir una solicitud de excepción] es un derecho.
> [*We are not very united. We should not be afraid. Asking for a waiver is our right.*]
> Parent4: Sí tengo miedo.[*I am afraid.*]
> Parent3: ¿Quién no quiere dos idiomas? [*Who doesn't want two languages?*]
> Parent4: Todos lo quieren pero tenemos miedo.[*We all want it but we're scared.*] (interview, 02/02/04).

The two parents who supported the English-only instructional policy of the district did not report any fear.

Awareness. Parent1 and Parent4 were uninformed about their options and unsure even of which program their child was in. Parent2 was better informed and was even able to stand up to the principal and demand her right to waive SEI for mainstream placement. Both Parent1 and Parent2 had realistic ideas about the difficulties faced by parents who were Spanish monolingual rather than bilingual (e.g. being unable to help with homework). Parent3 and Parent4 believed that those opposing bilingual education must not be bilingual. Overall, the interaction with others was limited. Parent1 did not talk about programs at all and the rest of the parent participants only mentioned conversations with other parents.

Community Stakeholders

The community participants all identified as Hispanic/Latino of Mexican ancestry and were either bilingual or, in the case of Community3, understood some Spanish. Community1 and Community2 supported the district's English-only instructional policy. Community1 was a school board member. Community2 ran a local community center. Community3 and Community4, on the other hand, were deeply concerned about parents' rights to waive in favor of bilingual education. Community3 was an activist attorney assisting the waiver support group. Community4 founded the waiver support group.

Implementation from the Community Perspective. There was a clear division in perspective. Those supporting English-only instruction (Community1 and Community2) recognized the difficulty of creating new programs in response to Proposition 227 and were impressed with how the superintendent had met the challenge. In their perspective, this work was impeded by protest groups. Those protesting (Community3 and Community4) saw the implementation of Proposition 227 as created and imposed by the district upon everyone else. They wanted a bilingual option and respect for parents' choices.

Awareness. All community participants were aware of the history and implementation of Proposition 227, the programs offered, and the controversy in the district over the English only instructional policy. Those who supported the English only instructional policy (Community1 and Community2) felt that the controversy was mainly the work of outside agitators and were affronted by tactics they characterized as aggressive and rude. Community3 and Community4, while they supported bilingual education, felt that it was mainly an issue of parent rights. The two groups were aware of each other and attempted to counter the perspective of the other side in their interviews. The excerpt from Community4's interview below illustrates both the awareness and a rebuttal:

> Community4: [F]rom the school board's vantage point, I guess you could say, they've always identified any informed person as being an outside agitator. I think that that's always brought into this whole struggle. I find that very interesting because the school board can always find consultants but when the parents actively look for someone who can inform them about the things that the school district hasn't informed them, then they get labeled as the outside agitator, the person [who] is inciting them to go against the school board. That is very insulting from a certain standpoint because it assumes that the parents don't have the ability for themselves to determine that something is right or wrong, and that somebody else has to come over and tell them that this is not in your best interests. The parents very well know when some people are against their family interests or their beliefs or values. Just as anybody else, when you don't have some information, you go and find somebody who can provide you that information. A consultant, that is what it is. The school district has consultants; we have outside agitators. (interview, 11/15/03)

Community members interacted with all of the stakeholder groups. The group they interacted with most, however, was the parents.

Discussion

The main areas of discussion are (1) perspectives and positions, and (2) interaction and awareness. This sections ends with a policy recommendation based on the findings from the case study.

Perspectives and Positions

The majority of the participants, on both sides of the issues, were Latino, and bilingual. The key to the positions taken by the participants favoring English-only instruction seemed to be their beliefs — particularly their support for assimilation — rather than their ethnicity or language. On the other hand, Spanish monolingualism did appear to factor into support for bilingual education for the parents. This was a practical issue, particularly where homework was involved, as well as a question of belief.

Despite these patterns, what was most striking was the diversity of positions on all sides of the issue. While standard arguments and strategies were present, participants tended to hold a variety of beliefs. Standard arguments used by participants included references by those supporting English-only instruction to the ability to "make it" without bilingual education and references by those supporting bilingual instruction to the economic benefits of bilingualism. In addition, however, several participants crossed lines or brought up other issues.

Line crossing was particularly characteristic of the participants who supported English-only instruction. The superintendent who instituted the English-only instructional policy told an anecdote about students being able to read in Spanish because they had learned to read English. Both he and Community1 seemed to support Spanish for Spanish Speakers as an enhancement once students had learned English. Similarly, Community1 and Parent2, who supported the district's English-only instructional policy, maintained that they would be interested in well designed bilingual programs. This is consistent with findings by researchers such as J. Cummins (1999), who noted similar contradictions in statements by Unz. Community1 and Parent2 opposed bilingual education in the district because they doubted the district's ability to provide a well designed program. Community1, the school board member, considered it an issue of practicality. She felt that the district could not adequately staff a bilingual program and that the resources were insufficient. Parent2 had first hand experience with the poor bilingual abilities of many teachers. She didn't want her children learning Spanish from someone who translated "hand the papers back" as "darlos espalda" ("espalda" being "back" as in a body part). Under better circumstances, however, they both felt that bilingual education was worthwhile. While these participants may have been seeking common ground with their interviewer by expressing qualified support for bilingual education, their willingness to cross lines is still notable.

Despite the focus on Proposition 227 in the interviews, about half the participants brought up other concerns. Admin4 was most concerned with using data to find what worked for different types of students (leaving the door open to both SEI and bilingual depending on their needs). Her true goal was success for students in whichever education program they found themselves in. Admin2 felt that any program would be successful as long as it had consistency. Community3 was primarily concerned with parents' rights. Parent1 recognized the difficulties Spanish monolingual parents faced in trying to help their children in English. Several parents were concerned about what they identified as fiscal inequities affecting primarily Latino schools (limited computer and internet access, unsafe play equipment, etc.) and thought that energy would be better spent addressing these issues. Within this diversity of positions there is great scope for working together. Stakeholders can oppose each other on some issues while working together on others.

Interaction and Awareness

Cooperation, however, appeared to be an underutilized strategy. Many of the participants had trouble answering my question about cooperation. When they did answer, their examples were restricted to their own spheres, e.g., teachers cooperated with each other rather than any other group.

Awareness of the positions taken by others varied among the participants. There were several misapprehensions on each side about the positions and actions of those on the other side. Two parents thought that the opponents of bilingual education must be monolingual. Although they couldn't conceive of someone who was bilingual opposing bilingual education, most of the participants supporting English-only instruction were both bilingual and Hispanic/Latino. As mentioned above, ethnicity and language were not key factors in the position taken.

There were also misapprehensions among the administrators and community members. Those supporting the district's policy found the protestors rude, and attributed the controversy, at least in part, to troublemakers from outside the district. The protestors, for their part, felt that they had exhausted polite options to no avail. While there were, indeed, outsiders involved, they had been invited. There were some teachers and parents from within the district who feared repercussions and kept a low profile by declining to state who they were, testifying in private, and/or using those with less to lose (outsiders) as their representatives. This low profile protected protestors within the district but also reinforced the idea that the controversy was spawned outside of the district.

Other misapprehensions centered on the reasons there were so few waiver requests (over a hundred the first year but under twenty or sometimes none in subsequent years). The administrative, teacher, and community members supporting the district's English-only instructional policy maintained that parents did not apply for waivers because they were not interested. While some or even most parents may have been uninterested, the two pro-bilingual parents I interviewed mentioned fear and failure as the chief reasons they were not applying again. It is very difficult to go against an established program. Despite a clear belief that parents had the right to speak, those supporting the district's policy did not seem to feel a corresponding necessity to listen. Parents petitioning for waivers had the sense that they were engaged in an undesirable activity. This was supported both by their experiences (such as the resource teacher who wanted to know why they were petitioning for waivers and had arguments against every reason they gave her) and by testimony in the interviews. To circumvent their fear, some parents requested that the community group supporting parent waiver requests send someone to accompany them to the office to fill out the waiver petition. The parents in the waiver support group also requested that someone else come to distribute waiver information as they did not want to be seen distributing it themselves. These parents eventual decided not to re-apply for waivers, judging that they were bound to be denied again.

Lack of information was a recurring theme throughout the parent interviews (other stakeholders were well informed about programs and policies). Two of the parent participants did not know what program their children were in and the other two found out only incidentally. Parent2, for example, mentioned seeing all of the Hispanic names on the roster and realizing that her children had been placed in SEI despite her preference for mainstream education. Because the default placement is SEI, parents who prefer mainstream and parents who prefer bilingual both find their students placed in SEI unless they take assertive action. The difference is that those waiving SEI for mainstream have the legal right to do so (and in fact an average of 110 parents in Case

Unified have done so each year) while those trying to waive for bilingual education can only petition. The district has rejected the grand majority of petitions.

Lack of information can also be inferred from the low turn-out at the program meeting I attended. The seven parents were almost out numbered by teachers there to explain the district's SEI program. This could be interpreted as apathy or busy parents or both. The fact remains that as a means of disseminating information, it was a failure due to low turn-out.

Awareness (of positions and of information) depends on interaction. The interviews suggest that some of the participants had very little interaction with other stakeholder groups. Based on their responses, community members were most likely to interact with parents and the administrators with teachers. The teacher participants cooperated primarily with each other. The parents were most likely to react as individuals. Students, while they showed up in anecdotes, were rarely referred to as a group. A possible interpretation of the absence of references to students as a group is that the controversy was primarily over, and was not about students, but who would control policy and program placement: the school or the parents.

Policy Recommendation

One of the chief findings concerned the status of the parents. In the interviews, the parent participants appeared less informed and had less interaction than the other stakeholders. One explanation is that this reflected their lack of power and position within the district. The fact that the administrators were the best informed and most aware tends to support the link between power, interaction, and position.

To enhance the parents' position, I recommend greater interaction, more information, and stronger rights. Teachers are the natural conduit for information (for good and ill) and they should be encouraged to discuss programs with parents. The key to more interaction is multiple sources and an assurance of respect. The routine rejection of waivers, albeit via the use of a highly comprehensive procedure of review, only reinforces the parents' sense of fatalism. The burden of proof needs to be on the district to prove why a waiver should be rejected rather than on a parent to prove why it should be granted. In other words, parent requests should be routinely approved in the absence of a compelling reason to reject them. With these reforms in place parents such as those participating in this study will be better informed and have more decision making power. Although these policies are directed at a specific situation in Case Unified, they could be applied in any district with similar issues.

Conclusion

We each have visions for the future. Some dream of everyone be coming equal while others dream of everyone's differences being valued. We will only achieve our visions by working with and through people. This is why it is important to understand how various groups see the issues and how they work or fail to work together. This chapter contributed to that understanding by examining the perspectives of different district stakeholders and some of the dynamics between stakeholder groups within the context of the implementation of Proposition 227. Not surprisingly, a chief finding was the need for better dissemination of information to parents as well as increased cooperation between groups. Part of the dream to value people, whether on an equal standing or through their differences, is to give all the opportunity to participate. Then the vision for the future becomes one not of apathy but of action and results.[oo]

Appendix A: Interview Guide

All topics will be covered, but questions will vary.

Background
- What should I know about you?
- What experiences have you had that helped shape your point of view?

Possible Questions (The intent is to get the participants talking, to tell their stories.)
- What has happened in this district since Proposition 227 passed in 1998 and the district officially went English-only? (A summary from your perspective.)
- What are different ways this story might be told?
  - How do you think the Superintendent would tell the story?
  - How do you think bilingual activists would tell the story?
- Tell me about the programs your school(s) have.
- Tell in your own words about the resistance or conflicts (if any) there are in the district or at your school site over these programs?
- How do people work together to help English Learners? What do you do?
- What language and educational challenges do you face at home? At school? In the district?
- Do you talk to people about the programs? What sort of things do you say? Try to re-create a conversation.
- Is there anything else you think I should know?

References

Alschuler, A. (1980). *Socially literate methods*. New York: Mc Graw-Hill.

Baker, C. (2001). *Foundations of bilingual education and bilingualism, 3rd edition*. Clevedon, England: Multilingual Matters Limited.

Ball, S. J., & Bowe, R. (1991). Micropolitics of radical change. In J. Blase (Ed.), *The politics of life in schools: Power, conflict,, and cooperation*. (pp.19-45). Newbury Park, CA: Sage Publications.

Berends, M., Nataraj Kirby, S., Naftel, S., & McKelvey, C. (2001). *Implementation and performance in New American Schools: Three years into scale-up* (Rand Publication No. MR-1145-EDU). Rand Educational Research Institute. Retrieved August 29, 2004 from http://www.rand.org/publications/MR/MR1145/

California Department of Education. (1998-2005) *Webquest reports*. Last retrieved February 16, 2005 from California Department of Education Website: http://cde.ca.gov

Collier, V. P., & Thomas, W. P. (2002). *A national study of school effectiveness for language minority students' long-term academic achievement* (ERIC Publication No. ED475048). Retrieved Oct. 20, 2004 from Education Research Information Clearinghouse (ERIC) document reproduction service.

Cummins, J. (1999). The ethics of doublethink: Language rights and the bilingual education debate. Posted in 1999 at *I teach I Learn . com: Educational Ideas and Solutions*. Retrieved March 17, 2005 from http://www.iteachilearn.com/cummins/researchbildebate.html .

Freire, P., & Macedo, D. (1987). *Literacy: Reading the word & the world*. South Hadley, MA: Bergin and Garvin.

Grissom, J. B. (2004, July 30). Reclassification of English learners. *Education Policy Analysis Archives, 12*(36). Retrieved August 6, 2004 from http://epaa.asu.edu/epaa/v12n36/ .

Macedo, D. (2000, April). The colonialism of the English only movement. *Educational-Researcher, 29*(3), 15-24.

One Nation. (1998). English for the Children home page. One Nation / One California web site. Retrieved in 1998 from http://www.onenation.org. [Note: "End of Bilingual Education" title is no longer posted.]

Palumbo, D., & Calista, D. J. (1990). *Implementation and the policy process*. NY: Green wood Press.

Parsons, W. (1995). *Public policy: An introduction to the theory and practice of policy analysis*. Brookfield, U.S.: Edward Elgar.

Patton, M. (1990). *Qualitative evaluation and research*. Newbury Park, CA: Sage Publications.

Rossell, C. (2002). Dismantling bilingual education; Implementing English immersion: The California initiative. (Research project funded by the Public Policy Institute of California.) Revised and posted 8/20/2002. Retrieved May 4, 2003 from http://www.bu.edu/polisci/CROSSELL Dismantling%20Bilingual%20Education,%20July%202002.pdf

Tashakkori, A., & Teddlie, C. (1997). *Mixed methodology. (Applied social research methods series, 46)*. Thousand Oaks, CA: Sage Publications.

U.S. Census (2000). *Demographic trends in the 20th Century*. Washington, D.C.: U.S. Government Publication issued November 2002. Retrieved June 3, 2003 from http://www.census.gov/prod/2002pubs/censr-4.pdf

Unz, R. (1999, November). California and the end of White America. *Commentary*. November 1999. Cover story. Retrieved January 2003 from http://www.onenation.org/article.cfm?ID=1704

Yettick, H. (2002, October 7). Four years, no answers: California's Prop. 227, akin to Amendment 31, spurs varied reactions. *Rocky Mountain News*. Retrieved from archives March 15, 2003 at http://www.RockyMountainNews.com/ .

Yanow, D. J. (1987). Toward a policy culture approach to implementation. *Policy Studies Review*. 7(1): 103-115.

Chapter 8
Indigenous Language Loss and Revitalization: Social, Economic and Political Variables In an Amerindian Community

by Paula L. Meyer
San Diego State University /
Claremont Graduate University
and Jon Meza Cuero
Kumeyaay Community
Tecate, Baja California

Abstract

In looking for an approach to language revitalization, this chapter explores the reasons languages of Indigenous peoples are resistant to revitalization efforts. We look at the social, political and economic factors contributing to the demise of these languages and that continue to affect any revitalization attempts. The chapter describes an Indigenous community in Baja California and the many types of loss that this community has suffered and continues to suffer. We conclude that without meaningful dialogue among the community and significant people from outside the community, these losses will continue to impede language revitalization efforts. Through genuine dialogue, the community will pave the way to the power they need to revive their language and their culture. They can then affirm their positive identity separate from the dominant society, and thus be able to participate as equals in the larger society.

Introduction

Indigenous language revitalization efforts usually have come about and are supported by majority populations only when Indigenous languages are hopelessly near extinction. In reality, Indigenous language revitalization projects pose no threat to the dominant societies, either economically or culturally because many of the communities involved have assimilated and are marginalized to the point that they have little power. The revitalization movement came to life in the 1990's when many Indigenous languages disappeared, were moribund or well on their way toward being extinct. Given this reality, how does an Indigenous community, working with outside facilitators and/or funding agencies, approach language revitalization?

Besides reporting on our approach to language revitalization, this chapter explores the reasons languages of Indigenous peoples are resistant to revitalization efforts. We look at the social, political and economic factors that have played a part in the demise of these languages and that continue to affect revitalization attempts.

Recognition of the rights/values of Indigenous peoples

The government of the state of Baja California in Mexico has officially recognized the existence of Indigenous people only in the last 30 years, even though they were there before the establishment of the current US/Mexico boundary. In fact, they are considered to have been there since time immemorial. The co-researcher of this work, Jon Meza Cuero, in 1969 confronted the governor of Baja California when he went to Mexico City to report to the President that there were indeed Indigenous communities in the state. He reports the following,

> *Y entonces, quise pelear en Baja California. En Baja California decían que no había indios. [Decían que no había indios] porque el gobernador del estado quería que no hubiera indios en Baja California para poder él vender todo Baja California; él quería quitarle la tierra a los indígenas. Y por eso fue el problema que tuve muy grande con el gobierno del estado, con Baja California, porque cuando yo pasé a México D.F. fui a reportarlo a él, y era cuando se enojó conmigo. Se enojó mucho conmigo, que mandó tres personas a matarme. Antes de todo eso me fui a México. Yo me fui a México representando las tribus Kumeyaay de Baja California.*

> [And then, I wanted to fight in Baja California. In Baja California they said that there weren't any Indians. [They said that there were no Indians] because the governor of the state wanted to not have any Indians in Baja California so that he could sell all of Baja California, take the land away from the Indians. And that was the reason for the very big problem I had with the governor of the state, with Baja California, because when I went to Mexico City, I went to report him, and that was when he got angry with me. He got so angry with me that he sent three persons to kill me. Before that I went to Mexico City. I went to Mexico City representing the Kumeyaay tribes of Baja California.]

Mr. Meza met with officials, including the President of Mexico, Luis Echevarría and he speaks of his meeting:

"¿Así que usted es de Baja California, señor?" "Sí, señor," dije. Estuvimos platican-
do con él. Yo platicando con él. Dijo, "Señor," dijo, "Mire," dijo, "Ahora que usted
dice que hay indios en Baja California, pongo una oficina allá. Yo estoy ordenando....
Quiero que vea a, todos los indios de Baja California, quiero que los registren bien,
que revisen bien, para ver cuántos indios hay en Baja California para poder poner una
oficina," dijo.

["So you are from Baja California, sir?" "Yes, sir," I said. We were talking with him. Me--talking with him. He said, "Sir," he said, "Look," he said. "Now that you say that there are Indians in Baja California, I'll put an office there. I am ordering....I want them to see, all the Indians of Baja California, I want them to register correctly, they should check well, to see how many Indians there are in Baja California, to be able to put an [Indian] office," he said.] This was the first official recognition of Indigenous people in the state of Baja California. But it was not without serious repercussions for Mr. Meza. The governor put out a contract on his life. The first two contractors had lost their lives trying to run him off a mountain road. This left one:

Y el tal Mocho Serranos, era muy bravo el amigo. Yo creo que era muy matón el cuate.
No más que yo tenía mucha amistad con él; tomábamos juntos todo el tiempo. Enton-
ces le dieron el trabajo a él, para que me matara a mí. Dijo, "¿Sabes qué? Juan," dijo,
"Te quiero decir algo," dijo. "No me animo, pero te lo voy a decir. Tú para mí eres
como un carnal," dijo. "Mira qué tengo para ti: una orden para matarte. Son cin-
cuenta millones de pesos tu cabeza. Y en una cruda, sí te mato, carnal."... "¿Sabes
lo que debes hacer? Juan," dijo, "Irte para Estados Unidos. Tienes oportunidad allí.
Véte. Aca, no eres de aquí," dijo. "Véte pa'tras. Véte con tus tías. Recógete con tus
tías. Diez, quince años, se va a calmar esta cosa." Entonces, con más derecho, vine a
Estados Unidos yo. Y aquí me quedé durante muchos años.... casi unos veinte años.

[And that Mocho Serranos, he was really tough, that guy. I think he was a real killer. The only thing was, we were really good friends; we used to drink together all the time. Then they gave the job to him, to kill me. He said, "You know what, Juan?" he said. "I want to tell you something," he said. "I don't really want to, but I'm going to tell you. You are like a brother to me," he said. "Look what I have for you: an order to kill you. There's 50 million pesos for your head. And hung over, I really will kill you, brother." "Know what you should do, Juan?" he said, "Go to the United States. You have opportunity there. Go. Here, you're not from here," he said. "Go back. Go to your aunts'. Stay with your aunts. Ten, fifteen years, this thing will calm down." Then, I came straight to the United States. And I stayed for many years....almost some 20 years.]

In those days not only was it shameful to speak Kumeyaay, it was life-threatening just to claim to be Kumeyaay! This kind of oppression caused Mr. Meza to move to San Diego and leave his advocacy work behind--just like people, who are in oppressive situations in general, sometimes have to flee or else be murdered. Today, the Indigenous communities of Baja California retain some, but not many, of their original institutions, including extended-family ties, songs, dances, pottery and some language, this last, however, is rapidly disappearing.

In the contact I (the author) have had through the years with these indigenous people, I felt an urgency to stop and reverse the language shift I observed. However, I perceived that my concern was not matched by the people involved. My frustration caused me to push language revitalization on people. I told them about language-teaching methods and connected people with language projects. Of course, all this met with absolute failure. Why? I knew that reversing-language-shift efforts had to come from the community and not from outsiders. But why weren't these efforts coming from the community?

People talked with me about the problem. Obviously they recognized it. I began to get a clue when I constantly met with the response, "How much will you pay me?" when I asked people if they were interested in reclaiming their language. Undoubtedly I needed to change course. I needed to discover their point of view, and I needed to investigate the "why." I needed to work <u>with</u> them, the people themselves, to investigate this question (Cameron, et al., 1992). "[E]very human being, no matter how 'ignorant' or submerged in the 'culture of silence' he or she may be is capable of looking critically at the world in a dialogical encounter with others" (Shaull, 2002 p. 32). So, I am now trying to work against the prejudices and misconceptions I carry as a member of the oppressor class. I am trying to facilitate real dialogue between the community and myself and among other community members. Although I thought I was working on the side of the people, I think I fit into what Freire (1970/2002) describes:

> [C]ertain members of the oppressor class join the oppressed in their struggle for liberation, thus moving from one pole of the contradiction to the other. Theirs is a fundamental role, and has been so throughout the history of this struggle. It happens, however, that as they cease to be exploiters or indifferent spectators or simply the heirs of exploitation and move to the side of the exploited, they almost always bring with them the marks of their origin: their prejudices and their deformations, which include a lack of confidence in the people's ability to think, to want, and to know. Accordingly, these adherents to the people's cause constantly run the risk of falling into a type of generosity as malefic as that of the oppressors. The generosity of the oppressors is nourished by an unjust order, which must be maintained in order to justify that generosity. Our converts, on the other hand, truly desire to transform the unjust order; but because of their background they believe that they must be

the executors of the transformation. They talk about the people, but they do not trust them; and trusting the people is the indispensable precondition for revolutionary change. (p. 60)

I recognize that this is a description of me, which I am working to change. I see it also as a description of various other people from outside the community who are working very hard to better the conditions endured by the community members. Indigenous persons perceive a lack of trust and confidence on the part of well-meaning people who genuinely want to work together to effect change. There can be a lot of animosity on both sides, which obviates real change.

> Liberating work can be carried out only through genuine dialogue. Critical and liberating dialogue, which presupposes action, must be carried on with the oppressed at whatever the stage of their struggle for liberation. The content of that dialogue can and should vary in accordance with historical conditions and the level at which the oppressed perceive reality....Attempting to liberate the oppressed without their reflective participation in the act of liberation is to treat them as objects which must be saved. (Freire, 2002, p. 65)

What, then, is the role of persons from outside the community? Freire (2002) says we are to be coordinators and at times give direction. We cannot impose our word for theirs. "If [we] are truly committed to liberation, [our] action and reflection cannot proceed without the action and reflection of others" (p. 126).

The Revitalization Project

We (Jon Meza Cuero and Paula Meyer) discussed all of this. We decided that the best way to go about dealing with it would be to have a short (two-day) language camp with planning and follow-up sessions for Mr. Meza's family in which we could begin to facilitate real dialogue while also developing a language project. Furthermore, we decided to begin with one single extended family because we observed that in this community people work well within family groups, whereas cross-family relations are often rife with envy and mistrust. Mr. Meza was well aware of this fact. power is the determining factor when it comes to language and/or culture revitalization. Traditionally, language-revitalization projects in Baja California have taken a depoliticized approach. They have, for the most part, not been very successful.

A depoliticized approach to language revitalization includes a concentration on methods and materials, or corpus planning as opposed to status planning (cf. Fishman, 1991) and, furthermore, outside the framework of the "other," ignores the "why" questions, which are not a part of a positivist research paradigm. The depoliticized approach excludes "the broader power issues" (Skutnabb-Kangas, 2000, xxii), and with this in mind, we used the planning sessions to reflect on the family's position vis à vis the dominant society. We had dialogues about the situation in which people find themselves, and we made concrete plans for the camping experience. This process took advantage of the planning ability of some family members and gave us a concrete objective to work with while at the same time raising consciousness about social, political and economic factors as well as linguistic aspirations.

Social, Political and Economic Factors

Investigation of the social, political and economic factors inherent in Indigenous-language decline and revitalization exposes nine types of loss brought about by continued colonization. They are loss of life, loss of culture, loss of livelihood, loss of health, loss of land, loss of freedom, loss of self-respect, loss of family and loss of trust. The multiple losses add up to an overall loss of power.

Loss of Life

Genocide. In the conquest of America, and of many other lands, physical genocide was and continues to be a common tool. Genocide is the first cause of language demise. Loss of physical life, however, continues in Indigenous America, both north and south of the Mexico/US border. We discussed how it is brought about by several causes related to the people's lack of political, social and economic power. A great many of the people whom have suffered untimely loss of life were fluent speakers of their endangered Native language.

The Healthcare System. Formal health care for Indigenous people and other people living in poverty in Baja California is poor to nonexistent. It is, however, all that is left after the Native health care was purposely destroyed by the missions because it was deemed pagan superstition. Even in San Diego, people have died from obvious refusal on the part of the health care system to treat them. Trina Antonia Cuero, late wife of Jon Meza Cuero, died of stomach cancer. As early as ten years prior to this, Trina went to the doctor complaining of pain in the stomach. She was "humored" and turned away because she had no health insurance or money. Trina and her husband did not know where to turn so they gave up. I visited Trina in the hospital, when she was finally admitted through Emergency services because of a huge tumor in her stomach, causing the removal of virtually all of her stomach. She finally starved to death. Trina was one of the most fluent and most creative speakers of Kumeyaay, and she was also a talented teacher of the language.

Suicide . The loss of culture—or, rather, the destruction of the culture— is one factor that seems to have an effect on the suicide statistics. In a handbook printed by the Indian Health Service, Villanueva (1989, p. 30, as cited by Duran and Duran) observes:

> The more recent literature shows both the suicidal adult and the suicidal adolescent as holding rapidly eroding tribal tradition; the developmental social structure which for centuries established roles and expectations and guided both through the life span is tottering—for many Native Americans it is no longer applicable, for others it is non-existent. For those pueblos, tribes and individual Native American families in cities for which their traditions are viable and workable, the suicide rates are the lowest. In other words if the culture would have remained intact, we would not be experiencing the devastating problems being faced. The responsibility should be place[d] in the right place and some honesty shed on the issue and then perhaps we could begin to ameliorate the problem. (p. 177)

Among the local Indigenous population, suicide takes many lives, especially young people. Finding themselves bereft of their traditions, without any moral or spiritual guidance, unable to communicate with or respect their elders and having internalized the violence of the conquerors, young people give way to violence and neglect of their persons. Suicide may be obvious or not. Many suicides involve substance abuse, another way to obliterate the intolerable state of anger from living in an imposed culture without any reliable means of monetary support, frequently at the edge of starvation. We have known young people who have shot themselves, those who set themselves on fire, those who died of pneumonia from passing out in freezing weather, and those who defied medical advice and died of preventable diseases. Young adults who should be becoming the leaders of their people have gotten themselves into dangerous situations and have been shot or died in car accidents. It is impossible to know which of these deaths were on purpose and which were truly accidental. Most of these people were speakers of their Indigenous languages.

Loss of Culture (More Genocide)

"When languages cease to be spoken (are pushed into not being spoken), there is the separate issue of researchers disagreeing about the relative role played by outside agents and by the group itself" (Skutnabb-Kangas, 2000, p. xxxi). Children are required to be sent to public schools in which the only language allowed is that of the dominant society. The policy in Mexico, and so in the schools, is that all people in the country are "Mexican." Moreover, in a state that denies the existence of Indigenous people, how can there be Indigenous languages? Furthermore, the culture, history and language taught to children as being "theirs" are the majority culture, history and language. "This, in fact, means that 'children from one group have been forcibly transferred to another group'—and this is part of [the] UN's definition of genocide" (Skutnabb-Kangas, 2000, p. 115). In the Indigenous community of Tecate, forced transfer of Indian children to the dominant group has been the case for about 50 years.

Denigration and the imposition of shame are further means of control over the dominated population. Families whose older children were ridiculed at school for speaking Kumeyaay stopped speaking the language to the younger children, and they do not know the language. When we ask people why none of their (grown) children know the Kumeyaay language that they speak so well, they tell us that they wanted them to do well in school and be successful. Also, they stopped speaking their language from the "shame."

Genocide was easily accomplished by the assimilation practices of the public schools and the other dominant society institutions. The result of a submersion "sink-or-swim" public education is a generation of people completely dominated by the majority society. The result is also young people who do not know their Indigenous language or culture. There have been two more generations in this community, and poverty is still rampant, despite everyone's fluency in Spanish and their adherence to Mexican customs, which were supposed to make them "successful." The only difference is that the people have lost their language and much of their culture, and they are at the bottom of the ladder socially, politically and economically.

Loss of Land/Environment

With the establishment of the missions began the appropriation of Indigenous lands and habitat in San Diego County and Northern Baja California. The land grab has continued. Indigenous people in Baja California have faced the loss of their lands from corporations, ranchers and "ejidos." The government has been turning many traditional Indian areas into cooperative communities of Mexicans. In these communities, control of the land is vested in majority vote, and there are more Mexicans than Indians. These lands are called "ejidos." Over and above these consequences, but related to the loss of land, there is a major culture shift which has promoted Kumeyaay language loss and prevents or makes attempts at language revitalization very difficult.

The Kumeyaay people originally lived in extended family groups. Each group involved communication with a large number of people of all ages. Thus, language was passed from parents, elders and others to young children, who had the opportunity to talk with people of all ages. Since the land robbery, people have been, for the most part, forced to find homes wherever they can afford. In order to have access to consumer goods, which are necessary because of the lack of original habitat, and access to schooling, which is required and deemed necessary for the "success" of their children, any Kumeyaay families live in urban "colonias."

The extended families are split apart, and the smaller units are surrounded by Spanish-speaking neighbors who would ridicule them if they talked Kumeyaay. Most Kumeyaay people are frequently at great distances from other Kumeyaay people. Communication is difficult and infrequent because of a lack of cars and telephones, and much less computers, which require power and phone lines. Extended families try to get together about once a month, but even this is difficult. The language, therefore, is not spoken.

Loss of Freedom (Incarceration)

The violence of invasion is internalized by the invaded. "Once a group of people have been assaulted in a genocidal fashion, there are psychological ramifications. With the victim's complete loss of power comes despair, and the psyche reacts by internalizing what appears to be genuine power—the power of the oppressor" (Duran & Duran, p. 29). This despair sinks into self-hatred. "When self-hatred is externalized, we encounter a level of violence within the community that is unparalleled in any other group in the country. Native Americans have the highest rate of violent crimes of any group, with homicide and suicide rates that are almost double the U.S. all-races rates" (Abbas 1982; French and Hornbuckle 1982, as cited by Duran & Duran, p. 29).

"[C]ultural invasion is…always an act of violence" (Freire, p. 152). In The Wretched of the Earth Franz Fanon (1963) discusses the violence of the colonizer which is internalized in the colonized. This violence is initially pitted against the fellow colonized, who are more accessible than the colonizer. "[T]he last resort of the native is to defend his personality vis à vis his brother" (Fanon, 1963, p. 52). The internalized oppression manifests itself in other destructive and self-destructive ways, also. Because of the oppressed person's lack of power, s/he is controlled by the majority society by means of the law enforcement system. Indigenous people spend a lot more time in prison.

Despite being the smallest segment of the population, Native Americans have the second largest state prison incarceration rate in the nation, according to a recent review of prison statistics. "….[A]cross the board, Natives are being sent to state prisons at increasingly higher rates. In 1980, there were 145 per 100,000 Indians in California's prisons, a rate which jumped to 767 per 100,000 in 2000" (Toward Freedom, p. 1). More specifically, "[a]ccording to US Department of Justice statistics, American Indians had a per capita rate of prison incarceration about 38% higher than the national rate. At the same time, the per capita rate of Native Americans on parole is about the same as that of the general population" (Steinberger, p. 4). So we see that Indians are incarcerated more but paroled less. Indigenous people are angry at what has been perpetrated upon them by the dominant society, represented by the legal system, law enforcement and the prison system. Native Americans frequently do not feel that they share in the dominant society. Therefore, they do not see any reason to cooperate with it.

In our discussion of the intergenerational nature of posttraumatic stress disorder (Duran & Duran, 1995), we were struck with the idea that anger, which many times can easily lead to incarceration, can be passed from father to son. We surmised that this is the case with people we know, persons who are working on controlling their anger. Intergenerational PTSD (post traumatic stress disorder) is explained by Duran and Duran (1995) as resulting from enforced assimilation and passed from generation to generation, as has been documented in the case of Nazi concentration camp survivors and their descendants. Mr. Meza, at the age of five, witnessed the hanging of his uncle by the federal police. There had been a spate of cattle rustling in the area, and the police were looking for a scapegoat. They looked for it among the Indians, people with little power.

> *Yo estaba chiquillo cuando colgaron a mi tío Benito…. Pues una tarde llegaban allí. Llevaron a mi tío Benito a colgarlo. Entonces la gente no me dejaba ir para allá, mis tías no querían que fuera a ver para allá…[pero] me fui corriendo. Entonces cuando fui corriendo a ver … a mi tío con la lengua aquí abajo [signals down to his waist], muy larga la lengua. Estaba muriendo él pues. Entonces me enojé con el señor ese. ¡Que lo bajaran! ¡Que no lo colgaran allí! "No, …muchacho mocoso, mugroso, vete a la fregada," me dijo groserías, ¿verdad? No quiero decir las groserías. Entonces le dije, "Algún día, cuando yo esté grande, voy a matarlo a usted."*

> [I was a boy when they hanged my uncle Benito….Well one afternoon they came there. They brought my uncle Benito to hang him. Then the people wouldn't let me go there, my aunts didn't want me to go over there…[but] I went running. Then when I went running to see…my uncle with his tongue hanging down to here [signals down to his waist], his tongue really long. He was dying. Then I got really angry with that man. Take him down! Don't hang him there! "No, snotty kid, dirty kid, get the hell out of here," he said obscenities to me, right? I don't want to say the obscenities. Then I told him, "One day, when I'm big, I'm going to kill you."]

When this child saw his uncle hanged, he felt a great rage and vowed to get revenge. Eight years later, he stole a gun and threatened to shoot the same police agent. He did not follow through with his threat, but he shot another officer in the foot. The thirteen-year-old later turned himself in and was jailed. He was let go after a month because of his young age. Of course, the police agent was not charged with any crime. Mr. Meza, and other persons in this community, have myriad stories of infuriating and traumatizing injustices. He feels that the characterization of anger passing down the generations is accurate.

Many persons who would be leaders in language revitalization could work on this with their elders, who are fluent in Kumeyaay and have a great deal of traditional knowledge. Unfortunately, they are not often free to do this. Their anger gets them into sticky situations which preclude their working on the language. Their inability to participate in language revitalization efforts is just one example of the obstacles in Native language retrieval.

Loss of Self Respect (Substance Abuse)

As an extreme example of loss of self respect, the drunken Indian is a stereotypical image of the Native people of this continent. Unfortunately, substance abuse really is common, with alcohol being the drug of choice of some people. Alcoholism and drug abuse are rampant and interfere in an obvious way with language revitalization. Many persons in the Baja California community who still know their traditional language also have spent a large part of their lives unconscious from alcohol or other drugs and have also acquired serious health (including mental) problems related to their use. Many deaths have been caused by substance abuse. This has reduced the number of possible language bearers capable of working to revive their language.

Substance abuse, in particular alcoholism, is, of course, related to shame, poverty and loss, and anger, which leave little room for language learning. One of the factors behind the abuse of alcohol is the oppression visited upon Native people when they use their language. Closely related to alcoholism is shame. The use of the Indigenous language continues to be a great source of shame to the generation that still knows the language.

Loss of Family Through Language Loss

There is a good deal of circularity in this study. For example, as the drinker said in *The Little Prince* (St. Exupery, 1994, p. 193), "I drink because I am ashamed....I am shamed because I drink." Another circular phenomenon is that of language loss related to loss of family. The breakup of families causes the language not to be passed on to the children. By the same token, families are broken up by the lack of communication that results from children not being able to communicate with grandparents and other relatives. This is brought about by the children not speaking the same language as the older generations. The language mismatch works its way up the generations, and there is a resulting lack of communication and of continuity among them.

The lack of respect for elders on the part of children and the lack of self-esteem and self-confidence that comes from an intergenerational culture and language split contribute to substance abuse and other health problems, violence, incarceration and language loss. All the factors that are brought up in an argument for bilingual, multicultural education today, including intergenerational communication, respect for elders, self respect and esteem, superior cognitive functioning and improved school performance, were present when the Kumeyaay language began its decline, and there were no advocates to fight for the affected children and their families. We are reminded constantly that the consequences of language loss that are put forth by bilingual educators as reasons for minority-language preservation were present generations ago, and the Kumeyaay people of Tecate never had a chance.

Loss of Trust/Belief in the Future

In order to work on a project that will affect future generations, one must trust in the successful results of one's efforts. There are various sources of funds and support for the revitalization of North American Indigenous languages. The granting of these minimal) funds assumes that the people involved look toward the future with some sort of plan to work on the language. This planning, however, depends on a trust in positive results. Following through with language learning depends on believing that you can accomplish the task. At first, it looks easy. But language learning/teaching is hard work and requires persistence, patience and trust in yourself and your teacher/student. Rather than drop out of the particular program, people do the paperwork necessary to show that they are working, and then they don't do the work. The language does not get passed on.

The other side of this coin is that when people do follow through and do the required work, no one in the community believes them. They are discredited in the community because they have apparently made themselves rich. This is related to the ubiquitous envy found among communities such as the Kumeyaay of Baja California. It is just not believed that anyone would do anything involving money for anything other than personal monetary gain. Furthermore, many Kumeyaay people do not believe that any outsider would become involved with the community for anything other than personal gain.

Opportunities, including language opportunities, are passed up because it is generally accepted that the person proposing the plan, an activist, is out to rob the community. So Kumeyaay people are passing up opportunities to revitalize their language. If we think about what Freire (2002) has to say about activists, we can understand this situation on a different level. Freire speaks of activism as being action without reflection. Action without reflection happens when people see themselves as advocates for the community. They are to be admired for the volume of work that they have done *on behalf of* the Indigenous people. "They see themselves as 'promotors' [sic] of the people. Their programs of action, which might have been prescribed by any good theorist of oppressive action, include their own objectives, their own convictions, and their own preoccupations" (Freire, 2002, p. 155). What is missing is the realization that "liberation is not a gift bestowed by the revolutionary leadership, but the result of the people's own *conscientização*" (Freire, 2002, p. 67) (conscientization).

There is pedagogical work to be done in the form of problem posing: "Problem-posing theory and practice take the people's historicity as their starting point" (p. 84). Magnificent projects "given" to the people do not work, although at this point, that is what they ask for. We have heard Kumeyaay leaders in Baja California say to those deemed to be in power, "Just give us a project; we don't care what it is." They do not see themselves as the decision makers; not trusting their own ability, they ask for the truth that is envisioned by the powerful, not as that which they themselves possess; they do not know, or do not express, their own aspirations; they have their own limitations (Freire, 2002, p. 107) which have to be perceived and understood. Activists who have come from outside to help do not see the Indigenous people as decision makers. "[To] alienate human beings from their own decision-making is to change them into objects" (p. 85), and objects do not take the initiative necessary to teach and learn languages. Language work will follow, not precede, *conscientização*. Raised consciousness will lead to hope for the future, which will make possible the will to do the hard work of language maintenance.

Conclusion: Power Through Dialogue and Language

We have outlined nine types of loss brought about by continued colonization: loss of life, loss of culture, loss of livelihood, loss of health, loss of land, loss of freedom, loss of self-respect, loss of family and loss of trust. The multiple losses add up to an overall loss of power. Power, which, according to Young (1990, p. 56f.), is the ability to contribute genuinely to one's society in a meaningful way, to make full use of one's talents, can only really be regained, with great difficulty, through genuine dialogue, dialogue among the members of the community and dialogue outside of the community with persons truly willing to engage in substantive and purposeful give-and-take with them.

The Tecate Kumeyaay people need to affirm a positive identity. The affirmation of a positive identity is a steep hill to climb, given these obstacles, and given the smallness of the Kumeyaay population. Nevertheless, they need to understand that their position is a result of social processes. The Kumeyaay community needs to identify itself as separate from the mainstream Mexican culture. Language revitalization can be part of this process. A symbolic level of language competence is reached way prior to the acquisition of total language proficiency and so is more attainable than fluency. The symbolic level of language competence serves to reinforce the identity of the language group and foster cohesion and self esteem (Meyer, 2006). Eventually it can help lead to the power needed to overcome oppressive conditions. People in the community need to stop looking elsewhere for solutions and look to their own people. There are other communities who have used language and culture revitalization to recoup their identity, with a resultant diminution in the volume of substance abuse and other health risks and a raising of self esteem and productivity among the young people.

How does the Tecate Kumeyaay community create the initial commitment? Who starts the dialogue? The people themselves need to act, as well as reflect, upon the reality of their situation and how to transform it. Individuals in the community need to learn how to engage in real dialogue: "Because liberating action is dialogical in nature, dialogue cannot be a *posteriori* to that action, but must be concomitant with it. And since liberation must be a permanent condition, dialogue becomes a *continuing* aspect of liberating action" (Freire, 2002). Community members have to have dialogue before they can engage in any action, and the dialogue has to continue throughout any action.

The people need to look clearly at their situation, at all the types of loss they have suffered and are still going through. They must face the loss of life, of culture, of livelihood, of health, of land, of freedom, of self-respect, of family and of trust. They need true dialogue through which they will come to an awareness of their situation and so begin to emerge from the oppression of loss, poverty and envy. Dialogue leading to *conscientização* is the path toward the healing of this community, so that they free themselves from the oppression that they have been under for so long and go on to revitalize their culture and their language. Starting with the language-camp meetings and dialogue as steps toward *conscientização*, we will work together toward the rescue of one family's heritage language and the healing of their oppression, and we have hope that the rest of the community will become aware of our success and join the dialogue. We have a big job ahead of us—and with success will come pride, self respect, freedom, and full humanity (Smith, p. 26) for the Kumeyaay people of Tecate, Baja California.

References

Behind bars: Native incarceration rates increase. <u>Toward freedom magazine</u>, August/ September 2001. <u>http://www.towardfreedom.com/2001/aug01/ nativeprison.htm</u>.

Cameron, D, Frazer, E., Harvey, P., Rampton, M.B.H., & Richardson, K. (1992). R e searching language: Issues of power and method. London & New York: Routledge.

Duran, E. & Duran, B. (1995). Native American postcolonial psychology. Albany, NY: State University of New York Press.

Fanon, F. (1963). The wretched of the earth. New York: Grove Press.

Fishman, J.A. (1991). Reversing language shift: Theoretical and empirical founda tions of assistance to threatened languages. Clevedon, UK: Multilingual Matters.

Foucault, M. (1977). Discipline and punish: The birth of the prison. New York: Pan-theon Books.

Freire, P. (2002). Pedagogy of the oppressed. New York: Continuum.

Meyer, P.L. (1999). Revitalization of Tiipay Kumeyaay in Tecate, Baja California: Four scenarios. Unpublished manuscript.

St. Exupery, A. (1994). El principito/The little prince. Mexico: Enrique Sainz Editores, S.A.

Shaull, R. (2002). Foreword. In Freire, P., <u>Pedagogy of the oppressed</u> (pp. 29-34). New York: Continuum.

Skutnabb-Kangas, T. (2000). Linguistic genocide in education—or worldwide diver-sity and human rights? Mahwah, NJ: Lawrence Erlbaum Associates.

Smith, L.T. (1999). Decolonizing methodologies: Research and Indigenous peoples. Dunedin, New Zealand: University of Otago Press.

Steinberger, R. (n.d.). Incarcerated Indians and the disparity of the legal system (Part 1 of a continual series originally published in the <u>Lakota Journal</u>, Rapid City, SD). http://www.okit.com/Justice4parts/justice1.html.

Young, I.M. (1990). Justice and the politics of difference. Princeton, NJ: Princeton University Press.

Chapter 9
A Useful Symbology for Modeling Critical Interactions among Stakeholders in Education
by Georges Merx, Ph.D.

Abstract

Human ability to process large amounts of complex structured data is limited. An approach proven successful in professional fields such as architecture and engineering is visual modeling, using a standardized modeling language of recognized symbols, annotated as needed. This article proposes the application of this approach to complex projects in education. Especially, research projects that primarily use qualitative data can benefit from visualizing study results. The benefits of modeling and graphical visualization include the obvious richness of information content in images; the efficient conveyance of complex relationships between data elements; effective abstraction and generalization of large amounts of data; and ease of access for the information consumer.

This article proposes a standard set of symbols to use in modeling and visualizing qualitative education research findings, such as results from focus groups, interviews, and literature searches. This work is based on widely accepted processes developed as Design Patterns in architecture (Alexander, 1977) and software engineering (Vlissides 1995) and the Unified Modeling Language used in software engineering (Kruchten, 1999; Object Management Group, 2004).

Qualitative information, such as field observations, interviews, literature searches, and case studies, is most useful when it can be effectively generalized. The generalization of information depends on abstraction. Specific anecdotes themselves are of little value, but when viewed together, information from anecdotes can become recognizable patterns of behavior and interaction. These patterns are open to interpretation and can be used for educational improvement. This chapter describes a methodology for extracting useful patterns from complex qualitative interaction data. The methodology uses a formal structure and syntax or symbolic system that makes the process generalizable and reliable. The methodology was applied to a sample of field observations conducted by the author at three Southern California high schools in 2001-2002 (Merx, 2003) to demonstrate the processes and utility of the methodology. These observations recorded interactions between parents and educators during meetings at the school sites to discuss student progress. The study examined the impact of cultural, language, and socio-economic differences between stakeholders (parents and educators) on the quality of their interactions during meetings.

Patterns – A Cross-Disciplinary Approach

The approach discussed in this chapter details a methodology that can be applied for the analysis of educational interactions. This approach is suitable for complex, multi-dimensional interactions such as parent-educator meetings. The tensions and conflicts that arise when parents and educators of differing backgrounds interact and attempt to collaborate are often complex, subtle, and difficult to discern outright (Merx, 2003; Macedo, 1994). Applying a pattern recognition, description, and visualization process aids in distilling and documenting relevant core issues and the causes of miscommunication or disconnections in these parent-educator interactions. However, the methodology can be applied to a wide range of complex, qualitative educational scenarios.

The methodology pursued in this chapter is based on design processes well-accepted in architecture and software engineering (Alexander, 1977; Kruchten, 1999): Design Patterns were originally popularized by Christopher Alexander, a successful urban architect, and adapted to the software engineering industry by Gamma et al. (1977). Alexander defines design patterns as follows:

"Each pattern describes a problem which occurs over and over again in our environment and then describes the core of the solution to that problem in such a way that you can use this solution a million times over, without ever doing it the same way twice." (Alexander, 1977)

This straightforward perspective developed and applied by Alexander and his colleagues for architecture was adapted to the design challenges in computer software engineering by Erich Gamma et al. as described below.

"A design pattern names, abstracts, and identifies the key aspects of a common design structure that make it useful for creating a reusable object-oriented design." (Gamma et al., 1995)

In software engineering, design patterns are used extensively to capture reusable practices, the industry's most successful approaches to solving complex software development problems. Instead of solving similar problems repeatedly, design patterns provide a "recipe" for how to deal with a particular design challenge in a way already proven to work by experienced practitioners.

Focusing on patterns in complex processes allows for the generalization of actions, interactions, and connections, which in turn allow for the extraction of Best Practices that apply to these activities. These best practices can then be applied in other, similar situations. The purpose of this chapter is to adapt these concepts proven effective in other disciplines to the description and abstraction of complex, dynamic educational processes.

Capturing qualitative information associated with human interactions – in our case, educational stakeholders – involves structured, detailed descriptions. Surrounding the information with a structure ensures consistency among patterns, improving accessibility and reuse. In addition, enhancing the verbal description of pattern elements with graphical visualizations enriches the information content of the pattern. After the pattern description, the second major application of this methodology is a graphical syntax language represented by a collection of diagram elements that allow for the visual representation of relationships, interactions between constituents over time, and interconnections between process elements.

Combining a structured documentation approach with a standardized graphical representation of multilevel interactions, collaborations, and tensions has worked well for other industries with complex, interactive processes. Its adaptation to educational processes is a natural step forward in improving the analysis of qualitative data such as observations, interviews, and case studies, and the application of discernable patterns to the potential improvement of critical educational processes. The development of reusable, generalized patterns is aided by examining the process being modeled from multiple perspectives.

Perspectives

An important way to validate the interpretation and generalization of complex educational processes is to examine them from multiple perspectives. Multiple viewpoints provide more comprehensive and more objective patterns as they account for the interests and priorities of more stakeholders.

In developing the content for the upcoming pattern description, it is helpful to consider the situation from these or similar related perspectives; this approach helps account for differences in priorities, values, and beliefs, as well as the impacts from different cultural, language, and socio-economic origins. The perspectives identified here may change for different situations; but the principle of seeking multiple viewpoints is a common engineering best practice of general validity, because it encourages mutual understanding and empathy, increases the bandwidth of information input, and promotes a multidimensional approach to human interaction and project execution. (Kruchten, 1999; Merx, 2003).

Figure 1: Perspectives on Interactions in Education

Pattern Structure

In defining educational interaction patterns, it is helpful to follow a standard documentation outline that standardizes the description of each aspect of the interaction pattern. Patterns are useful if their description is detailed, but general enough to be representative of a reasonable variety of similar situations or scenarios. The following outline provides the headings and brief descriptions for each major descriptive component of an educational interaction pattern.

Table 1: Pattern Name and Classification

- **Pattern Name and Classification**
  - *Name:* should describe the pattern's core purpose and be action-oriented
    - Examples: *Parent Meeting Setup; Parent Meeting Action Plan; Staff Meeting; …*
  - *Classifications:* describes the type of pattern
    - Examples: *Information Exchange; Conflict Resolution; Planning; Emergency Management; …*[1]
- **Also Known As**
  - Alternate name or designation, possibly in another context
- **Intent**
  - Definition of purpose and scope
    - Example: *This pattern describes the interaction between teachers and administrators on the subject of measurable student learning outcomes*
- **Actors**
  - An *actor* is an active participant/stakeholder
  - Most patterns have one primary or sole actor
- **Interactions and Collaborations**
  - Description of the pattern structure
    - Scenarios (step-by-step descriptions)
      - Primary (best-case)
      - Secondary (zero or more) (obstacles, problems, disconnects)
    - Diagrams
      - Visualizations
- **Application**
  - How this pattern can be applied to improving the type of situation captured by the pattern
    - Known uses
    - Suggested uses
- **Consequences**
  - Results anticipated from the application of the pattern
- **Extensions**
  - Potential future enhancements or extensions
- **Artifacts**
  - Any written outcomes, such as action/project plans, reports, minutes, …
- **Related Patterns**
  - Other patterns which potentially interact with this pattern or enhance it
- **Comments**
  - Any additional unstructured information that needs to be recorded in conjunction with this pattern
- **Examples**
  - Concrete examples of the application of this pattern

This outline provides the structure for the detailed documentation of an educational process or interaction, ensuring that all relevant information is included with the pattern description. Adherence to this structure ensures consistency and synergy across multiple related patterns.

Visualization Language

Engineering disciplines use graphical representation extensively to describe complicated structures and interactions. In computer software engineering, for example, the graphical representation of complex component interactions is provided by a standardized graphical language called the Unified Modeling Language™ (Fowler, 1999; UML, 2004) – or UML™. The different diagram types provided in the UML allow the software designer to model completely all the necessary features and interfaces of even a very sophisticated software solution. The importance of modeling is two-fold: it captures and visualizes the essence of the planned solution without requiring the detailed design of all the technical components; and it preserves flexibility in the overall project as it delays implementation until all critical design issues are worked out.

This approach translates effectively to intricate educational interaction processes and serves as a model in this chapter for the definition of a set of three diagram categories and their associated diagram syntax components that can be used to model educational situations that have been generalized into educational interaction patterns. The field of education does not traditionally use sophisticated modeling techniques, but there are many benefits associated with adopting some of the best visualization practices from architecture and engineering. Among these benefits are the development of shared understanding of educational processes among diverse stakeholders; the power of images to convey multi-dimensional, fluid interactions, tensions, and relationships; and the very concept of learning from other professional disciplines and adapting their best practices to educational situations. The representation of the information captured from these various perspectives can be augmented through the use of diagrams as described in the next sections.

Diagram Categories

For the purpose of modeling educational processes and interactions, the following three diagram types are defined:

- System diagram
- Interaction diagram
- Process diagram

The visualizations for educational interaction patterns fall into one of these three categories. (Other practitioners may justify the definition of additional types, but this should be done conservatively to maintain simplicity and avoid a proliferation of similar categories.)

System Diagram

The System Diagram category includes those pattern visualizations that describe relationships and interactions at the "system" level. These diagrams provide a macro-level view of constituent components.

Interaction Diagram

Interaction Diagrams graphically describe the details of interactions, including the participant actors, their relationships, and their generalized exchanges. They are similar to traditional flow charts.

Process Diagram

Process Diagrams focus on the time and sequence element of interactions. They map conceptually to sequence diagrams in the UML but use a simpler Gantt2 chart representational syntax.

Graphic Modeling Syntax

The diagrams in these categories used to model educational interactions are constructed from simple geometric shapes and lines annotated with three types of readily available fonts: *Times-Roman, Arial,* and *Courier.*[3] It is important to follow the graphical syntax for these visualizations to ensure that meaning and form are preserved across patterns and representations. The following table summarizes the graphical syntax used for visualizing educational interaction patterns.

Table 2: Visualization Symbology

Symbol	Purpose	Example
System or Subsystem (ellipse)	Is a container for process components or participants; can be nested or intersecting to represent inclusion, exclusion, or union. Applies to system interaction, and process diagrams	**Administration** — **Principal**, **Vice-Principals** (nested ellipses)
Scenario (rounded rectangle)	Captures a sequence of events. Applies to interaction and process diagrams	Initiate parent meeting → Student present?
Decision (diamond)	Allows for a decision branch. Applies to interaction and process diagrams	Let student summarize current status / Explain current student status
Integration (thick bar)	Combines multiple paths. Applies to interaction and process diagrams	Parents respond to information
Label — **Labeled Directional** (triangle)	Shows directional trend or force. Applies to system, interaction, and process diagrams	School: Institution Regulations Priorities — Family: Values Origins Socio-Economic Status; School Officials, Expectations, Tension, Expectations, Employers, Parents
Stakeholder (figure)	Represents a project stakeholder. Applies to system, interaction, and process diagrams	

Table 2: Visualization Symbology (continued)

Symbol	Purpose	Example
Actor	Represents a project actor (actively involved stakeholder). Applies to system, interaction, and process diagrams	
Beginning Date / End Date / 1/1/2005 / 3/5/2005 / **Duration (incomplete)** / **Duration (complete)** / **Milestone (incomplete)** / **Milestone (complete)**	Provides standard symbols for timeline project representation (Gantt-style). Applies to process diagrams	Schedule parent meeting / Plan meeting / Hold staff pre-meeting / Parent meeting / Plan dev./documentation / Plan due
Connected To / **Leading To** / **Associated With** / Derived From	Provides connecting arrows for various meanings. Applies to process diagrams	Campus violence incident report / Initiate parent meeting / Student Saturday class detention / Disciplinary action / *may include suspension*
Times-Roman annotation / ***Times-Roman Italic*** annotation-emphasis / **Arial** descriptive / ***Arial Italic*** descriptive-emphasis / `Courier` technical / `Courier Italic` technical-emphasis	Times-Roman, Arial, and Courier fonts (normal and italic) are used for the different purposes described at left. Applies to all diagrams	**See above**
This is a typical annotation / **Note**	All symbols and connections may be annotated	

These symbols are combined into system, interaction, and process diagrams that graphically represent the various aspects (perspectives) associated with educational interactions and processes. They provide for ways to represent relationships, interactions, information flow, and time-sequenced activities.

Procedure for Creating a Process Model

The translation of information about an educational process into a useful model and visualization involves a process of *organization, abstraction* and *generalization*. Fundamental to the process is a clear, detailed, structured understanding of the requirements that the project's stakeholders have for the project. The purpose of most valuable processes in any discipline, including education, is to *create value* for stakeholders. Value is created when existing processes are improved in terms of speed, quality, or cost, or when new processes are created that enable new capabilities or create better access to existing capabilities.

A reasonable, systematic process for creating a useful process model and visualization can be described as follows:

1. Identify process stakeholders
2. Collect requirements from stakeholders and document them in a structured, organized document
3. Analyze the requirements in the context of the desired value creation (e.g. process creation/improvement)–extract and generalize key critical elements and relationships
4. Use the visualization syntax provided earlier to draw the process components in terms of their temporal and semantic relationships
5. Critically evaluate the patterns emerging from the visualization of the model and seek incremental improvements until the information and control flows appear optimized
6. Expose model to stakeholder scrutiny and obtain critical feedback; fold in feedback in ongoing improvement cycle

This sequence helps ensure that the model and visualization (1) encompass the current span of knowledge about the process; and (2) are subject to iterative improvement over time, with feedback from the project stakeholders.

The next section examines the specific example of Parent-Educator Interaction, based on sixty observations conducted in three Southern

California public high schools in 2001-2002 (Merx, 2003). It shows how the pattern structure and graphical modeling language support the description, the abstraction, and generalization of these observations.

Example: Parent-School Communications Patterns

In 2001-2002, the author conducted approximately sixty observations of meetings between parents and educators (counselors, administrators, and teachers) in three public high schools in Southern California with diverse populations: one predominantly suburban/latino; one predominantly inner-city/African-American; one predominantly suburban/white. Each school had additional minority groups of students from a wide range of cultural and socio-economic backgrounds (Merx, 2003). The observations were conducted during meetings between parents and educators, recorded in writing, and then transcribed into categorized matrices.

Table 3:   Sample Observation Matrix (Merx, 2003)

Meeting Type	Overt Agenda	Covert Agenda	Expected Outcomes	Level of Formality	Issues of Power	Sources of Tensions	Political, Cultural, Socioeconomic Factors
Academic Performance	Parent: obtain educator input about student performance Educators: present student problems – at times, convince student and parent to move to an off-campus program (ECC or JobCorps)	Parent: sometimes vent frustration, present excuses, more often, accept educator input Educators: fulfill administrative requirement to present student problems to parent; sometimes, provide last warning, or move student off-campus	Parent: any workable solution Educators: improved student performance; sometimes alternative education program for student	Depending on factors: Number and type of educators present Similarity between educators and family in terms of culture, language, and SES- generally relatively informal at this campus	Most educators at this school are members of disenfranchised group, mostly African-American, more aware of the issues of power, and more sensitive to parent and community collaboration. Not as competent in dealing with cultures other than African-American, however	In extreme cases, parent upset at school involving Child Protective Services or police. Some educators aggressive in their tone. Parents often no-shows at important meetings. Some students in severe trouble with crime or drugs	Range of socio-economic, cultural, and language diversity in this community – educators most comfortable with traditional low-SES African-American population – struggle with Latino, Laotian, and scarce low-SES white population

Actors and Roles

Meeting Type	Participants	Perceived Roles	Actual Roles	Institutional Roles	Interests	Significance
Academic Performance	Parent, student, 1-3 counselors, rarely a teacher	Parent: provide home environment conducive to learning; keep control of student learning. Educators: get and maintain student on an acceptable academic track	Parent: often just keep a dysfunctional family operating as well as possible. Educators: perform administrative ritual; find alternative program for student if necessary	Parent: abide by laws, including enforcing school attendance. Educators: avoid student failure; enforce regulations including using Child Protective Services or police	Parent: keep student functioning, advocate for student, support school in finding workable solutions. Educators: mediate between student and family, encourage and exhort	When severe family problems exist, the school is at a loss on how to proceed – this often results in students with all failing grades due to problems outside of school; these problems are largely ignored as the school is not equipped to deal with them

Initial Setting

Meeting Type	Physical: Time, Geography, Room, Space, Temperature	Representational: Significance, Group Composition
Academic Performance	Meeting takes place in the counseling office's conference room, a cluttered, musky room also used for storage. This inner-city school has vastly outdated facilities, which are due to be rebuilt in the coming years as a new multi-purpose high school.	The poverty of the school is an example of how inner-city, non-anglo-majority schools are burdened with fewer resources and substandard amenities. Most of the educators at this school are African-American, while the student body is increasingly non-African-American, with an influx of Latinos and Laotians – the school has shrinking attendance and resources and is not equipped to deal with the growing diversity

Verbal Interactions

Meeting Type	Predominant Statement Types	Purpose/Length/Speed of Statement	Voice Tone, Intensity, Variation	Vocabulary Level	Silence Intervals	Listening
Academic Performance	Parent: some ranting and raving about own problems, others intimidated or disengaged from process, but all parents committed to student success Educators: factual suggestions, admonitions, questions; some just quiet	Parent: sometimes endless tirades, wanting attention, validation, and sympathy; sometimes short questions; sometimes Spanish only; communicating via translator only Educators: exhortations, suggestions, recommendations – often more engaged than at large suburban schools as student body has dire need for personal attention often not available at home	Parent: at times dramatic, plaintive; others monotonous or quiet Educators: all-business, even-toned, "professional"; exhortative if particular engaged in a particular case(special interest in athletes – this campus has produced a long string of football and basketball professionals)	Parent: from elementary school level to college level Educators: counselors in tune with working class-level language typical for community; other staff use jargon at times	Few – focus on dialogue more common here than at other campuses	Often, educators here are more interested in exhorting than in listening as they are used to problems, dysfunction, and excuses

Facial Expressions

Meeting Type	Type of Expression	Intensity/ Frequency	Perceived Significance	Alternative Meanings
Academic Performance	Educators: one counselor has the habit of raising her eye brows when she makes a point; others are relatively impassive Parent: sometimes dramatic grimaces and faces accompanying other body movements; others stoic or slightly intimidated or uneasy	Educators relatively subdued Parent: sometimes dramatic performance, usually rather low key, in receptive mode	Educators are expected to "keep their cool" as educational professionals Parents view these meetings as vital to their child's academic recovery	Educators don't always know how to deal with particularly theatrical displays by parent. They tend to be most engaged with parents of similar background and demeanors as themselves

Emotional Expressions

Meeting Type	Tears, Crying, Anger	Sighing, Other Non-Verbal Sounds	Expressions of Joy	Gestures Expressing Emotions	Other Emotions	Perceived Significance
Academic Performance	Sometimes a student cried during a meeting, or a parent had an outburst – but dramatic emotional expressions are rare and unseen from educators, with the exception of the school nurse who was angry to be interrupted by a parent, "I am speaking now!"	One mother sighed frequently and loudly during the meeting, underscoring her travails with raising her difficult child – but this was an exceptional situation – most parents were calm during the meeting, as are the educators	These meetings were rarely cause for joy, and the meetings on this gloomy campus are usually rather subdued and even a little depressing	One parent gesticulated dramatically during much of her meeting, making wide-reaching movements with her arms, leaning on the table heavily, almost like a drunk person – but this was exceptional: most parents as well as educators sat rather still, with little movement	Some parents were very frustrated, others stoic, about their children's academic performance problems Counselors could be quite frustrated as they exhorted students to be responsible and to improve their attendance and school performance	When parents were too dramatic, educators didn't know how to react – but in general, more emotional engagement is a positive sign of effort and good will to effect positive change

Body Position and Movement

Meeting Type	From–To Position Change	Type/Speed/ Frequency of Movement	Repetitive Gesturing	Association of Movement With	Perceived Significance
Academic Performance	One particular parent shifted positions quite wildly at times which can be disconcerting to other participants, but most parents sat quite still, maybe at times leaning forward to listen Educators sat quite still and composed, maybe leaning forward to seek eye contact and make a point to a student; one educator habitually underscored her key points with a raised finger or raised eye brows	Typically quite subdued, with the exception of a particular parent who made many wide-flung moves during her meeting	Most participants sat rather still during these sessions, even the students	Those parents who actually attended meetings (many just don't show up) were actually keenly interested in their children's school success and paid close attention to what educators had to say – they typically sat still, leaned forward and listened carefully	When a parent got overly dramatic, educators tended to disengage somewhat, not knowing how to deal with such a display – in normal situations, the small movements associated with leaning forward to exhort or to listen signify increased engagement

Action-Reaction Sequences

Meeting Type	Action-Reaction	Frequency/Intensity	Context	Perceived Meaning
Academic Performance	The one parent's emotional antics got relatively little reaction from educators, as they did not know how to react – in other meetings, the typical exchange between parents and educators was mostly verbal, with a focus on questions-and-answers exchanges and the citing of academic problems and potential remedies	Low-key, cooperative exchange was the norm	When parents and educators were not on the same "wavelength", due to style, culture, language, or SES differences, the number of action-reaction sequences or events was reduced, often substantially	When there was genuine engagement between parents and educators, it was reflected in verbal and non-verbal interactions, often in barely noticeable movements or sequences

Other Non-verbal Behaviors

Meeting Type	Description	Frequency/Intensity	Context	Cultural Component	Perceived Meaning
Academic Performance	In awkward meetings, educators tend to cluster at one end of the table, and parent and child at the other Some parents try to show affection towards their troubled children Some students show anger, frustration with parent and/or school	Throughout the meetings	The stresses of dysfunctional family life in a troubled community often adversely affect student performance	Low-SES families seem to have the most problems engaging the school in a cooperative effort to help students succeed Differences in culture and language also play a role as opportunities to establish genuine cooperation between parents and educators are rare and short in duration	Even without prejudice or racism, differences in culture, language, or SES have a subtle, but clearly noticeable impact on meeting participants being able to closely engage each other as strangers on the topic of their shared responsibilities

Outcomes – Action Items

Meeting Type	Description	Written/Oral	Ownership Established	Follow-Up	Final Tone/Level of Tension
Academic Performance	Plans were typically established in writing – often to move the student to an off-campus facility (ECC or JobCorps) – in reality, these approaches have a high rate of failure as they require the heretofore irresponsible student to very quickly become accountable and responsible for attendance and academic work	Recorded in writing as part of the meeting documentation; typically up to student to take initiative	Student has the responsibility to pursue, usually not clear if school would help manage, or not Parents rarely engaged explicitly	Follow-up usually not discussed or planned – parent role not clarified – as at other campuses, there seemed to be a preference to hold student accountable and deal with student directly	While meetings ended politely, there was rarely a shared feeling of accomplishment after these meetings – they often served mostly administrative purposes and allowed educators to clarify their positions and concerns

One of the challenges of this fieldwork was how to extract useful information that could be generalized from the large volume of anecdotal events. This is where the application of a pattern-based visualization approach provides substantial benefit, because it allows for the structured extraction and representation of generalizable elements.

In the following sections, the diagrams and graphical artifacts introduced earlier will be used to describe a sample pattern applied to these observations. Patterns are discerned based on a critical analysis of repetitive behaviors and outcomes on the part of the meeting participants. While these abstractions may have a subjective component, their validity would be tested in a next step (beyond the scope of this chapter) to ensure that they were reusable and applicable to similar situations in the field. This type of empirical validation is typical of the development and application of patterns in the various disciplines where they are in practical use (e.g. architecture; computer software engineering).

The first step in generalizing a subset of repetitive behaviors or interactions observed during the meetings between parents and educators is to capture the patterns of abstractable behaviors. For the sake of this example, we will showcase a single pattern description. The selected pattern addresses the interaction between stakeholders from differing socio-economic and/or cultural backgrounds in a school with a diverse but primarily African-American population situated in an economically depressed urban neighborhood.

Table 4: Sample Pattern Description

Pattern Name and Classification	High-Tension Student Performance Intervention Student Performance Review
Also Known As	Parent Emergency Meeting
Intent	Inform parent of serious student performance problems and discuss causes and options; establish plan of action
Actors	Student; parent(s), sometimes other family/caretaker(s); educators (one or more of the following): principal; vice-principal; counselor(s); teacher(s)
Interactions and Collaborations	Primary Scenario Positive/constructive: relationship building; listening; shared vocabulary; empathy; connection;conflict management
	Secondary Scenarios Unproductive/potentially destructive: disconnection; language/vocabulary differences/use of professional terminology; avoidance; time pressure; lack of regular contact except for crisis mode; judgmental approach/preconceptions
Influencing Factors	Socio-economic status; culture, values, beliefs, origins; language; degree of difference in these factors between educators and family
Application	Problem resolution meetings with parents of different cultural, language, and/or socio-economic origins
Consequences	Improved awareness of tensions negatively affecting critical parent-educator meeting
Extensions	Follow-up meetings
Artifacts	Agenda; plan-of-action
Related Patterns	Low-Tension Student Performance Review
Comments	Attention to documentation critical to productive outcomes
Examples	Meetings called as a result of student truancy; low academic performance; altercations; drug use

Visualization diagrams would typically be included with the pattern description, but they are separated out in the following sections for the sake of clarity. Diagrams are useful not only for the visualization of the specific pattern of interaction observed, but also for documenting the context of the project. The first diagram in this sample series shows the system level environment associated with the project in question (Figure 2).

Figure 2: School System in the Context of Family Interaction

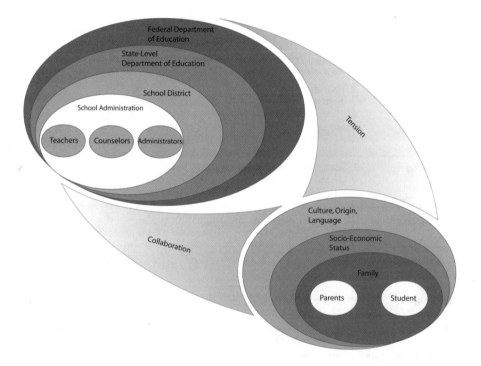

This simple system-level diagram illustrates the relationships between educational stakeholders in the wider context of their positions and roles. It shows the potential dichotomy between desired collaboration and tensions based on conflicting positions and priorities. This high-level visualization provides a context for the scenario-oriented diagrams illustrating the specifics of the pattern and promotes a critical viewpoint of the structures that influence the nature of parent-school interaction across cultural and socio-economic boundaries.

Figure 3: Process Diagram for Example Pattern

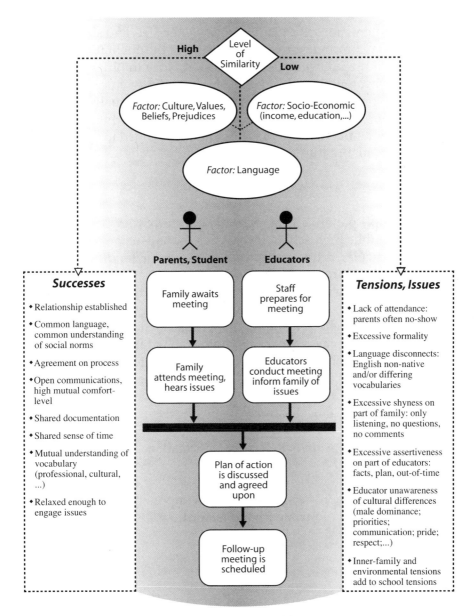

Bridging Opportunities

This process diagram captures the main issues, tensions, relations, and interactions in the observation series cited above. While patterns and associated diagrams by definition do not capture every detail of the original interactions, they summarize, generalize, and abstract these observed behaviors and capture the essence of the qualitative information central to the interpretation of the field work in order to increase stakeholder awareness and develop process improvement strategies.

The very process of constructing patterns and visualizations contributes to the structured analysis of qualitative data while more effectively preserving the richness of information contained in these records than a purely quantitative study could.

Additional Comments

The example pattern and associated field study were based on work done at the public high school level where parent-school communications are particular brittle and prone to misunderstandings and conflicts due to the scarcity of face-to-face contacts between parents and educators. However, the overall approach can certainly be applied to other educational scenarios.

Also, it can be helpful to supplement the visualization process with carefully selected images, such as photographs taken in conjunction with the process being modeled. In another context, for example, a variation of the approach described in this chapter is also being applied to the visualization of Student Learning Outcomes (SLOs) at San Diego Mesa College in California.

Author Reference Information

Dedication
Work on special projects like this one is impossible without the loving, patient support of my smart and beautiful wife Jin.

References

Alexander, Christopher. (1977). A Pattern Language: Towns/Buildings/Construction. Oxford University Press, Inc. Oxford, UK.

Fowler, Martin. (1999). UML Distilled: A Brief Guide to the Standard Object Modeling Language (2nd Edition). Addison-Wesley, Boston, MA.

Joyce, Bruce, Marsha Weil, and Emily Calhoun. (1972). Models of Teaching. Allyn & Bacon, Needham Heights, MA.

Kruchten, Philippe. (1999). The Rational Unified Process - an Introduction. Addison-Wesley-Longman, Reading, MA.

Macedo, Donaldo. (1994). Literacies of Power. Westview Press, Boulder, Colorado.

Merx, Georges. (2003). Parent-School Interaction Patterns at Three California Public High Schools. Ph.D. Dissertation. San Diego State University/Claremont Graduate University. UMI Dissertation Services.

Object Management Group. (2004). Introduction to OMG's°Unified Modeling Language™ (UML®). Available: www.omg.org/gettingstarted/what_is_uml.htm.

Vlissides, John, Erich Gamma, Richard Helm, and Ralph Johnson. (1995). Design Patterns. Addison-Wesley, Boston, MA.

Footnotes

[1] *Classifications* should be defined for an organization and used consistently by all organization members.

[2] For more information, visit http://www.ganttchart.com

[3] Visually equivalent fonts may be substituted.

[4] It is beyond the scope of this chapter to cite all relevant references associated with this example. The reference information is available in (Merx, 2003).

Chapter 10
Operationalizing a Transformational Paradigm of Parent Involvement: Parent Voice and Participation

by Edward M. Olivos
California State University, Dominguez Hills
and Alberto M. Ochoa
San Diego State University

Abstract

The following chapter outlines what the authors describe as a *Transformational Paradigm of Parent Involvement*. The authors argue that despite education research supporting parent involvement as proactive means of supporting bicultural student achievement and parent empowerment, most school efforts aimed at bicultural parents tend to be geared towards mere volunteerism and low-impact rhetoric which lead to superficial engagement. They propose that efforts must be made to critically analyze the current modes of engagement that exist in the school system in an attempt to move parent involvement toward a more transformational orientation. The authors therefore suggest that bicultural parents can be transformational agents of school reform/change and cultural democracy and offer examples of parent work in San Diego County, California.

The Need for Transformational of Parent Involvement

There is a clear consensus among many in the field of education that involving parents in their children's formal education is beneficial to their success, particularly if they come from historically disenfranchised groups. They argue that the "evidence is consistent, positive, and convincing: families have a major influence on their children's achievement in school and through life" (Henderson & Mapp, 2002, p. 7). Yet, why is it that the public school system has consistently been unsuccessful in establishing an authentic relationship with the communities it serves, particularly "hard to reach parents," namely African-Americans, Latinos, immigrants, and low-income parents? And why is it that teachers who work in many urban and bicultural school settings still find themselves asking: why aren't these parents more involved? Or, why don't these parents care? And, finally, why do bicultural parents who *do* participate often feel that their participation is meaningless or disingenuous?

As parent involvement advocates, this chapter will serve to operationalize and promote a more genuine, authentic, and meaningful form of democratic parent participation. This model of parent involvement is what we refer to as a *Transformational Paradigm of Parent Involvement* (Olivos & Ochoa, in press). Also included within this chapter is a critique of traditional models, mindsets, and policies which dictate how bicultural parents are to function, and have functioned, within the school system at the level of low-impact rhetoric and volunteerism. We conclude by laying out what we feel is a possible model of parent involvement, one which seeks a more democratic form of parental participation and voice. In our minds, the model we propose will serve to not only transform the parents' personal self-perception of efficacy and empowerment but the schools and the school system as well.

Issues in Bicultural Parent Involvement

Parent involvement has been characterized by three issues that make general assumptions about its effectiveness problematic, particularly when referencing bicultural parents and communities. The first issue involves the "perceptions of appropriate roles of family and community members in connections with the schools" (Jordan, Orozco, & Averett, 2001, p. viii). In other words, what "rights" do parents legally and morally have in regard to how the school system functions? This question has often led to a "functional and conceptual gap," in thinking and in practice, between the home and the school; particularly in relation to how far reaching the influence of the parents should be in how the schools choose to educate children and whose responsibility (or fault) it is when educational attainment is unsuccessful (Cutler, 2000).

The second issue is the emphasis placed on school-centered definitions of "family and community involvement." Family and community involvement has frequently meant helping "reach goals defined by the schools (administrators and teachers) that reflect only school values and priorities" (Jordan, et. al., 2001, p. viii). This has been particularly problematic in districts and schools which serve large numbers of bicultural parents in that the goals have often been defined quantitatively rather than qualitatively. That is, administrators and school personnel have often been satisfied with the number of parents in attendance at open houses, on fieldtrips as volunteers, and at assemblies rather than on the effectiveness of parents' participation in more meaningful roles such as decision makers and advisors in school governance committees.

The third issue is the "multiple definitions" given to parent involvement, definitions which are at times vague, overlapping, or even contradictory. The vague definitions used to describe parent involvement have affected measuring its effectiveness as well as the possibility of replicating "successful" programs or practices (Jordan et. al., 2001). These multiple definitions have also allowed many educators to assume that parent involvement is only "successful" when it meets their particular definition of the term, a definition which frequently has meant superficial parent participation under the watchful eye of professional educators.

A significant layer of complexity is added to the issues raised by Jordan et. al. (2001) when the families in question are from bicultural backgrounds and/or low-income (Boethel, 2004; Compton-Lilly, 2004). This, of course, is of particular importance in contemporary urban school settings in which a higher ratio of ethnic, racial, linguistic, economic, and religious diversity is found, and where failing schools have brought on the urgency of school reform and accountability.

Therefore, a crucial area of attention for parent involvement supporters and advocates is the dynamic nature of how these diverse parent populations relate to their children's schools and the education system in general, particularly given the issues raised earlier. By the same token, attention must also be paid to how the school system relates to them. In other words, educators must not only attempt to understand more clearly how bicultural parents perceive their roles in the education of their children but also how school personnel treat and interact with family members who are non-middle-class and non-white. This reflection process will mean that school personnel will have to critique traditional practices found in parent/school relationships, even if it means changing their entire conception of what it means to involve parents in a meaningful and effective manner.

Parent Involvement Models

Our purpose here is to propose a more functional and transformational form of parent involvement, one that offers historically disenfranchised parents the opportunity to become meaningful participants in the formal education of their children. We offer this parent involvement paradigm with the purpose of moving bicultural parents from the passive roles they have generally had in the school system to that of action researchers and decision-makers. It is our belief that these new roles will help transform the schools so that they become more receptive and accountable to the needs of bicultural parents and their children. To do this, however, we must first provide a critique and overview of what we call "traditional parent involvement models." These "models" form the foundation of where we have been with parent involvement and where we continue to struggle. Here it is also important to note that the vast majority of parent involvement activities and literature used to promote participation in the schools has consistently been based on the archetypal, middle-class Euro-American family. Therefore, the consequences for those parents who are living out a bicultural experience in the U.S. are often completely different.

We identify the four parent involves models as: *The Family Influence Model, The Alternative School Reform Model, The Cooperative Schools Model,* and *the Transformative Education Context Model.* In the examination of these parent involvement models it is possible for common practices from one model to carry over to others. Likewise, it is possible that these models be implemented in various ways according to the school administrator and the particular schools' culture. Nonetheless, using these four models, previously identified by Delgado-Gaitán (1990) and McCaleb (1997), one can recognize the underlying theory and/or outcome of each. Each of the four models also has assumptions that perceive parents as either having a passive or active voice or role in the school context, which we will point out.

The Family Influence Model (I), also referred to as the Schools Transmission Model (McCaleb, 1997), employs techniques and strategies that work to change the family and the home. As Delgado-Gaitán (1990) notes, "[academic] deficiencies are presumed to be corrected by school-designed interventions that make home socialization congruent with the school culture" (p. 50). Thus, school personnel see the deficiency in learning as originating in the home. Their belief is that the home culture of the student is somehow inadequately supporting their academic progress; therefore it must be changed and/or corrected so that the child's life chances are improved.

The Family Influence Model is founded on the principals of the deficit theories, theories which view bicultural communities as "lacking" or deficient in either intelligence, culture, and/or social adjustment (Barrera, 1979). The underlying assumption of viewing the bicultural parents as a hindrance instead of an asset can be seen in the parent education classes that are often offered by the school in which "parents are given guidelines, materials, and/or trainings to carry out school-like activities in the home" (McCaleb, 1997, p. 7). Equally popular are efforts of teaching parents about "effective" parenting and the legitimacy of the school culture. For bicultural parents, this model is an effort to "assimilate them" into the school culture.

The overall goal of this model is for the school to provide opportunities for the parents to improve their home condition in order to mirror that of the school culture. No attention is paid to other factors (both outside and inside the school) that contribute to limiting the bicultural community's ability to effectively participate in the schooling process of their children. Furthermore, school personnel are seen as the owners and purveyors of legitimate knowledge and culture, thus putting forth the notion that bicultural communities have nothing of value to offer. Ironically, despite the obvious shortcoming and disrespect this model has for all communities, particularly bicultural, it continues to be the most commonly accepted among America's pubic schools.

Alternative School Reform Model (II): This second model provides a shift in paradigm to the Family Influence Model in that the parents and the community try to change the schools to make them more responsive to them and their children (Delgado-Gaitan, 1990). That is done by parents exercising their power at the school, challenging school personnel to be more accountable to their children's needs. It is important to note however that this model is more prevalent, and more effective, amongst communities from the dominant culture. That is, middle-class and upper-class Euro-American parents have more success in demanding their children's educational rights than do bicultural parents of lower resources. This, of course, is due to the fact that there is a closer symmetrical power and status relationship between the school and the home community. Furthermore, school personnel have historically been more inclined to respond to the needs of those parents who they feel are their equals, or their superiors; in other words, high status parents who have the power and resources to hold school personnel accountable for their children's learning (Fine, 1993; Shannon, 1996).

The Cooperative Systems Model (III): This model is all-encompassing and general in that it integrates the parents into various roles within the school, even as employees (lunch duty helpers, teachers' assistants, etc.). The philosophy behind this third model argues that "factors in the home, school, and community are interrelated" (Delgado-Gaitan, 1990, p. 54). It sees the parent as a: volunteer, paid employee, teacher at home, audience, decision-maker, and adult learner. The Cooperative Systems Model therefore attempts to integrate the economic, social, and educational interests of the parents under one general umbrella term of parent involvement. These multiple roles, particularly that of a paid employee, makes direct parent advocacy less likely however since those who are working in the school have developed an economic interest in the continuation of the status quo education system since it is the source of their livelihood. Furthermore, parents who challenge the school system and are active players in school activities are often co-opted by becoming employees of the school who then must adhere to its existing practices.

The Transformative Education Context Model (IV): This fourth model is based on the notion that knowledge is socially constructed between participants, and as such, all are equally responsible and capable of contributing, understanding, and transforming the educational process (McCaleb, 1997). This model is also sometimes referred to as Family Literacy. Influenced by the work of Freire, Giroux, Cummins, and other critical pedagogues, this model's philosophy argues that "through analysis and critique, all people are capable of engaging in actions that may transform their present realities" (McCaleb, 1997, p. 26). Parent involvement is therefore seen as a process of transformation in which social literacy and consciousness raising is achieved by all the participants for the benefit of student literacy, academic achievement, and school transformation. This process of transformation, or critical literacy, is possible via the Freirian principles of dialogue and problem-posing education that seeks to name the problem, understand the conditions creating the problem, and offering alternatives and solutions to the problems.

Darder (1991) writes about the "unwavering support that critical educators have for the Freirian notion of dialogue as an emancipatory educational process" (p. 94). Such support is grounded in the notion that dialogue is important in that it provides the generative themes, or the dominant school community issues, that are necessary for relevant learning as well as a vehicle for consciousness raising (Freire, 1973, 1993). In addition, dialogue promotes a language of not only resistance but of possibility. The possibility for positive change is rooted in the belief that collaboration within the entire school population will build a community of learners in which learning is not isolated, but collective, historical, social, authentic, and transformational. Thus, bicultural parents act to promote their interests, those of their children, and those of other people's children, while at the same time participating in the political process of changing their lives from objects to subjects —e.g., from passive to active involvement.

By now, the questions raised by the reader might be: how is this model of parent participation different from the previous models, besides the rhetoric? And, is this model possible?

First and foremost, the importance of this model is its ability to take into account the social, cultural, and economic factors impacting the quality of life of the school community. The Transformative Education Context Model addresses the issue of how knowledge is constructed and normalized based on an individual's or group's position in society. Additionally, it does not ignore or conceal the strong political interests found in schooling. Therefore, parent involvement is seen as political and empowering (Núñez, 1994; Olivos, 2003, 2004). In other words, parent involvement is a political process in which parents from diverse backgrounds (including middle-class Euro-Americans) work to transform a system that engenders subordination and stratifies students. Additionally, it presents a counter-perspective which views the home knowledge and culture of the participants as equally valid and powerful for social change. It is this "model" that forms the basis of our paradigm, a paradigm that seeks to transform parent involvement into a meaningful act of empowerment and political involvement with the goal of making education a democratic and reflective action.

A Transformative Paradigm of Parent Involvement

We argue that there is a need to develop a transformative paradigm of parent involvement, one that will work to not only transform the parents' self awareness and self-efficacy in regard to school related matters, but to transform the school system into a democratic community.

Over the past thirty years, the persistent achievement gap between students of color and middle- and upper-class Euro-American students demonstrates the need to improve the existing practices of our education system. We believe that it will be the parents of these low-performing children who serve as the catalyst and/or trigger that transforms the school system to meet the needs of their children and their communities.

We believe that a transformative paradigm of parent involvement will provide parents and parent advocates the necessary tools to confront the social injustices currently taking place in the public education setting. This will become possible when parents begin unmasking and understanding the contradictions that are found in the current system and by developing a social consciousness along with their fellow parents and communities (Olivos, 1993).

The Parent Involvement Paradigm, as depicted in Table 1, illustrates a formula we propose for analyzing progressive levels of parent involvement in a democratic social and educational context. Democratic education, as defined by Pearl & Knight (1999), is both a means and an end. The means is informed debate leading to reflective action; the ends are a society where decisions are made on the basis of universal participation in informed action; where the majority rules only to the extent that specified rights of minorities are respected; and where the decisions made equally encourage all members of the society to fully participate in every facet of the society. Four levels of analyses are suggested.

The paradigm assumes that movement from one system to another is driven by the social commitment and developmental consciousness of its participants and communities. The paradigm provides a progressive and developmental course towards socio-economic-political consciousness. The paradigm begins and moves from a functionalist philosophical/ideological perspective (level I), to a structural functionalism (level II), to a conflict theory (level III), and finally to a combined use of *conflict theory & interpretivist social constructionist* perspectives to create socio-economic political pluralistic school communities.

Level I of parent involvement centers on ensuring that the parent community conforms to the dominant values of the school's culture or in support of the status quo (functionalist). Feinberg and Soltis (2004) define the functionalist perspective as serving to socialize parents and students to adapt to the economic, political, and social institutions of that society. In this perspective, functionalists suggest that we view social institutions as analogous to the parts of the body. Each part func-

Table 1 Parent Involvement Paradigm

Level	Theoretical /Social Focus	Parent Involvement Models	Perception of Parents as Contributors to Schools
I Status Quo	Functionalist(Conformity)	Family Influence: Change bicultural parents —"improve" home condition for participants to acquire preferred behaviors and values	Superficially connecting parents to school culture (I)
II	Structural Functionalist(Social control and harmony)	Cooperative systems: parents participate within the school culture to assimilate to school practices and behaviors	Parents as collaborators of school culture (II)
III	Conflict Theory(Equity and power relations)	Alternative school reform: Parents challenge schools to be more responsive, inclusive and equitable	Parents as co-participants in the decision-making process (III)
IV Open Democratic System	Conflict theory, social constructionist & interpretivist (Transformational change towards cultural and economic democracy)	Transformational education: Problem posing that seeks solutions enabling inclusion, voice and representation in decision making	Cultural democracy, parents as action researchers, agents of transformative change in the school and community (IV)

tions to serve the needs and purpose of the whole. Thus, Level I is simply concerned with superficially connecting the parent community to the school in order for them to conform to its culture.

Level II of the paradigm of parent involvement is guided by the focus on assimilating the parent community to the dominant values of the school's culture or in support of governing rules (structural functionalist). Under this perspective, schooling is seen as a means of socialization for molding the school community to fit existing social practices and requirements. The perspective here is to view equity as simply providing the same resources to all participants without concern for its benefits or utility. This view's only concern is thus providing limited resources and it is the responsibility of the participants to fit the institutions' available resources. Quality, relevance and meaningfulness are not criteria for determining benefit or utility of access. Thus, Level II is simply concerned with working with the parent community to collaborate in support of the school's culture in order to take advantage of its available services and without questioning its policies, programs, staffing practices, or standards (Compton-Lilly, 2004).

Level III of the paradigm of parent involvement focuses on addressing social and educational inequities that have been created by the dominant culture and embedded in the practices of the school's culture (conflict theory). Under this perspective, the view of schooling is seen as a social practice supported and utilized by those in power to maintain the culture of dominance in the social order. This perspective questions the inequitable class relations in society and urges social action to undue schooling as an instrument of class domination and serving to produce the workforce and maintain class relationships (Feinberg & Soltis, 2004). From a legal perspective, the conflict theorist perspective represents legal and civil rights legislation that advocates for eradicating past discriminatory practices through social and educational institutions that seek to actualize the principle of "equal benefits." This principle is not only concerned with access to resources but also in the quality of services to develop the human condition. The responsibility shifts from the individual to institutional services to fit the needs of its participants. Quality, relevance and meaningfulness become the criteria for assessing benefit or utility of access. Thus, Level III is concerned with the parent community becoming a co-participant in the decision making process of the school, or "having a piece of the pie" while seeking the full benefits of the educational system and special programs which are created to provide equal benefits.

Level IV of the paradigm combines the equity focus of the conflict theorist perspective (Feinberg & Soltis, 1992), the emphasis of the constructivist perspective in seeking an involvement process that promotes parent and student participants in the construction of knowledge, dialogue, and as agents of creating and recreating meaning in the improvement of the school community (Macedo, 1991), and the interpretivist perspective that sees the social world as a world made up of purposeful actors, who acquire, share, and interpret a set of meanings, rules, and norms that make social interaction possible (Feinberg & Soltis, 2004). The focus is on creating culturally democratic participation in developing and implementing social and educational policy that develops social responsibility and the human condition-socially, cognitively, and politically.

Participants in this level have a deep understanding and social justice orientation in seeking to act on social injustice at the personal and community level. From a legal perspective, the combined perspectives seek to operationalize cultural democracy (equal representation, equal participation, equal access, equal encouragement, and the right to social mobility) while directly addressing practices that eliminate racial and class preference. This perspective also seeks to transform the school community to ensure that its values and practices are congruent with the pursuit of cultural and economic democracy. Thus, Level IV is concerned with creating a school community for the "collective we."

Level I to level IV suggest educational practices (parent involvement) that move from an authoritarian model of governance to a democratic model of governance and work. The paradigm also places the parent involvement models mentioned earlier into a context that will serve to propose the direction that we need to direct our efforts as we seek socio-economic-political pluralism in our democracy.

The objective of the Olivos and Ochoa (in press) parent involvement paradigm is to reach the fourth level of transformational education that is guided by parental participatory involvement. Such involvement ensures the participation of low-income parents and can be viewed as consisting of three interrelated parts. First it is initiated through a problem posing that forms the basis of our inquiry and work. Secondly, through this process of inquiry and dialogue participants learn about the world and about themselves, thus engaging in a transformative educational experience. Thirdly, through personal and individual and collective reflection, action is taken towards resolving the issues that initiated the problem posing process (Freire, 1982).

It is through the act of questioning and inquiry that a true educational act occurs, and knowledge is invented or re-invented in community with others. According to Freire (1982), "Education as a practice of freedom - as opposed to education as the practice of domination-denies that [we are] abstract isolated, independent and unattached to the world...." (p. 69). Figure 1 provides the circular process of problem-posing and reflection.

Figure 1: Problem Posing and Reflection

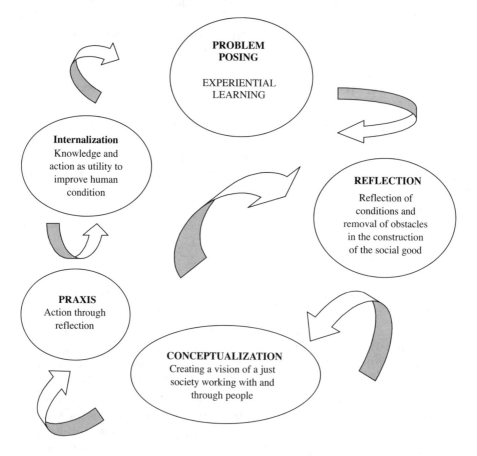

In problem posing dialogue, participants come to recognize their ability to know and to reflect. Parent involvement is based on empowerment that leads to action and further reflection, which, in turn, leads to further questions for inquiry and action research (Ada, 1988). We see knowledge in its action, practice and reflection. In the words of Maturana and Varela (1987), "Reflection is the process of knowing how we know. It is our only chance we have to discover our blindness and to recognize that the certainties and knowledge of others are, respectively, as overwhelming and tenuous as our own" (p. 24).

This paradigm on parent involvement therefore ultimately seeks to pursue the ideal of cultural democracy. Such an ideal exits where the principle of equal encouragement is institutionalized in policies and practices that unmask and eliminate discriminatory racial and class institutional policies and practices. The institution attains cultural democracy when its infrastructure is reflective of the total community at all structural levels of the organization. At this point, multi-racial competency becomes the norm. Cultural democracy recognizes the existence of racial and class tensions as a necessary condition of its existence and for actualizing democracy (Lindsey, Robins & Terrell, 1999).

Another essential process of transformational education in the paradigm is participatory research as a way for researchers and disempowered people to meet in collaboration to address concrete and specific problems and situations. This participatory research means working with and through people as a viable tool in discussing issues of social justice and equity through the following:

1. The active participation of the individuals or groups who have an interest in changing the conditions in which they live or work.
2. The researcher (parent/teacher/administrator/university faculty) and the participants collectively exploring those conditions, which may be oppressive in nature and promote a lack of equity in education.
3. Through this process the researchers do not maintain a position of power over the participants or promote his/her ideas about the world.
4. The researcher does not define knowledge for the participants; rather knowledge is derived from the collective activity of dialogue and work.
5. The researchers and the participants engage in dialogues to facilitate both a deeper understanding of the problems surrounding the

research and an exploration of some type of solution or structural change.

6. The process calls for engagement and working with and through people.
7. The researchers and the participants constantly reflect on the challenges of current educational and social problems.
8. The researcher and the participants engage in dialogical activity that explores the question of research, its use and how it serves to support the selected communities.
9. The researchers and the participants work with communities to improve the human conditions through transformational approaches that do not blame but rather seek structural solutions. The result is a dynamic process in the development of a plan of action for the participants to transform their world.
10. Transformation will not occur unless the co-researchers name their realities and then take action to improve them for themselves and others with similar realities. The act of taking theory, critical reflection through engagement in a free and open manner with social action is defined as praxis.

The outcome of participatory research is to engage researchers and community in the process of praxis-to transform oppressive conditions into opportunities to recreate conditions of hope, love, humility, and social justice. Therefore, the objective behind this parent involvement paradigm is to examine the nature and cause of poverty, oppression and exploitation and to seek action to resolve the problems and empower the participating community and transform social realities in order to achieve social justice.

Parents Transforming the School System

The greatest challenge of operationalizing a model such as the one we propose is visualizing its possibilities. To visualize these possibilities one must understand that there are many parents and parent groups currently out in the public school system that have already taken their own individual steps towards a transformational view of being involved in their children's schools. These movements demonstrate how bicultural parents have come to understand their position in society and to pose problems and questions as to why these inequities exist. This problem posing is done with the purpose of seeking solutions that will benefit the entire school community. We conclude by demonstrating some of the possibilities that exist for taking the first steps toward a transformational paradigm of parent involvement.

Ochoa (1997) documents some of the work done by the Parent Institute for Quality Education (PIQE), an organization established on the premise that "no force on earth is as strong as that of a parent determined to get a fair break for his or her child" (p. 45). This organization, founded in San Diego, acknowledges the sincere and profound impact low income and bicultural parents have on their children's education. It works to create conditions that will help parents connect to their children's schools and establish an effective home/school learning environment. This is an important first step for many immigrant and bicultural parents who are generally unaccustomed to actively participating in their children's schools.

PIQE's work in low-income schools which have "a history of very low parent participation" uses a problem-posing approach "to design and provide workshop experiences generated by parents" (Ochoa, 1997, pp. 45-46). For bicultural parents this marks a significantly different approach from the traditional "parent education classes they have been subjected to which are usually designed to teach them 'parenting skills' or other strategies for overcoming their children's deficits,'" (Cummins, 1996, p. 8). This problem-posing approach to issues and concerns that are most familiar to them help the parents "conceptualize problems and then ways of acting on them ("praxis")" (Ochoa, 1997, p. 46).

Our work with Latino parents in San Diego County has clearly demonstrated to us the important foundation PIQE has provided many of them for understanding the school system. Many of the most active parents we have encountered are "graduates" of the program. Where PIQE leaves off, however, many parents have continued through their own personal struggles to understand and transform the school system. Two particular case studies in San Diego demonstrate how Latino parents have organized themselves in the face of injustice to work for a more equitable school system.

Núñez's (1994) study about the empowerment process of Mexican origin parents demonstrates some of the issues that most concern these parents and how they perceive their political efficacy and self-esteem within a school system characterized by "embedded racism." Núñez documents how a group of Mexican-origin parents worked together to organize themselves as the *Asociación de Padres Hispanos*. Núñez calls this group a "quasi-autonomous parent organization" whose members "regularly involve themselves in some facets of the schools [*sic*] operation" (p. 104). Significant in this study is how Núñez, himself an active participant of this group, uses a participatory and critical approach to help the parents understand the underlying political foundations of the problems at their school. This participatory research creates a generation of themes which leads to new knowledge as these once "isolated" parents begin to understand their critical role in the transformation of their children's school.

Olivos' (2003) work with parents seeks to understand the tensions that lead to conflicts between Latino parents and their children's schools and why these parents at times resist the efforts of the schools. Significant in both Nuñez's and Olivos' work with parents is the self-organization of Latino parents into autonomous parent groups which struggle to hold their children's schools more accountable. Nuñez's parents work within the school system, however, while those in Olivos' effort work "outside" of it.

In Olivos' (2003) study, he documents how a small group of Latino parents form a parent organization independent of the school. He details how after repeated attempts to dialogue with the school administration on meaningful topics and to have a say in the decision-making process at the site, these particular parents started having their own education meetings off campus. At these meetings the parents would openly discuss concerns they had with the school, and certain members of the personnel, and strategize how they could go about rectifying them, i.e. problem posing and praxis.

These parents' hard work, persistence, and political understanding of the problem at hand, led them to become action researchers and advocates, thus able to document the problems at their site, using methods and tools (such as writing letters to create a "paper trail") accepted by the dominant society. In time, "this group became so powerful and "well-connected," despite being small in numbers, that the principal at the site was eventually replaced upon the parents' continuous urging." These parents "even went on to form an autonomous parent organization that published a monthly newsletter on the critical situation of Latino students in their district" (Olivos, 2004, p. 30-31).

Conclusion

We contend that there is a need to transform the schools so that they meet the needs of all children, particularly those who have historically been neglected by the school system. Understanding the important role parents play in their children's lives, we have attempted to demonstrate the urgency of developing a transformational paradigm of parent involvement using a participatory and problem-posing approach. We believe that parents hold a fundamental interest in having the schools succeed: the academic and social success of their children. Thus, we offer a critique of how parents, particularly bicultural ones, have been asked to participate in their children's schools.

Traditionally, parents have been invited into the schools using models and approaches which have been contradictory to their authentic involvement. We put forth in this chapter that until parents are invited into the schools with the understanding that they and the school share the equal responsibility and power to transform the schools so that they meet the educational and social needs of all children, the school system will continue to confront what is quite possibly this nation's greatest contradiction, the inability to close the educational achievement disparity between specific social groups. Therefore, we propose a transformational paradigm of parent involvement that must be actualized so that parents, teachers, and community can work together to generate the conditions that will create an equitable and democratic schooling experience and society.

References

Ada A. F. (1988). Creative readings: A relevant methodology for language minority children. In M. Malwe (Ed). NABE '87. Theory, research and applications: Selected papers (pp. 97-111). Buffalo, NY: State University of New York Press.

Barrera, M. (1979). Race and class in the Southwest: A theory of racial inequality. Norte Dame: University of Norte Dame.

Boethel, M. (2003). Diversity: School, family, & community connections. Austin, TX: National Center for Family & Community Connections with Schools.

Compton-Lilly, C. (2004). Confronting racism, poverty, and power: Classroom strategies to change the world. Portsmouth, NH: Heinemann.

Cummins, J. (1996). Education for Empowerment in a diverse society. Ontario, CA: CABE.

Cutler, W.W. (2000). Parents and schools: The 150 year struggle for control of American education. Chicago: University of Chicago Press.

Darder, A. (1991). Culture and power in the classroom: A critical foundation for bicultural education. Westport, CT: Berson & Garvey.

Delgado-Gaitán, C. (1990). Literacy for empowerment: The role of parents in children's education. New York: The Falmer Press.

Feinberg, W. & Soltis, J. F. (2004). School and society. New York: Teachers College Press.

Fine, M. (1993). [Ap]parent involvement: Reflections on parents, power, and urban public schools. Teachers College Record. 94(4), 682-710.

Freire, P. (1973). Education for critical consciousness. New York: Continuum Publishing Company.

Freire, P. (1982) (Ed.) Dialogue is not a chaste event: Comments by Paulo Freire on participatory research. University of Massachusetts: Center for International Education.

Freire, P. (1993). Pedagogy of the oppressed. New York: Continuum Publishing Company.

Henderson, A.T. & Mapp, K.L. (2002). A new wave of evidence: The impact of school, family and community connections on student achievement. Austin, TX: Southwest Educational Development Laboratory.

Jordan, C., Orozco, E. & Averett, A. (2001). Emerging issues in school, family, & community connections. Austin, TX: National Center for Family & Community Connections with Schools.

Lindsey R.B., Robins, K. N., Terrell R.D. (1999) Cultural proficiency: A manual for school leaders. New York: Corwin Press, Inc.

Macedo, D. (1991). The politics of power: What Americans are not allowed to know. San Francisco: Westview Press.

Maturana, H. R. and Varela. F. J. (1987). The tree of knowledge. Boston: New Science Library.

McCaleb, S. P. (1994). Building communities of learners. New York: St. Martin's Press.

Núñez, R. (1994). Schools, parents, and empowerment: An ethnographic study of Mexican-origin parents participation in their children's schools. Unpublished Doctoral Dissertation, San Diego State University/Claremont Graduate School, San Diego, CA/Claremont, CA.

Ochoa, A.M. (1997). Empowering parents to be teachers of their children: The Parent Institute for Quality Education. <u>Learning communities' narratives: Learning from our differences: Color, culture, and class. Part two.</u> 2 (2).Cleveland, OH: Learning Communities Network, Inc.

Olivos, E.M. (2003). <u>Dialectical tensions, contradictions, and resistance: A study of the relationship between Latino parents and the public school system within a socio-economic "structure of dominance."</u> Unpublished Doctoral Dissertation, San Diego State University/Claremont Graduate School, San Diego, CA/Claremont, CA.

Olivos, E.M. (2004). Tensions, contradictions, and resistance: An activist's reflection of the struggles of Latino parents in the public school system. <u>The High School Journal: Chicana/o Activism in Education: Theories and Pedagogies of Trans/formation.</u> 87(4), 25-35.

Olivos, E.M. & Ochoa, A.M. (In press). Voice, Access, and Democratic Participation: Towards a Transformational Paradigm of Parent Involvement in Urban Education. In J. Kincheloe, P. Anderson, K. Rose, D. Griffith, and K. Hayes <u>Urban education: An encyclopedia.</u> Westport, CT: Greenwood Publishing Group.

Pearl, A. & Knight T. (1999) <u>The democratic classroom.</u> Cressskill, New Jersey: Hampton Press, Inc.

Shannon, S. (1996). Minority parental involvement: A Mexican mother's experience and a teacher's interpretation. <u>Education and Urban Society.</u> 29(1), 71-84.

About the Authors

Cristina Alfaro is an Assistant Professor in the Department of Policy Studies in Language and Cross-Cultural Education at San Diego State University. Her research interests center on home/school cross-cultural languages and literacy practices. As a teacher researcher she has examined the role of teachers' *ideological and political clarity* related to teaching practices with language minority and other subordinated student groups. Email Address: calfaro@mail.sdsu.edu

Karen Cadiero-Kaplan is Assistant Professor at San Diego State University in the Department of Policy Studies in Language and Cross Cultural Education. Her research interests include literacy in the arts and technology, democratic practices for teacher development, and policy that impacts programming for biliteracy and English language development. Recent publications include a book titled: *The Literacy Curriculum and Bilingual Education: A Critical Examination.* Email Address: kcadiero@mail.sdsu.edu

Shu-ching (Michele) Chu is an associate professor at Wenzao College of Foreign Languages in Taiwan. She earned her Ph.D. in education from the Joint doctoral program at San Diego State University and Claremont Graduate University. Her research focuses on English teacher education and English instruction to speakers of other languages. Email Address: ching.chu@gmail.com

Tamara Collins-Parks teaches a Language Issues course for the Policy Studies Department at SDSU. She also helps teacher candidates improve their writing skills. She is currently completing a case study of district politics in the implementation of Proposition 227. Her son attends a dual language school. Email Address: biliterate@cox.net

Antonella Cortese. Born in Canada, having grown up in Michigan, her family originally immigrated from Italy where she lived and studied for many years. Her research interests include after-school programming, educational technology and is currently working on issues around multiculturalism and literacy development. She is affiliated with the Center for Research in Teacher Education and Development at the University of Alberta, Edmonton, Canada. Email Address: acortese@mac.com

Jon Meza Cuero is a leader in the Indigenous community of Baja California. He is one of few native speakers of his heritage language. Jon is also the only living singer of the wildcat genre of Indigenous songs and is greatly sought after to perform and teach the songs and the language. You may contact the author through Paula Meyer. Email Address: pmeyer@sdcoe.k12.ca.us

Larry W. Emerson, Diné, is an activist, living in Shiprock, NM, Diné Nation. Presently, Emerson is a post doctoral research fellow at the Native American House, University of Illinois Urbana-Champaign, furthering research work on Diné decolonization theory and practice. Email Address: emerson714@froniternet.net

Yvette V. Lapayese is assistant professor in the School of Education at Loyola Marymount University. She received her Ph.D. from the University of California, Los Angeles. She formerly served as an elementary school teacher and is extensively involved in research on critical educators in the classroom. Professor Lapayese's other research interests include race and feminist methodologies and critical theory and practice as it relates to marginalized teachers and students of color. Email Address: ylapayes@lmu.edu

Georges Merx is an Associate Professor in Computer and Information Sciences at San Diego Mesa College and a Visiting Professor in Computer Science and Engineering at the University of California, San Diego. He holds a Ph.D. in Education from San Diego State University/Claremont Graduate University (joint program) and a Master of Science in Information and Decision Systems from San Diego State University. Dr. Merx specializes in modeling and visualization of complex social processes; he teaches software engineering and object-oriented programming languages and is currently working on a college textbook for Pearson/Prentice-Hall with co-author Dr. Ronald Norman on the topic of *Software Engineering with Java.* He developed his professional experience in various technical and management positions in high-technology software development companies and organizations in San Diego, California, and Zürich, Switzerland, before turning to education as a full-time career. Dr. Merx lives in San Diego, California, and is a native of Luxembourg. Email Address: gmerx@georgesmerx.com

Paula Meyer has a background in linguistics and language teaching. She has been involved with the Indigenous communities of Baja California for many years. Paula has extensive experience as a bilingual teacher. She is currently coordinating a project for the maintenance of Spanish among Spanish-language students in a public school. Email Address: pmeyer@sdcoe.k12.ca.us

Alberto M. Ochoa is Professor and Chair of the Department of Policy Studies in Language and Cross Cultural Education in the College of Education at San Diego State University. Since 1975, he has worked with over 60 school districts in providing technical assistance in the areas of: language policy and assessment, bilingual instructional programs, curriculum programming, staff development, community development, organizational development and school climate, program management, monitoring and evaluation. His research interests include public equity, school desegregation, language policy, critical pedagogy, student achievement, and parental leadership. Email Address: aochoa@mail.sdsu.edu

Edward M. Olivos is Assistant Professor in the Division of Teacher Education at California State University, Dominguez Hills. A former classroom teacher in San Diego, his research interests include: bilingual education, Latinos and education, critical pedagogy, policy studies, and (bicultural) parent/community involvement. He is currently writing a book about parent communities and parental voice. Email Address: emolivos@cox.net

Index

❧ Notes

❧ Notes